REVELATION

THE – RAPTURE – EQUATION

Not For one single
moment, did il ever
Stop loving you ♡

Sincerely.

WA4-5292

Revelation

—

The
Rapture Equation

ABIDE Ministries
KPFM2018@gmail.com
Philadelphia, PA 19124
www.rapture2061.org

Revelation: The Rapture Equation — Revised 2nd Edition

All scriptures are in King James Version 1611, unless otherwise noted.

Contents

Foreword

Every once in a while, a book appears on the shelves that deeply impacts the lives of everyone who reads it.

Reader be warned; If you are comfortable and complacent about what is happening in the world today and want it to stay that way, do not read this book.

This book will heighten your awareness of the two spiritual forces in this world; Good and Evil.

Get ready to go on a spiritual journey guaranteed to change your life and your world forever.

Brother, I am so thankful to God for choosing you to reveal these things at this hour in biblical history. I admire your position in Jesus Christ.

I love you and may God continue to bless you and others as they read this book.

—Evangelist Harriet James—

Acknowledgment

I want to thank my God and my Lord; King Jesus for opening my eyes and giving me the Spirit of Understanding and Interpretation. I can take no credit for this book. The Holy Ghost deserves all the credit; as I was only used as a conduit.

"Knowing this first, that no prophecy of the Scripture is of any private interpretation. For the prophecy came not in old time by the will of man: but holy men of God spake as they were moved by the Holy Ghost." – II Peter 1:20-21

Introduction

Jesus Christ revealed to his Apostle John what would occur in the last days. John would see events that would occur more than 2,000 years into the future. John could only use the terminology of his times to explain what he saw.

The Book of Revelation seems mysterious, but it is not. False teachers spreading their false doctrines make the Book of Revelation appear mysterious. Nowadays, many Christians do not know what to believe, so they adopt and adhere to preconceived ideas. Many Christians hold themselves back from fully understanding the Revelation of Jesus Christ because they hold onto their deeply engrained preconceived notions. Deeply engrained preconceived notions are often distorted opinionated beliefs that will eventually steer you away from the fully understanding the Bible. Once you get past this, the Book of Revelation will become clear.

The Book of Revelation has many symbols, figures of speech, and allegories. Revelation is a book of after-thoughts, metaphors, perspectives, idioms, and tenses. Revelation has many vantage points: historical, imagery, spiritual, comparative, descriptive, literal, parenthetical, and at times narrative. It has many layers, and layers within layers.

The hardest part for me was to know how and when to apply these vantage points in contrast to what is being relayed by its writer. To properly interpret the Book of Revelation, all vantage points must be applied within context at the proper time. When John is describing or using a metaphor, it should not be taken as literal, and vice versa. Revelation has several perspectives:

- Earthly & Heavenly
- Self-Explanatory
- Past Events
- Present Events
- Future Events

For many years I did not read the last book of the Bible, because there were so many different interpretations. When I began to study the Book of Revelation verse by verse and scripture by scripture, I realized its' text is comprehensive, but not impossible to understand. The Book of Revelation is so interwoven with prophetic nooks and crannies it is impossible to see the big picture from a one-dimensional simplified approach.

Therefore, we cannot lump the entire Book of Revelation together as some do, regarding what they term as the Seven Year Tribulation period. What does the Bible actually teach about the Pre, Mid and Post Tribulation theology? I will discuss that in my book.

Upon further study I discovered most of what is taught today is completely off the mark. It is as though teachers are getting this hearsay doctrine from one another because it sounds good, and authors are making millions of dollars selling people these feel good books about the end times. I did not write this book to make you feel good. I do not care about money; I care about truth.

My book is not like other books you have read about end-time prophecy. Unlike other books on Revelation you may have read, my book takes you in a completely different direction. My book hermeneutically, systemically, and mathematically dismantles the nonsensical babel that has infiltrated church doctrine and end-time prophecy.

This book will change your viewpoint on what has been taught in most Christian churches for years, about what the Bible actually teaches. Come with me as I explain Revelation verse by verse and unravel the mystery of – The Rapture Equation.

"...Go thy way Daniel: for the words are closed up and sealed till the time of the end." – Daniel 12:9

Chapter One
The Exalted Christ

"The Revelation of Jesus Christ which God gave unto him, to show unto his servants things which must shortly come to pass; and he sent and signified it by his angel unto his servant John. Who bare record of the word of God, and of the testimony of Jesus Christ, and of all things that he saw. Blessed is he that readeth, and they that hear the words of this prophecy, and keep those things which are written therein: for the time is at hand." – Revelation 1:1-3

Revelation is the showcase of the risen Christ. Jesus Christ is revealed as the First and Last, Beginning and Ending, Kings of Kings, Lord of Lords, Judge and Ruler of Heaven and Earth. It is God the Father who gives Jesus his commission. In turn Jesus reveals himself to his servants (**the Elect**), primarily to John on the Island of Patmos by an angel. Those who read, study, and understand the words of this prophecy, and keep these words in their heart and mind are blessed of God.

The Seven Churches

"John to the seven churches which are in Asia." – Revelation 1:4

John is writing to the Church of Ephesus, Smyrna, Pergamos, Thyatira, Sardis, Laodicea, and Philadelphia. In John's time these were the seven major churches of early Christianity. Some believe the seven churches represent different periods in history. This is not the case due to verse four which states, *"To the seven churches which are in Asia."* 'Are' is present-tense in John's time.

In this portion of scripture Jesus is addressing the pros and cons, admonitions, and commendations of the seven churches that were in Asia Minor. If you were raised up in church as I was, there were lessons to be learned from Christ's commendations and rebukes on these seven churches. Over the years I have attended many churches and have seen characteristics of all seven churches to one degree or another. Jesus pointed out several of these churches that allowed false teachings into them. The infiltration of false doctrine among the congregation of Christ has been going on since the inception of Christianity.

The Elect must know how and when to recognize false doctrine, and confront it. Christ's rebuke of yesterday's Church should be a warning for all believers today. The Apostle Paul's first letter to the Corinthians, speaks of Israel's wilderness experience. They wandered forty years in the wilderness always murmuring and complaining against Moses until God destroyed that wicked generation except Caleb and Joshua. Paul accentuates that we identify and flee this attitude.

1

As we discuss the pros and cons laid out by the Exalted Christ, you must compare it to the church you are attending. There have been many times when I have heard motivational preachers put the congregation into a frenzied uproar only to leave the Word of God out of the message. It was a great atmosphere if you wanted to be entertained, but there was no spiritual milk or meat in the message.

"Grace be unto you, and peace, from him which is, and which was, and which is to come: and from the seven Spirits which are before his throne. And from Jesus Christ, who is the faithful witness and the first begotten of the dead and the prince of the kings of the earth. Unto him that loved us, and washed us from our sins in his own blood." – Revelation 1:4-5

John salutes the seven churches, honors the risen Christ, and recognizes the Seven Spirits before God's throne. Revelation 4:5 describes the Seven Spirits of God as seven lamps of burning fire. Jesus Christ was anointed with the Seven Spirits of God. Isaiah 11:2 tells us exactly what the Seven Spirits of God reference. John goes on to recognize Jesus' sacrifice, resurrection, and authority as the Prince of Kings.

"And hath made us kings and priests unto God and his Father; to him be glory and dominion for ever and ever. Amen. Behold, he cometh with clouds; and every eye shall see him, and they also which pierced him."

"All kindreds of the earth shall wail because of him. Even so, Amen. I am Alpha and Omega, the beginning and the ending, saith the Lord, which is, and which was, and which is to come, the Almighty." – Revelation 1:6-8

Because of His resurrection, Christ can resurrect all those who believe in Him (even in his name) and make us Kings and Priests of God forever. On the Day of the Lord when Christ returns in the clouds, every eye will see his true power. Jesus is Alpha: The Word is the beginning of all things. Jesus is Omega: The Word is the finality of all things. Jesus is that which was, is, and is to come. The Word exists through time, space, and all realities. The Word is the Almighty God: Beginning and Ending. Amen.

"I John, who also am your brother, and companion in tribulation, and in the kingdom and patience of Jesus Christ, was in the isle that is called Patmos, for the word of God, and for the testimony of Jesus Christ." – Revelation 1:9

John was exiled to the Island of Patmos for his belief in the risen Savior, and gives us a short bio of the sufferings of the early Church. The Roman Empire under Caesar with the Jewish leaders persecuted Christians by imprisoning, and killing them. Christians were sport for gladiators, fed to the lions, tortured to death, beheaded, crucified, and even buried alive.

"I was in the Spirit on the Lord's Day, and heard behind me a great voice, as of a trumpet." – Revelation 1:10

"I am Alpha and Omega, the first and the last; and what thou seest, write in a book, and send it unto the seven churches which are in Asia; unto Ephesus, and unto Smyrna, and unto Pergamos, and unto Thyatira, and unto Sardis, and unto Philadelphia, and unto Laodicea." – Revelation 1:11

God gave John a vision. John heard a great voice of authority behind him. This great voice uttered, *"I am the beginning of all things. I am the finality of all things. What I am going to reveal to you write in a book."* Send one copy to the Church of Ephesus; one copy to the Church of Smyrna; one copy to the Church of Pergamos; one copy to the Church of Thyatira; one copy to the Church of Sardis; one copy to the Church of Philadelphia; and one copy to the Church of Laodicea.

"And I turned to see the voice that spake with me. And being turned, I saw seven golden candlesticks; and in the midst of the seven candlesticks one like unto the Son of man, clothed with a garment down to the foot, and girt about the paps with a golden girdle. His head and his hairs were white like wool, as white as snow; and his eyes were as a flame of fire; and his feet like unto fine brass, as if they burned in a furnace; and his voice as the sound of many waters." – Revelation 1:12-15

John turned towards the voice and saw Jesus surrounded by seven golden candle sticks. Jesus had on a full length robe with a golden belt. His head and hair is white like wool and snow. His eyes were as a flame of fire. His feet were like fine brass burning in a furnace, and his voice as the sound of many waters.

There is a misconception by some about John's description of Jesus. I often hear people debate Jesus having wool-like hair. Jesus' hair is not wool. One must understand that John is describing a heavenly encounter. John is comparing the Exalted Christ by his limited understanding. So this portion of scripture is descriptive by comparison. Notice the phrases John uses: 'Voice **as** the sound of many waters', 'White **like** wool', 'White **like** snow', 'Eyes **as** a flame of fire', 'Feet **like** fine brass'.

If a person runs fast **like** a gazelle, the person is not a gazelle. If a guy has the agility **like** Spiderman, the guy is not Spiderman. If a woman punches **like** the Incredible Hulk, is she the Incredible Hulk? Jesus' eyes burning like flames of fire are not literal. John's description of the glorified Christ is metaphorical because there are no words to describe what John saw.

"And he had in his right hand seven stars: and out of his mouth went a sharp two-edged sword: and his countenance was as the sun shineth in his strength." – Revelation 1:16

Jesus had seven stars in his right hand and a sharp two-edged sword proceeded out of his mouth. His face shined **as** the sun. This portion of scripture is also metaphoric.

- Shineth as the Sun = Glory of God
- Sharp two-edge sword = Word of God

"And when I saw him, I fell at his feet as dead. And he laid his right hand upon me, saying unto me, Fear not; I am the first and the last. I am he that liveth, and was dead; and behold, I am alive forevermore, Amen; and have the keys of hell and of death. Write the things which thou hast seen, and the things which are, and the things which shall be hereafter." – Revelation 1:17-19

When John saw the Exalted Christ, he became paralyzed with fear. Jesus touched John with His right hand and told him not to be afraid. Jesus was alive with The Father, but was separated from The Father when he died for our sins. When Jesus became the propitiation for our sins, The Father could not allow sin in his presence.

"And at the ninth hour Jesus cried with a loud voice, saying, Eloi, Eloi, lama sabachthani? which is, being interpreted, My God, my God, why hast thou forsaken me?" – Saint Mark 15:34

Jesus died for our sins and was buried, but marvel now, for surely Jesus arose from the dead and is alive eternal, and he holds the keys of Hell and Death in His hand. Jesus told John to write in a book the things that have already happened in the past, the things that were happening in John's time, and the things that would happen in the future.

"The mystery of the seven stars which thou sawest in my right hand, and seven golden candlesticks. The seven stars are the angels of the seven churches: and the seven candlesticks which thou sawest are the seven churches." – Revelation 1:20

Jesus reveals the mystery of the seven stars which are the seven angels of each church in Asia Minor. Angel (Aggelos–Greek), not of nature, but of office, refers to a human messenger (Pastor). The seven golden candlesticks (Menorah) represent the seven churches or the seven locations where the Christian congregation gathered.

Not merely a location or a building, the Church is the Christian community. Notice in verse 13 how Jesus is present in the midst of the church. Christ is in the midst of the Church through his omnipresence.

<u>To the Church of Ephesus (Chapter 2:1–7)</u>

"Unto the angel of the church of Ephesus write; These things saith he that holdeth the seven stars in his right hand, who walketh in the midst of the seven golden candlesticks; I know thy works, and thy labor, and thy patience, and how thou canst not bear them which are evil: and thou hast tried them which say they are apostles, and are not, and hast found them liars: And hast borne, and hast patience, and for my name's sake hast labored, and hast not fainted." – Revelation 2:1-3

I commend your efforts and I know your works. I know your labor and patience. I know that you are virtuous, always aware of evil infiltrating the Church, because you have tested them which say they are apostles and are not. You labored through long patience and did not faint.

Works or 'Ergon' in the Greek means any matter, performance, or the result of performance. The Church of Ephesus recognized false doctrine and false teachers. They stood against those claiming to be teachers and preachers of Christ, and found them to be liars (antichrists). Jesus commends them for their long-suffering, endurance, and patience through hard circumstances.

"Nevertheless I have somewhat against thee, because thou hast left thy first love." – Revelation 2:4

Jesus also pointed out that their first love for him dwindled. Whatever you and I do for Christ must be motivated by our love for Him. We should never get into a religious mode of working for God, or think that we are doing God's will out of habit. Let me give you an example. A middle aged woman was, as she called herself a minister of the Lord, visited a home several times. Each time she came to this particular home the occupants never wanted to hear her message. Eventually the owner erected a fence around his yard, bought a dog, and posted a no trespassing sign to keep this woman out.

One day this self-appointed minister felt she could walk through the gate (because she was doing the Lord's work) and once again, pester and force the gospel down this man's throat. The result was, she was attacked by the owner's dog, and had the nerve to sue the homeowner in court. Well, her case was thrown out. I ask, *"Was she doing the Lord's work or her own work?"* To rephrase the question, *"Was she doing the work of God or the work of self?"*

5

Jesus adopted and loves you. Remember when you first met Jesus. You had zeal so great that you wanted to preach to everything that moved. You remember that do you not? I am taking this to heart because I see God talking to me in this scripture. We must be careful what motivates us in the service of God. Is it money, fame, praise, bravado, or love? What motivates you? Do the first works. Repent and fall in love with Jesus again. If not, He will remove His spirit from you.

"Remember therefore from whence thou art fallen, and repent, and do the first works; or else I will come unto thee quickly, and will remove thy candlestick out of his place, except thou repent." – Revelation 2:5

"But this thou hast, that thou hatest the deeds of the Nicolaitanes, which I also hate. He that hath an ear, let him hear what the Spirit saith unto the churches; to him that overcometh will I give to eat of the Tree of Life which is in the midst of the paradise of God." – Revelation 2:6-7

According to Bible Study tools.com, the Nicolaitanes were a religious sect that held the doctrine of Balaam. Though Jesus scolds the Church of Ephesus, he does commend them in verse six as – 'Hating the deeds of the Nicolaitanes'. In the Book of Numbers Chapters 22-24, Balak, a king of Moab sent for Balaam the Seer (prophet) to curse the Children of Israel. The Moabites hated the Children of Israel and seduced them into all sorts of idol worship. Balaam had personal motivations because he asked the Balak for a house filled with silver and gold. I see this religious activity in many high profile churches today. Some will charge thousands of dollars to go speak at church seminars. When did Jesus, Paul, Peter, or any other apostle ever preach for money? I am not saying do not give your tithes and offering to your church in the name of Christ. What I am saying is discern between those who preach for monetary gain.

The Balak and Balaam's plan to curse the Children of Israel did not come to fruition. God had other plans for Balaam and the Moabites. According to Numbers 24:1-9; Balaam blessed the Children of Israel. God's judgment came against Moab, and the Moabites were eventually wiped off the face of the earth as a nation.

Listen and understand what the Spirit of God is saying to you. To him that overcomes I will give the right to eat from the Tree of Life which is in the midst of the Paradise of God.

To the Church in Smyrna (Chapter 2:8–11)

"And unto the angel of the church in Smyrna write; these things saith the first and the last which was dead, and is alive." – Revelation 2:8

Unto the Pastor of the Church of Smyrna, I am before matter, space, energy, time, and reality. I am the Judge. I finalize all things. I died a natural and spiritual death, but I came back to life never to die again, ever. As the First and the Last, I possess power and authority to bring others back to life.

- First (Proton–Greek) Before anything created or designed
- Last (Eschatos–Greek) The one that make all things final
- Dead (Nekros–Greek) Natural death, Spiritual death
- Alive (Zao–Greek) Come back to life to exist eternal

"I know thy works, and tribulation, and poverty, (but thou art rich) and I know the blasphemy of them which say they are Jews, and are not, but are of the synagogue of Satan." – Revelation 2:9

The Synagogue of Satan is religion that pushes works of salvation. Jesus referred to these types of people as tares. Tares look, walk, and talk like Christians, but their actions, deeds and motives do not line up with the fruit of the Holy Spirit. It does not matter if you are a Jew or Gentile, because synagogue is synonymous with worship. A person is not a Jew outwardly, but inwardly. These are religious people that persecute those that uphold the truth of Jesus Christ in virtue. They believe they are the seed of faith, but in reality, they are the seed of Satan. Jesus knows those attending church who say they are believers, but are not. Jesus scolded the religious leaders in his day for this reason.

"Ye are of your father the devil, and the lusts of your father ye will do..." – Saint John 8:44

"And I will put enmity between thee and the woman, and between thy seed and her seed..." – Genesis 3:15

- Between thy seed or the seed of religion
- And her seed or seed of faith

Jesus complimented the Church of Smyrna for their service, tribulation, and poverty for His name sake. Faced with impoverishment, religious opposition, and persecution from the unbelieving Jews, some were sent to prison and others martyred. In the eyes of the world the brethren at Smyrna seemed like outcasts and materialistically poor, but in the eyes of God they were rich in faith. The Jewish leaders of that day who were in league with Rome were the main persecutors of Christians. What is interesting to me is Christ made a distinction between real Jews and fake Jews.

7

When we go back before the Law of Moses and the Hebrews, God called Abram (Abraham) from the land of Chaldea (Genesis 11:31). Abram turned away from the pagan gods of that land and made a choice to follow Yahweh. Abram's belief in God was counted to him as righteousness. The lineage of the Hebrew nation sprang from the seed of a man from a pagan land. It is not about heritage, the language you speak or the religion you are born into. It is our faith in Jesus that makes us real Jews. We are not natural Jews outwardly, but we are spiritual Jews inwardly (Romans 2:28-29).

"Fear none of those things which thou shalt suffer: behold, the devil shall cast some of you into prison, that ye may be tried; and ye shall have tribulation ten days; be thou faithful unto death, and I will give thee a crown of life. He that hath an ear, let him hear what the Spirit saith unto the churches; He that over cometh shall not be hurt of the second death." –
Revelation 2:10-11

Christ encourages all believers who may find themselves in this situation, not to be afraid of facing imprisonment, persecution, and possibly death for His name sake. Christ encourages us to be faithful unto death. Christ promises to reward those with an eternal crown of life. If you lose your life because you love Him, you will be resurrected back to life never to die again. Listen and understand what God is saying to you. Whoever overcomes and is faithful to the bitter end, God will save this person from eternal death.

To the Church in Pergamos (Chapter 2:12–17)

"And to the angel of the church in Pergamos write; These things saith he which hath the sharp sword with two edges; I know thy works, and where thou dwellest, even where Satan's seat is: and thou holdest fast my name, and hast not denied my faith, even in those days wherein Antipas was my faithful martyr, who was slain among you, where Satan dwelleth." –
Revelation 2:12-13

The sharp two-edge sword is the truth and word of God proceeding out of the mouth of Jesus Christ. This phrase *"Sharper than any two edge sword."* implies Christ's power to know the thoughts and intents of the heart (Hebrew 4:12).

I am aware of your struggle. I am also aware the devil has seated himself in Pergamos because it is a city of secularism and watered down religion. In the days when my faithful servant Antipas was alive, the congregation of Pergamos upheld my name even in a society pushing for quasi religion. I commend Antipas because he was martyred on my behalf.

"But I have a few things against thee because thou hast there them that hold the doctrine of Balaam, who taught Balak to cast a stumbling block

before the children of Israel, to eat things sacrificed unto idol, and to commit fornication." – Revelation 2:14

"So hast thou also them that hold the doctrine of the Nicolaitanes, which thing I hate. Repent, or else I will come unto thee quickly, and will fight against them with the sword of my mouth." – Revelation 2:15-16

But I have a few things against you because you allowed the doctrine of Balaam to infiltrate my Church. The doctrine of Truth and doctrine of Balaam cannot be combined. It was Balaam who taught Balak to cast a stumbling block before the Hebrews causing them to eat foods sacrificed to idols. No man can serve two masters. You are committing spiritual fornication. Just as the Nicolaitanes, you have allowed riches and money to motivate your actions. I really hate this!

Repent or I will come quickly and fight against them which hold this doctrine. Get your priorities straight. Turn away from this false belief or I will become your enemy.

"He that hath an ear, let him hear what the Spirit saith unto the churches; To him that over cometh will I give to eat of the hidden manna, and will give him a white stone, and in the stone a new name written, which no man knoweth saving he that receiveth it." – Revelation 2:17

Listen and understand what the Spirit of God is saying to you. Whosoever over-comes will I give spiritual bread no one knows about. I will also give that person a white stone. In that white stone will be a new name customized only for that individual.

'Over cometh' is a present participle that refers to unwavering faith, continuity, or continuous action. Hidden refers to something that has not been revealed yet. Manna refers to life giving bread which can only come from God. This white stone is something incredibly special. It will be a gift given to you by the person that created you. The person that created the trillion trillions stars in the billion billions galaxies wants to give you a white stone. I do not think it is going to be an ordinary stone. There are many white stones from jade, to jasper, to quartz, but more than likely it may be a quartz crystal. What I am about to say is not Bible, but I am going to give you one possible scenario on what I think this stone is.

The word 'New' or 'Kainos' in Greek denotes qualitative. Some American names have zero meaning. However, in the Old Testament names were full of meaning. Adam (Awdam) means ruddy man. Eve (Chavvah) means life giver. Moses (Mosheh) means draw out. Jacob (Yaagob) means heel catcher. In biblical times names (Onomas–Greek) meant identification by characteristics or purpose.

9

Back in the 1980s, B-bop crews were made up of rapper musicians, MCs, and break-dancers. They took on names that described their talents and abilities. For example, a group called the Fat Boys made crazy fresh sounds acappella called beat-boxing. MCs would blend several different sounds to make new music. Breaker dancers would perform special moves called poppin', lockin', and breakin'. Break dancers took on special names that described their dancing abilities. My breakin' name was Kosmoe.

I watch a television series titled 'The Flash'. This male goes by the name Barry Allen. He can move faster than the speed of sound and light. This television series introduce individuals that were affected by a particle accelerator device, endowing these superheroes or supervillains with supernatural abilities. They then take on a name that characterizes their special abilities.

Just like superhero shows we watch in the movies and on television, we will similarly have abilities in heaven. God is holding back a myriad of gifts and abilities from us because we are in these weak sinful bodies. Even after we are saved, we still battle the sin nature every day. It would be suicide to have our full abilities because these abilities would corrupt us absolutely. Rewards in heaven will not be given out until after we receive our glorified body. Then and only then will we know how to use our gifts properly.

From God's perspective making it into heaven is a big deal. When one sinner repents the angels in heaven rejoice. The gifts and rewards that will be given to us will just blow our minds. This special stone may endowed its owner with some type of ability. The other scenario is it may increase the owner's ability 10, 50, or 100 fold. If your ability in heaven is speed, strength or super hearing, this special stone will increase your ability 10, 50, or 100 fold. Imagine if your ability in heaven was wisdom, knowledge, or the ability to move a small moon. This stone is a big deal!

"And I will give unto thee the keys of the kingdom of heaven..." – Saint Matthew 16:19

Jesus promised to give us the keys to the Kingdom of Heaven. Heaven is the universe and these keys will unlock the mysteries of the universe. With our new-found gifts and life eternal, the universe will be our playground. Similar to the Witness Protection Program here on earth, we will be given a new life, a new identity, and a new name. Our new abilities and gifts will not be used for personal gain, but to serve Jesus Christ and God the Father throughout all eternity. The stone that Jesus will give to a person is an added bonus. How awesome is that? We do not have the slightest clue what awaits us on the other side.

"But as it is written, eye hath not seen, nor ear heard, neither have en-tered into the heart of man, the things which God hath prepared for them that love him." – I Corinthians 2:9

To the Church in Thyatira (Chapter 2:18–29)

"And unto the angel of the church in Thyatira write; These things saith the Son of God, who hath his eyes like unto a flame of fire, and his feet are like fine brass; I know thy works, and charity, and service, and faith, and thy patience, and thy works; and the last to be more than the first." – Revelation 2:18-19

Before Jesus gave the message to the pastor of the Church in Thyatira, he asserts the seriousness of the matter by confirming his status as 'Son of God', his Lordship, and his exalted state. Jesus commended this church for its labor of love, assertion of divine truths, endurance under negative circumstances, and continuous work in the ministry.

"Notwithstanding I have a few things against thee, because thou sufferest that woman Jezebel, which calleth herself a prophetess, to teach and to seduce my servants to commit fornication, and to eat things sacrificed unto idols. I gave her space to repent of her fornication; and she repented not." – Revelation 2:20-21

In First Kings Chapter 16, Ahab the King of Israel did much evil in God's sight, even marrying a Phoenician princess named Jezebel. She was literally the driving force of Ahab to do away with the worship of God, and to erect altars in Israel making way for Baal worship. Jezebel was a false accuser, idol worshiper, liar, gossiper, and maniacal sociopath that wanted praise as a prophetess instead of giving all praise to the God of heaven.

In Leviticus 18:21, 20:2-5, and First Kings 11:7, the Bible spoke of the pagan deity Molech (loosing associated with Baal the god of fertility). The nations of the world worshiped many pagan deities, but Molech and Baal required human sacrifices, which were strictly forbidden by God. These forbidden practices sprang from the Canaanites and were adopted by many other nations including the Ammonites and Phoenicians. It was Jezebel that re-introduced and brought these false teaching to the Israelites in the 9th Century BC.

Christ hated the false teachings of Baal worship. The Church of Thyatira allowed theses false teachings in the city without putting up a fight or even protesting against it. These false ideologies caused some servants of God to err from the truth and to commit spiritual fornication (worshiping God and pagan deities).

"Behold, I will cast her into a bed, and them that commit adultery with her into great tribulation, except they repent of their deeds." – Revelation 2:22

"And I will kill her children with death; and all the churches shall know that I am he which searcheth the reins and hearts; and I will give unto every one of you according to your works." – Revelation 2:23

Jezebel established her own religious prophets. She ushered in a cultural shift of serving other gods and eating foods sacrificed to idols. God in his love and mercy gave Jezebel years to see the error of her ways without even chastising her, but her wickedness increased, and she did not repent. For Jezebel and all who follow her ways and teachings, Jesus will cast on them grievous afflictions unless they repent. For all those that follow Jezebel, her ways, and teachings they will be killed with death; then the churches will understand that Jesus knows the innermost thoughts of the heart. God will pay every man and woman according to their works.

The devil is not original. In fact, he uses the same tactics against human beings over and over again. People think times have changed. Times have not changed. There is nothing new under the sun. All the deities of yesteryear are still here today, but wearing a different mask. Organ harvesting is the techno ritualistic human sacrifice to the pagan god Molech, and abortion is child sacrifice to the pagan god Baal. It is still not too late for our nation to repent.

"And if the people of the land do any ways hide their eyes from the man, when he giveth of his seed unto Molech, and kill him not: then I will set my face against the man, and against his family, and will cut him off, and all that go a whoring after him, to commit whoredom with Molech, from among their people." – Leviticus 20:4-5

"But unto you I say, and unto the rest in Thyatira, as many as have not this doctrine, and which have not known the depths of Satan, as they speak; I will put upon you none other burden. But that which ye have already hold fast till I come. And he that overcometh, and keepeth my works unto the end, to him will I give power over the nations:" – Revelation 2:24-26

To those in Thyatira that have not heard of these matters and do not know the shrewdness of the devil, I will bring none other burden on them. But hold fast that doctrine that you do have inside your hearts until I come. To the person that keeps my words until the bitter end, I will give that person power over the nations.

"And he shall rule them with a rod of iron; as the vessels of a potter shall they be broken to shivers: even as I received of my Father. And I will give

12

him the morning star. He that hath an ear; let him hear what the Spirit saith unto the churches." – Revelation 2:27-29

Jesus will rule the nations with a rod of iron in his millennial reign. As the vessel of a potter shall the nations be broken to shivers. Jesus is the Morning Star. He will share his throne with them that overcome. During Jesus' Millennial Reign he will make us mayors, governors, senators, ambassadors, cabinet members, dignitaries, princes, judges, and kings. Listen and understand what the Spirit of God is saying to you.

To the Church in Sardis (Chapter 3:1–6)

"And unto the angel of the church in Sardis write; these things saith he that hath the seven Spirits of God, and the seven stars; I know thy works, that thou hast a name that thou livest, and art dead. Be watchful, and strengthen the things which remain that are ready to die:" – Revelation 3:1-2

"For I have not found thy works perfect before God. Remember therefore how thou hast received and heard, and hold fast, and repent. If therefore thou shalt not watch, I will come on thee as a thief, and thou shalt not know what hour I will come upon thee." – Revelation 3:2-3

I know your works and your great reputation of being a living church, but you are dead as bones. You are in dire straits, because none of your works are worthy before God. Go back to the original message of God and remember, understand, and hold fast to it. Repent and wake up, for you do not know when I will come upon you as a thief in the night.

"Thou hast a few names even in Sardis which have not defiled their garments; and they shall walk with me in white: for they are worthy. He that overcometh, the same shall be clothed in white raiment. And I will not blot out his name out of the Book of life, but I will confess his name before my Father, and before his angels. He that hath an ear, let him hear what the Spirit saith unto the churches." – Revelation 3:4-6

Even in Sardis some have keep their dignity and not defiled themselves. These will walk with me, and I will make them pure. He that overcomes I will clothe with righteousness and will not blot out his or her name from the Book of Life. On the contrary, I will put in a good word for them before my Father and his Holy angels. Listen and understand what the Spirit of God is saying to you.

To the Church in Philadelphia (Chapter 3:7–13)

"And to the angel of the church in Philadelphia write; These things saith he that is holy, he that is true, he that hath the key of David, he that openeth and no man shutteth; and shutteth, and no man openeth; I know thy works: behold, I have set before thee an open door, and no man can shut it: for thou hast a little strength, and hast kept my word, and hast not denied my name." – Revelation 3:7-8

I am Holy and I cannot lie. I have the Key of David. I lock what no man can unlock and what I unlock no man can lock. I know your labors of ministry. I hold open a door before you that no man can shut. You have a little strength, yet with that little strength you have kept my word and not denied my name.

"Behold, I will make them of the synagogue of Satan, which say they are Jews, and are not, but do lie; behold, I will make them to come and worship before thy feet, and to know that I have loved thee.

Because thou hast kept the word of my patience, I also will keep thee from the hour of temptation, which shall come upon all the world, to try them that dwell upon the earth." – Revelation 3:9-10

Those religious liars who think they are devout Jews or Christians are of the synagogue of Satan. These will know that I love you. I will make these false believers come and worship before your feet. Because you held your ground and endured under negative circumstances, I will keep you from the Wrath of God.

"Behold, I come quickly: hold that fast which thou hast, that no man take thy crown. Him that overcometh will I make a pillar in the temple of my God, and he shall go no more out: and I will write upon him the name of my God, and the name of the city of my God, which is New Jerusalem, which cometh down out of heaven from my God: And I will write upon him my new name. He that hath an ear, let him hear what the Spirit saith unto the churches." – Revelation 3:11-13

Hold on to your faith. Do not allow anyone to stop you from entering heaven. Listen and understand what the Spirit of God is saying to you. Whoever overcomes I will make an upstanding child in God's house and give them a new name, and they will live with me forever in New Jerusalem.

To the Church of Laodicea (Chapter 3:11–22)

"And unto the angel of the church of the Laodiceans write; These things saith the Amen, the faithful and true witness, the beginning of the creation of God; I know thy works, that thou art neither cold nor hot: I would thou wast cold or hot. So then because thou art lukewarm, and neither cold nor hot, I will spew thee out of my mouth." – Revelation 3:14-16

I, who am the Trustworthy, True and Faithful witness, and the beginning of time; I know your lukewarm labors of ministry. It puts a bad taste in my mouth, so I will spit you out of my mouth.

14

"Because thou sayest, I am rich, and increased with goods, and have need of nothing; and knowest not that thou art wretched, and miserable, and poor and blind, and naked: I counsel thee to buy of me gold tried in the fire, that thou mayest be rich; and white raiment, that thou mayest be clothed, and that the shame of thy nakedness do not appear; and anoint thine eyes with eye salve, that thou mayest see." – Revelation 3:17-18

You say you are rich because you possess materialistic goods and need nothing, but spiritually before a Holy God you are wretched, miserable, poor, blind, and naked. Let me give you some good advice: Obtain my gold which is the purest, that you may be rich. Buy my clothes for they are righteousness.

Dress yourselves in white clothing to cover your shame and nakedness. Purchase my eye ointment so you will be able to see clearly.

"As many as I love, I rebuke and chasten: be zealous therefore, and repent. Behold, I stand at the door, and knock: if any man hear my voice, and open the door, I will come in to him, and will sup with him, and he with me." – Revelation 3:19-20.

"To him that overcometh will I grant to sit with me in my throne, even as I also overcame, and am set down with my Father in his throne. He that hath an ear, let him hear what the Spirit saith unto the Churches." – Revelation 3:21-22

I chastise and rebuke you not because I hate you, but on the contrary, it is because I love you. Be zealous and repent with great regret. See and understand my love for you. I am knocking on the door of your heart. If any man hear my voice and open his or her heart to me, I will reside there. It will just be us two as though we are having dinner together. To he or she that overcomes, I will allow that person to sit with me in my throne. Listen and understand what the Spirit of God is saying to you.

*"And they **overcame** him (the Devil) by the blood of the Lamb and by the word of their testimony; and they loved not their lives unto the death." – Revelation 12:11*

*"After this I looked, and, behold, a door was opened in heaven: and the first voice which I heard was **as it were** of a trumpet talking with me; which said, come up hither, and I will show thee things which must be hereafter." – Revelation 4:1*

The Exalted Throne (Chapter 4:1–11)

John looked up into the sky and saw a doorway open in heaven. A voice as a trumpet asked John to go up into heaven to be shown things that will happen in the future. 'As a trumpet' may represent a loud voice or a voice of authority. 'After this' – shows the Book of Revelation to be chronological.

"And immediately I was in the spirit: and, behold, a throne was set in heaven, and one sat on the throne." – Revelation 4:2

John did not go up into heaven physically because our sinful bodies are not allowed into heaven. Some believe this event in John's life symbolizes the Rapture of the Church. The Rapture is a bodily resurrection. John had a spiritual experience.

"For the Lord himself shall descend from heaven with a shout, with the voice of the arch angel, and the dead in Christ shall rise first: Then we which are alive and remain shall be caught up together with them in the clouds to meet the Lord in the air: and so shall we ever be with the Lord." – I Thessalonians 4:16-17

As you read Revelation 4:2, you do not see:

- Jesus descending from heaven into the clouds
- The voice of the arch angel
- All believers that die through the ages coming back to life
- Any meeting in the clouds
- No bodily resurrection

John did not ascend into heaven physically, but rather he ascended into heaven spiritually. Revelation 4:2 is the Holy Spirit summoning John's human spirit out of his physical body to go up into heaven to experience these mysteries. Human beings do not realize they have two bodies; a physical and a spiritual body.

- I was in the spirit = I was in my spirit body

This phenomenon is called bio-location. It means being in two places at one time. Your physical body is stationary, but your spirit body has the ability to travel outside your physical body to a different location. Believe it or not, some people have this ability. In John's case this ability was controlled by the power of God. I write about this phenomenon in my book entitled, *"The Bible and the Near Dear Experience"*, which is currently in revision.

16

Your physical body is made of physical material. Your spirit body is made of spiritual material. The dichotomy is the material from which each is derived, but a body is a body. Jesus mentioned we have two bodies.

"And fear not them which kill the body (physical body), but are not able to kill the soul: but rather fear him which is able to destroy both soul and body in hell." – Saint Mathew 10:28

When you die without Christ your physical body is still in the coffin while your soul goes to hell. Hell is a place within the earth's core. Even-though Hell has physicality it is a spiritual domain. Inference implies if your physical body is still in the coffin, then Jesus was referring to another body. If you were a fish, you would need fins, scales, and gills to exist in a freshwater or saltwater environment. If you were a worm, you would need a subterranean body to exist in that environment.

God is a spirit (Saint John 4:24), and he has a spirit body. Angels are spirits (Psalms 104:4) and they have a spirit body. Adam was created in God's image. That means we also have a spirit body. To live in the spiritual reality you need a spirit body.

John's physical body remained on the Island of Patmos while his spirit body traveled up into heaven. Because we have both a spiritual and a physical body we can interact in the spiritual and physical world simultaneously if God so chooses. This is how Adam and Eve were able to talk directly with God before the fall of humanity. So when you hear someone say unembodied spirit, there is no such thing. Some religions teach you cease to exist when you die. This is not true. God is eternal and mankind was created in his image. Thus, we are eternal beings. After we leave this world, we will continue to exist forever in some form or fashion. The spiritual body is eternal.

"Or ever the silver cord be loosed, or the golden bowl be broken, or the pitcher be broken at the fountain, or the wheel broken at the cistern. Then shall the dust return to the earth as it was: and the spirit (spirit body) shall return unto God who gave it." – Ecclesiastes 12:6-7

When John's human spirit ascended into heaven, he saw one being sitting on the throne. God's appearance was like jasper and sardine stone which is brilliant, beautifully colorful, and glossy. There was also an emerald colored rainbow encompassing the throne of God.

"And he that sat was to look upon like a jasper and a sardine stone: and there was a rainbow round about the throne, in sight like unto an emerald. And round about the throne were four and twenty seats: and upon the

seats I saw four and twenty elders sitting, clothed in white raiment: and they had on their heads crowns of gold." – Revelation 4:3-4

There are twenty-four seats and Twenty-Four Elders sitting on those seats dressed in white, each wearing a gold crown. The Bible does not give us any specifics about the Twenty-Four Elders. We can only speculate on what or who these beings are. I am not going to speculate, because I have not the slightest clue. I am not going to pretend that I know everything, because I do not. But what God reveals to me I will reveal to you. So let us move on.

Seven Spirits of God

"And out of the throne proceeded lightnings and thundering and voices: and there were seven lamps of fire burning before the throne, which are the seven Spirits of God." – Revelation 4:5

Multiple lightings, thunders, and voices emanated out of God's throne, and there are seven burning lamps of fire before God's throne. These lamps are symbolic of the Seven Spirits of God. To better understand the Seven Spirits of God, we could view them as the quantum of God. Isaiah 11:2 and Revelation 11:11 give us the Seven Spirits of God.

Spirit of the Lord (Spirit of Life)   **(Ruach)**
Anointed, endowed, or brought forth by God for his purpose

Spirit of Wisdom   **(Chokhmah)**
Foresight of knowledge, logic and good judgment

Spirit of Understanding   **(Binah)**
To grasp or comprehend the hidden secrets of God

Spirit of Counsel   **(Etsah)**
Render advice with a purpose and plan to benefit individuals, and to bring them into a closer relationship with God

Spirit of Might   **(Me'od) - (Chayil or Own)**
To vehemently exert spiritual force

Spirit of knowledge   **(Dha'ath)**
Foreknowledge, spiritual insight, intuition, discernment, acuity

Spirit of the Fear of the Lord   **(Yirah)**
A trembling awe of God mingled with reverence and respect

"And before the throne there was a sea of glass like unto crystal: and in the midst of the throne, and round about the throne, were four beasts full of eyes before and behind. And the first beast was like a lion, and the second beast like a calf, and the third beast had a face as a man, and the fourth beast was like a flying eagle. And the four beasts had each of them six wings about him; and they were full of eyes within: and they rest not day and night, say Holy, Holy, Holy Lord God Almighty, which was, and is, and is to come." – Revelation 4:6-8

Before you get to God's throne there is a sea of crystal glass and four beastly entities full of eyes all over their bodies. Each has six wings, and each was different in appearance. The first had the appearance of a lion. The second had the appearance of a calf. The third had the face as a man. The fourth was like a flying eagle. These four beasts are angelic in nature. It seems their main purpose is to exalt God with their chorus, "Holy, Holy, Holy, Lord God Almighty; the Omnipresent."

Seraphim have six wings, but based on God's creative power we must not assume these four beasts are seraphim. Just as there are different types of races, there are more than likely different types of angelic beings with six wings. Who and what these beings are would be pure speculation on my part. I am not going to speculate, because I have not the slightest clue. I am not going to pretend I know everything, because I do not. What God reveals to me I will reveal to you. I hope you see my point. God is so masterfully creative; we must not lock Him in a box and make assumptions. God tells us they are four beasts, so let us move on.

"And when those beasts give glory and honour and thanks to him that sat on the throne, who liveth forever and ever, the four and twenty elders fall down before him that sat on the throne, and worship him that liveth for ever and ever, and cast their crowns before the throne, saying, thou art worthy, O Lord, to receive glory and honor and power: for thou hast created all things, and for thy pleasure they are and were created." – Revelation 4:9-10

When the Four Beasts sang their chorus, the Council of the Twenty-Four Elders tosses their gold crowns from their heads and fall on their faces to worship the eternal God saying, *"You are the worthy one; glory and honor and power to your holy name. You do not need us, but you created all things for your good pleasure."*

The Book with Seven Seals (Chapter 5:1-14)

"And I saw in the right hand of him that sat on the throne a book written within and on the backside, sealed with seven seals. And I saw a strong angel proclaiming with a loud voice, who is worthy to open the book, and

19

to loose the seals thereof? And no man in heaven, nor in earth, neither under the earth was able to open the book, neither to look thereon." – Revelation 5:1-3

God had a book in his right hand. The book was sealed shut with seven seals. No man in heaven, earth, or hell could break the seven seals to open the book.

"And I wept much, because no man was found worthy to open and to read the book, neither to look thereon. And one of the elders saith unto me, Weep not: behold the Lion of the tribe of Juda, the Root of David, hath prevailed to open the book, and to loose the seven seals thereof." – Revelation 5:4-5

John was consumed by grief, because no man was able to break the Seven Sealed Book to reveal future events. One of the twenty-four elders told John not to worry because there was someone from the lineage of David powerful enough to break the seven seals.

"And I beheld, and, lo, in the midst of the throne and of the four beasts, and in the midst of the elders, stood a Lamb as it had been slain, having seven horns and seven eyes, which are the seven Spirits of God sent forth into all the earth." – Revelation 5:6

When John focused his attention where the Four Beasts and Twenty-Four Elders were, he saw standing in the center of the throne the Lamb of God with seven horns and seven eyes. The number seven in the Bible represents perfection or completion. A horn represents power or authority. The eyes of the Lamb represent all knowing and all seeing.

"And he came and took the book out of the right hand of him that sat upon the throne. And when he had taken the book, the four beasts and four and twenty elders fell down before the Lamb, having every one of them harps, and golden vials full of odors, which are the prayers of saints." – Revelation 5:7-8

"And they sung a new song, saying, Thou art worthy to take the book, and to open the seals thereof: for thou wast slain, and hast redeemed us to God by the blood out of every kindred and tongue, and people, and nation; and hast made us unto our God kings and priests: and we shall reign on the earth." – Revelation 5:9-10

When Jesus took the Seven Sealed Book from God, the Four Beasts and Twenty-Four Elders fell down in praise and worshiped Jesus with harps and vials of incense.

"And I beheld, and I heard the voice of many angels round about the throne and the beasts and the elders: and the number of them was ten thousand times ten thousand, and thousands of thousands; Saying with a loud voice, Worthy is the Lamb that was slain to receive power, and riches, and wisdom, and strength and honor and glory and blessing." – Revelation 5:11-12

Accompanied by the Four Beasts and Twenty Four Elders around God's throne was a great host of angels saying, "Worthy is the Lamb that was slain to receive power, and riches, and wisdom, and strength and honor and glory and blessing."

"And every creature which is in heaven, and on the earth, and under the earth, and such as are in the sea, and all that are in them, heard I saying, Blessing, and honor, and glory, and power, be unto him that sitteth upon the throne, and unto the Lamb forever and ever. And the four beasts said, Amen. And the four and twenty elders fell down and worshiped him that liveth forever and ever." – Revelation 5:13-14

John heard the voice of every creature in heaven, every creature on the earth, every creature in hell, and every creature in the sea say, "Blessing, and honor, and glory, and power, be unto him that sits upon the throne, and unto the Lamb forever and ever."

So let it be written, so let it be done.

Chapter Two
The Last Days

"But thou, O Daniel, shut up the words, and seal the book, even to the time of the end: many shall run to and fro, and knowledge shall be increased." – Daniel 12:4

The angel of the Lord revealed last day prophecies to Daniel the prophet (Daniel 10:14). Daniel was seeing events more than 2,500 years into the future. Daniel did not understand any of it. The last day prophecies were not meant for Daniel and his generation. The angel told Daniel to keep secret those things for now. The angel said last day prophecies would come to light with the last generation, and knowledge in the end times would increase.

'Knowledge shall be increased' is referring to technology. The time of the end would come when society would be technologically advanced. Today many people are in a rush to go nowhere. They are unaware society as they know it is coming to end.

The Seven Year Tribulation Period

Revelation Chapter 5:1 introduces the book with seven seals. Some Bible scholars teach each seal represents a one year period on earth, which is known as the seven year tribulation period. This idea is based on the belief seven sealed judgments in the Book of Revelation equates to seven years. This teaching is not biblical. Contrary to what is taught in most Christian churches as truth, the seven year tribulation period will not culminate within a seven year period. As a matter of fact Jesus never equated a seven year tribulation and seven prophetic years as being tantamount.

The seven years is based off of the Book of Daniel Chapter 9:24-27. God would be dealing with his people (Israelites) for seventy weeks. In reality each week represents one seven year period totaling 490 years. 483 years have already passed. There is one more prophetic week (seven year period) of Daniel remaining.

The seven year tribulation theology being preached to millions, and is the most accepted view regarding end time events. Christians accept views such as these because they are pounded into our heads, but no one bothers to check these things out. Just as some have accepted, we are living in the Church Age; some accept the seven year tribulation theory as well. The Church Age started with Moses. Yet, because everyone is jumping on the anecdotal bandwagon, then it must be correct doctrine. The Church Age is just a fancy phrase someone made up because it sounded good. The Church is throughout all ages.

"Unto him be glory in the church by Christ Jesus throughout all ages, world without end. Amen." – Ephesians 3:21

"This is that Moses, which said unto the children of Israel, A prophet shall the Lord your God raise up unto you of your brethren, like unto me; him shall ye hear. This is he, that was in the church in the wilderness with the angel which spake to him in the Mount Sinai..." – Acts 7:37-38

The last seven year period coincides with three main views based on when Jesus comes back to Rapture the Church. Although 'Rapture' is not in the Bible, teachers have coined it as such as a reference word to describe Jesus coming to gather all believers before God's wrath comes. The beliefs are: Pre-tribulation, Mid-tribulation, and Post-tribulation.

Pre-tribulationists believe the Church will be raptured bodily before the Great Tribulation begins. Those raptured will spend seven years in heaven eating grapes and drinking wine at the marriage supper of the Lamb.

Mid-tribulationist believes the Church will be raptured in heaven bodily half-way through the seven year tribulation period. Soon a man of great power and prominence will rise to power. The Bible refers to this man as the 'Beast' or 'Antichrist'. Antichrist will confirm a peace armistice with World Leaders for seven years (one prophetic week). At the mid-point or three and one-half years later Antichrist will break his promise and wreak havoc on the Israeli nation and declare himself as a deity. During this three and one-half year period Antichrist will wage war against Jews and Christians.

Post-tribulationist believe Christians will suffer throughout the entire seven year tribulation period and be raptured bodily after the seven years. When Jesus returns, they will be taken up to meet Jesus in the sky and immediately descend back to earth to rule and reign with Him a thousand years on earth.

After the **'Fall'**, Adam and Eve experienced tribulation when they were kicked out of the Garden of Eden. Joseph in the dungeons of Pharaoh experienced tribulation. Noah, during the one hundred twenty years building the ark, suffered tribulation through ridicule, sabotage, and terroristic threats. Lot was vexed from day to day in the land of Sodom and Gomorrah; experienced tribulation. John, who suffered in the dungeons of Herod Antipas, experienced tribulation. In the end John the Baptist lost his head.

The first century Christians who were fed to the lions for sport experienced tribulation. All around the world, at this very moment Christians are being killed for their belief in Jesus Christ. John's exile to the Island of Patmos was the only original apostle of Jesus that was not martyred; and they tried to boil him alive in oil. How we are different? We have the same eyes and ears as tribulation Christians. We have the same nose, feet, and toes as tribulation Christians. We have the same legs, arms, and hands as martyred Christians. I cannot tell you why we are so different. Do you know?

Whoever or whatever group of people conjured up this theory about seven seals and seven years is very imaginative. I do not know who made all this stuff up, but Jesus never said the tribulation would last seven years. Before we go any further, we must get the terminology correct. Jesus said there would be *"Great Tribulation"*. If anything, it should be called the seven year great tribulation period, but even that would not be correct. I have not read one single verse in the Book of Revelation that mentions a seven year tribulation period. Seven years of great tribulation? You also must leave room for God's wrath and not confuse one for the other. Some scholars have incorporated God's wrath into the great tribulation period and vice versa. The two are mutually exclusive.

Calculating a Jewish Month

The Jewish calendar is dynamic and does not change. Jewish holidays do not change even though their calendar operates on a lunisolar year. A lunar year (354 days) is about eleven days shorter than a solar year (365 days).

Every two to three years a leap year is added to the Hebrew calendar to sync solar and lunar years (lunisolar). Our Georgian calendar operates on a solar year. That is why Jewish holidays fall on different dates on our Georgian calendar every year. The Jewish leap year occurs seven times in a nineteen year cycle. The Jewish leap year begins with year 3, 6, 8, 11, 14, 17, 19, and will have thirteen months instead of twelve months.

Additionally, the Hebrew calendar still calculates about six minutes and thirty seconds longer every nineteen years. This means that every 216 years, one day must be subtracted from the Hebrew calendar. These are the three types of Hebrew years:

- Common Deficient 353 Days   *Leap Deficient 383 Days
- Common Regular 354 Days   *Leap Regular 384 Days
- Common Shlemah 355 Days   *Leap Shlemah 385 Days

A Hebrew year can range from 353 or 354 or 355 days, and a leap year can range from 383 or 384 or 385 days in a given year. To reiterate, this is done because the Jewish calendar is based on lunar years. An average Hebrew year is 360 days. Let us do the math.

To get the average Hebrew month we must add 353 + 354 + 355 + 383 + 384 + 385. This will give us a total of 2,214 days. We then divide 2,214 ÷ 6, giving us a total of 369 days in a twelve month period (369 ÷ 12 = 30.75; or 31 Hebrew days). But remember, over a period of **216** years the Hebrew calendar deviates ahead by **1** day. So we must subtract **1** day from **31** days, giving us an averaged **30** day Hebrew month.

The Jewish <u>Ecclesiastical</u> month is Nisan, but Jewish <u>Civil</u> month is Tishrei which normally occurs in September on Rosh Hashanah. The Jewish calendar is dynamic and does not change. Jewish holidays do not change even though their calendar operates on a lunisolar year.

- 30 Days × 12 Months = 360 Days (1 Hebrew Year)
- 360 Days × 7 Years = 2,520 Days or 7 Hebrew Years (1 Prophetic Week)
- 2,520 days = 7 years or 84 months (1 Prophetic week)

There are 42 Jewish months in a 3½ year period. 30 days × 42 Jewish months will get the total number of days in a 3½ year period, which 1,260 days. If the great tribulation period is going to be a seven year period, the number of days would be 2,520. Even if you wanted to call the last prophetic week seven years, it is not seven years. This period of time is measured in Jewish months or days, not years.

An average Hebrew month is 30 days. Seven Hebrew years is 84 months; 84×30 = 2,520 days. On our Georgian calendar there are 365.25 days in a year. When we multiply seven Georgian years (7 × 365.25 days), we get 2,557 days; not 2,520 days. By doing simple math, we understand the **'seven year'** tribulation theory is not actually seven years. 2,520 days equals 6 years, 10 months, and 25 days.

Now that I have disproven the fallacy of the seven year tribulation logically, I will disprove the fallacy of the seven year tribulation mathematically. To be precise and not to throw off the eschatological timeline, calculations in Revelation must be based on Hebrew days, because Hebrew calendar days overlap on our Georgian calendar. However, for arguments' sake, I will use seven years or three and one-half years whenever applicable.

"And he shall confirm the covenant with many for one week: and in the midst of the week he shall cause the sacrifice and the oblation to cease, and for the over spreading of abominations he shall make it desolate..." – Daniel 9:27

- Confirm the covenant or confirm the global peace armistice

25

- One prophetic week = 7 years or 2,520 Days
- In the midst of the covenant week is 3½ years later
- Sacrifice and oblation to cease means the Antichrist will desecrate the Jewish Temple
- Over spreading of abominations means Antichrist will setup idols in the Jewish Temple

According to Jesus, the Seventieth Week of Daniel starts with the desolation of Jerusalem and the Jewish temple three and one-half years after the global peace armistice is signed into legislation. If 3½ years have already passed, only 3½ years remain. How can the remaining 3½ years be 7 years of great tribulation? You cannot get seven years out of three and one-half years if it is only three and one-half years left. I do not want to sound condescending or offensive, but this is basic math. The remaining half of the peace armistice is actually the first half of Daniel's Seventieth Week. Thus, there is a gap in the last and final week of Daniel. In other words, there are two 3½ year periods that completes the Seventieth Week of Daniel.

The entire seven year peace armistice is not the Seventieth Week of Daniel, but does incorporate the latter half of it. Teachers are mistakenly starting Daniel's last prophetic week at the beginning of the seven year global peace armistice, when it should start three and one-half years after the global peace armistice is ratified. We must view the seven year peace armistice as a reference point or gauge for when the Abomination of Desolation would occur, how long it would last, and when the Rapture will take place. It is only mere happen-stance the seven year peace armistice will be set for a seven-year period. The seven year tribulation theory is predicated on this error. Daniel Chapter 9:27 clearly states, in the middle or halfway through a seven year period of a peace armistice the Abomination of Desolation would occur. If the entire seven year global peace armistice is Daniel's last **prophetic week**, the scripture would read like this:

*"And he shall confirm the covenant with many for one week: in the **beginning of that week** he shall cause the sacrifice and oblation to cease..."* – Daniel 9:27

If this were the case, the length of time would be seven years or 2,520 days or 84 months. If the sacrifice and oblation ceased in the beginning of that **seven year period,** the seven year tribulation teaching would be solid theology. Jesus also said the Abomination of Desolation is the Great Tribulation Period: *"When ye therefore shall see the **abomination of desolation,** spoken of by Daniel the prophet, stand in the holy place...Then let them which be in Judea flee into the mountains: Let him which is on the housetop not come down to take anything out of his house:"*

26

"Neither let him which is in the field return back to take his clothes. And woe unto them that are with child, and to them that give suck in those days! But pray ye that your flight be not in the winter, neither on the sabbath day; for then shall be **great tribulation***..." – Saint Matthew 24:15-21*

Revelation Chapter 12:6 confirms how long the Abomination of Desolation will last. The Abomination of Desolation is to the Jew what the Great Tribulation will be to the Christian. Great means global. At the time of the Abomination of Desolation it will be global tribulation for both Jews and Christians. Revelation 12:6 and 13:4-5 tells us how long Antichrist will rule during the Abomination and Great Tribulation Period.

The woman (which is symbolic) is fleeing into the wilderness to escape the wrath of Antichrist. As you can see, the scripture is quite clear the Abomination of Desolation **(Great Tribulation Period)** will only last for 3½ years or 1,260 days.

"And the woman fled into the wilderness, where she hath a place prepared of God that they should feed her there <u>a thousand two hundred and three-score days</u>." – Revelation 12:6

- A Thousand = 1,000 Days
- Two Hundred = 200 Days
- A Score = 20 × 3 = 60 Days

1,260 Days or 42 months or 3½ Years

"And they worshiped the dragon which gave power unto the beast: and they worshiped the beast, saying, who is like unto the beast? Who is able to make war with him? And there was given unto him a mouth speaking great things and blasphemies; and power was given unto him to continue forty and two months." – Revelation 13:4-5

Because seven years of tribulation is constantly pounded into our heads, over and over again, misinterpretation of the Daniel 9:27 passage is being taught incorrectly. This seven year misconception is just **bad theology**.

The devil knows repeated repetition is the key to brainwashing human beings. The person begins to believe that it is true even though they know it is not true. For example, a mother constantly tells her son that he will never amount to anything. Her child grows up and does not amount to anything. Another example is when law enforcement interrogators force the issue of a person's guilt without forensic evidence or witness identification at a crime scene. After four to six hours into the interrogation the person will falsely believe in and confess to a crime they know they did not commit.

These are the same tactics cult leaders employ. No one is immune to repetition. We must daily check our thoughts to make sure we do not come under its' spell. Because some teachers are mistakenly starting the Seventieth Week of Daniel at the beginning of the seven year global peace armistice and pounding it into our skulls, it is throwing off other eschatological events. I was so confused about when the Rapture would occur, the timing of the Marriage Supper of the Lamb, when God's wrath would occur, and how many resurrections there are. I once believed this false teaching, and it thoroughly confused me about other end time events. And it all goes back to that infamous seven year pre-tribulation teaching.

I was completely wrong in my interpretations of all end time events because of my misconceptions due to pre-tribulation theology. Then I asked myself, "How can all these end time events take place in seven short years? Something is not right!" When I stopped listening to all those end time preachers I began to pray earnestly and search the scriptures for myself. I began my studies in the Gospel of Saint Matthew to listen to what Jesus said regarding the last days.

"And as he sat upon the Mount of Olives, the disciples came unto him privately, saying; tell us, when shall these things be? And what shall be the sign of thy coming, and the end of the world?" – Saint Matthew 24:3

Jesus' disciples asked him three questions: What will spark the beginning of the end of the world? What will be the sign to let us know that you will come back a second time? When will this dispensation end?

What sparks the beginning of the end of the world?

"...Take heed that no man deceive you. For many shall come in my name, saying, I am Christ; and shall deceive many. And ye shall hear of wars and rumors of wars: see that ye be not troubled..." – Saint Matthew 24:4-6

"...For nation shall rise against nation, and kingdom against kingdom: and there shall be famines, and pestilences, and earthquakes, in divers' places. All these are the beginning of sorrows." – Saint Matthew 24:7-8

What will be the sign of your second coming?

"Then shall they deliver you up to be afflicted, and shall kill you: and ye shall be hated of all nations for my name's sake. And then shall many be offended, and shall betray one another, and shall hate one another. And many false prophets shall rise, and shall deceive many."

"And because iniquity shall abound, the love of many shall wax cold. But he that shall endure unto the end, the same shall be saved." – Saint Matthew 24:12-13

28

"And this gospel of the kingdom shall be preached in the entire world for a witness unto all nations; and then shall the end come. When ye therefore shall see the abomination of desolation, spoken by Daniel the prophet, stand in the holy place, (whoso readeth, let him understand.)..."

*"For then shall be **great tribulation**, such as was not since the beginning of the world to this time, no, nor ever shall be..." – Saint Matthew 24:14-21*

"Immediately after the tribulation of those days shall the sun be darkened, and the moon shall not give her light, and the stars shall fall from heaven, and the powers of the heavens shall be shaken: And then shall appear the sign of the Son of man in heaven." – Saint Matthew 24:29

"...and then shall all the tribes of the earth mourn, and they shall see the Son of Man coming in the clouds of heaven with power and great glory. And he shall send his angels with a great sound of a trumpet, and they shall gather together his elect from the four winds, from one end of heaven to the other." – Saint Matthew 24:29-31

When will this dispensation end?

"Now learn a parable of the fig tree; when his branch is yet tender, and putteth forth leaves, ye know that summer is nigh: So likewise ye, when ye shall see all these things, know that it is near even at the doors. Verily I say unto you, this generation (last future generation) shall not pass, till all these things be fulfilled." – Saint Matthew 24:32-34

Today we are amid global deception. False prophets, false doctrine and propaganda are part of everyday life. Wars, pestilences, famines, and earthquakes will intensify as we come closer to the end of the world. Before the world ends things will get much worse. Jesus never incorporated or equated God's wrath into the great tribulation period or the great tribulation period into the first Four Seal Judgments. Common teachings I have heard say all these events will happen in seven years culminating with the opening of seven seals. All these end-time events are separate. Jesus said end-time events would occur in stages, not in seven years. These stages are:

- Beginning Of Sorrows
- Great Tribulation Period
- The Rapture
- The End of our Era

Jesus specifically said there would be a period called the beginning of sorrows before the great tribulation period and before the Rapture.

The period known as the 'Beginning of Sorrows' will occur first. The Great Tribulation will occur second. The Rapture will occur third. And the end shall come with the return of Jesus Christ at his Second Coming. Many people are confused because they are not following the chronology of Saint Matthew 24:1-44. Stop believing these false teachings and believe what Jesus taught. Jesus means what He says and says what He means.

Many Christians are taught to look for the Rapture as the next event on the prophetic timeline. When the Rapture does not occur and the Saints are hurled into the great tribulation period, many will be seeking for answers. Many false predictors of Jesus' return and the end-times will once again lead many astray, probably to their demise. These false prophets will say Jesus will come back on a Monday and appear at Times Square, or Jesus will come back on a Friday and appear in the desert, and so on and so forth.

"Wherefore if they shall say unto you, Behold, he is in the desert; go not forth: behold, he is in the secret chambers; believe it not." – Saint Matthew 24:26

When the Rapture occurs believers will meet Jesus in the clouds and be taken into heaven during God's wrath. We will not immediately return to Earth. This is why post-tribulation is also false doctrine. After the Great Tribulation occurs, God's wrath will fall on all mankind. After the wrath of God is completed, the Elect will eventually return to earth with Jesus. I just want to say the correct view is mid-tribulationism. Even though mid-tribulationists have been duped by this seven year time frame, technically they are correct in the longevity of three and one-half years. The proper terminology to use is one thousand two hundred sixty (1,260) days of great tribulation.

Numbers do not lie or make mistakes, people do. Even though common sense, logic, math, and the Bible all agree the great tribulation period will last three and one-half years, many may still refuse to believe God's Word. People will believe a lie before they believe in the truth. I am no respecter of persons when it comes to God's Word. I am just giving you the truth. I do not base theology on hearsay. If the Bible states the great tribulation period will last for 1,260 days or 3½ years, then that is what it means. **#Either Believe the Bible or Don't.**

Jesus revealed to his disciples the last seven years of Daniel's prophecy is just a small portion of end time events. It is being preached as seven years, but it should be preached as end-times. When I omitted this fallible pretribulation teaching, the Book of Revelation began to make a lot of sense, and all the other eschatological events began falling into place.

If you are learning or teaching is built on this seven year theology, you are building your theology on sinking sand. Forgive my bluntness, but there is no way around sound doctrine. If the seven year tribulation theology does not fit, you must omit.

The Falling Away

There have been many stages throughout biblical history. Currently, we are in the Age of Grace, but also of great deception. The 'Falling Away' is the moral decline of humanity similar to Noah's time, and the infiltration of false prophets with their false doctrines, and cultural apostasy.

"This know also, that in the last days perilous times shall come. For men shall be lovers of their own selves, covetous, boasters, proud, blasphemers, disobedient to parents, unthankful, unholy, without natural affection, trucebreakers, false accusers, incontinent, fierce, despisers of those that are good, traitors, heady, high-minded, lovers of pleasures more than

lovers of God; Having a form of godliness, but denying the power thereof: from such turn away." – 2 Timothy 3:1-5

- Perilous – Full of danger. Unsafe. Treacherous
- Men will be lovers of themselves – Self Importance, Selfish, Self-Absorbed
- Covetous – Having or showing great desire to possess something or someone, especially if it belongs to someone else
- Boasters – Talk with excessive pride and self-satisfaction about one's abilities, achievements, possessions, whether real or imagined, while showing contempt for others
- Proud – People that show themselves over others. A high opinion of oneself
- Blasphemer – Slander or false witness especially against God
- Disobedient to Parents (Authority) - Refusing to respect the rules of authority
- Unthankful - Unwilling to show gratitude or appreciation
- Unholy - Wicked, Irreverent, Godless, Impious
- Without natural affection – Without brotherly love; No respect for anyone
- Trucebreakers – Irreconcilable attitude. Unforgiving. One who refuses to listen to terms of reconciliation; One who violates a covenant or agreement
- False accuser – To slander with the intent to wound
- Incontinent – Without self-control
- Fierce – Intense, Cruel, Violent, or Aggressive

- Despisers of those that are good – Hate others for doing the right thing
- Traitors –A backstabber
- Heady – Rash. Decisions made without considering consequences
- Lovers of pleasures more than lovers of God
- Having a form of godliness – Appear to be religious.
- Deny the Power – Contradict or reject the Word of Truth

Jesus warns us to watch for the signs of the end-times so we can prepare ourselves physically, emotionally, psychologically, and spiritually. People are running to and fro absorbed in the now, not discerning the times. Those who live haphazardly are ignoring the signs right in front of their eyes.

"Now the works of the flesh are manifest, which are these; adultery, fornication, uncleanness, lasciviousness, idolatry, witchcraft, hatred, variance, emulations, wrath, strife, seditions, heresies, envyings, murders, drunkenness, revellings..." – Galatians 5:19-21

- Adultery – Extramarital sexual relations
- Fornication – Sex out of marriage with multiple partners
- Uncleanness – Filthy, Dirty
- Lasciviousness – Uncontrolled sexual behavior. Reckless sexual pleasures
- Idolatry – Worshiping everything but God
- Witchcraft – The art of divination or control over other people
- Hatred – Intense dislike or ill will
- Variance – Contention, Debate, Strife, Drama
- Emulation – Desire to match or surpass others to make oneself standout
- Wrath – Outburst of anger
- Strife – Bitter disagreement over fundamental issues
- Seditions – Inciting rebellion
- Heresies – Belief in one's own religious opinion
- Envying – Desire to have something belonging to someone else. Jealousy
- Murder – Killing without cause. Includes to harm emotionally, mentally, or physically
- Drunkenness – Under the influence of any substance
- Revel-lings – Great pleasure from riotous living

This sounds like some of our favorite movies and television series. What is scary about Second Timothy 3:1-5 and Galatians 5:19-21, is I see many of these behaviors from Christians. We are constantly bombarded with these attitudes 24/7. Exposure to these types of attitudes will only desensitize us to corrupt morals. This strategy by the 'Powers that be' is, 'The Conditioning'. This influence does not discriminate, even hooking its' claws into the Church. We must not be conformed to the world and its' ways, but be transformed by the daily renewing of our minds in God's Word.

I have heard some ministers preach sermons without any biblical fortitude or spiritual meat: yet have its members in an uproar. They make their congregations feel good by telling them what they want to hear. They pick, choose, and incorporate folklore and fables into God's Word. They put and pull God out of their pocket at their leisure, and profit off the stupidity and gullibility of their members. Across the spectrums of religions many view their gods as an impersonal 'it', like a genie in a magic bottle waiting to be summoned to fulfill their desires. Herein is the problem with watered down Christianity.

There are many great pastors out there, but some congregations do not want the truth. They only pick and choose from the scriptures to condone their lifestyle. If the pastor speaks out against these sins, that pastor is fired. These Christians want things easy and convenient. The only time they open their Bible is when they attend church. They would rather have a seared conscience and hide their sin because these types of Christians want to live life their way.

"Now the Spirit speaketh expressly, that in the latter times some shall depart from the faith, giving heed to seducing spirits, and doctrines of devils; speaking lies in hypocrisy; having their conscience seared with a hot iron." – I Timothy 4:1-2

Some Christians like to play judge, jury, and executioner Old Testament style. People love the power and control they have over others. They look at your faults, exalt themselves above you, judge you, and condemn you, but become angry when you tell them the truth about themselves. Those who have the god-complex serve themselves when it is convenient because it is much easier to have a form of godliness. These people have itching ears, wanting only the good parts of the Christian life. People do not want the truth because they do not want to be told what to do. They do not want to be told what to do because they do not want their sins exposed. Sound doctrine exposes the truth.

"For the time will come when they will not endure sound doctrine; but after their own lusts shall they heap to themselves teachers having itching ears. And they shall turn away their ears from the truth, and shall be turned unto fables." – 2 Timothy 4:3 & 4

The god complex has deceived many people within the Church. They want to take the good convenient parts of God like blessing, wealth, health, comfort, etc., and ignore the ugly (I use the term loosely) parts of the Christian life, such as obedience, self-denial, sacrifice, and suffering. Believe it or not, the ugly parts of the Christian life help you grow. There is a popular saying; *"Whatever does not kill you will only make you stronger."* Jesus said as long as you live on earth you will have good days and you will have bad days, regardless of your religious status.

One can go to a church for one hundred years, get baptized every week, and even confess their love for Jesus, but these actions alone will not save a person. If doing works alone does not save a person, then what does? In Romans 10:9 Paul said, *"If you confess with your mouth and believe in your heart that God raised Jesus from the dead you will be saved."*

My fellow coworker is frustrated with the direction society is headed. He talks about how the world is coming to an end. I told him he could see what many people could not see. I told him he was not far from the kingdom of heaven and he needed the Bible to explain to him what he is seeing. My hope is he will understand that God is angry with this world and will soon judge this world. I told him he did not have to be a Jesus fanatic like me, but it is important to know what is in the Bible. If my fellow coworker responds correctly the next words spoken out of his mouth should be, *"God what do you want me to do?"*

Jesus, Servant of Man and Servant of God, is equal with and perfect with God, yet he said, *"Not my will, but thy will be done." (KJV – Saint Luke 22:42).* Being a Christian comes down to one crucial decision; *"God, what do you want me to do?"* I often ask myself, *"What would Jesus do?"* If Jesus did not say it, pray it, preach it, or do it, then you should not do it, say it, pray it, or preach it. Jesus is the epitome of our righteousness. Jesus told us he can only do what he sees the Father do. Likewise, we must follow suit. I can only do what I see Jesus do. If you follow this guideline, you will never go wrong.

Have you noticed in many religions, the gods require a sacrifice? Father God also requires a sacrifice. In the Old Testament it was lambs, goats, rams, and doves. In the New Testament we must give what Jesus gave. Jesus sacrificed his life. God does not want your religious sacrifices. God wants you. ALL OF YOU! Love God more than you love yourself; treat people as you want to be treated even if they are not treating you fairly. Be obedient even when it hurts. Be obedient even unto death and Jesus will give you eternal life. This decision may sound simple, but believe me, it is not. This is why carnal Christians fake it.

You must choose to obey God, and you must choose to deny yourself. Carnal Christians recreate God in their own image and bring Jesus down to their level (Romans 10:6). This is a grave error.

It is not easy being a Christian. If someone spat on and slapped you, could you honestly react in a Christ like manner? It is not enough to go to church and confess Jesus. It is not enough to be spiritual. You must live the life. If you talk the talk, you must walk the walk. It is about your love for God and your personal intimate relationship with Jesus Christ. If you love God, you will keep his commandments all the time, not when it is convenient.

There are times when we do not understand our trials and sufferings, but we must love God in the good, bad, and ugly times. Christians are bought with the highest price which is the shed blood of Jesus Christ. We no longer own ourselves. We are owned by Jesus, and we no longer have any rights to exercise our own will. We must operate in the will of Christ by following the Holy Spirit. An attitude of genuine sorrow and regret will lead you to genuine repentance and transform your mind to think like the mind of Christ. Believe me, it is not all peaches and cream. The truth hurts. It is not easy living the life of a true Christian, but the truth will set you free.

False Teachers

"Beware of false prophets, which come to you in sheep's clothing, but inwardly they are ravening wolves. Ye shall know them by their fruits. Do men gather grapes of thorns, or figs of thistles? Even so every good tree bringeth forth good fruit; but a corrupt tree bringeth forth evil fruit. A good tree cannot bring forth evil fruit; neither can a corrupt tree bring forth good fruit." – Saint Matthew 7:15-18

In 1844, William Miller prophesied Jesus would return October 22, 1844. The Rapture never occurred. October 22, 1844, is known as *"The Great Disappointment"*.

David Koresh – Leader of the Branch Davidian sect prophesied end time events. According to the ATF, Koresh and his members were storing up illegal firearms and explosives. On April 19, 1993, the Branch Davidian group was confronted by ATF authorities. The siege lasted almost two months.

According to news reports the Branch Davidian compound was set on fire by one of its members. When it was all over, David Koresh and 79 other people die in the fire.

Marshall Applewhite – In 1972 Marshall received a spiritual awakening and claimed he had a vision that explained mankind's purpose and destiny. Marshall soon meets a woman named Bonnie who was moderately involved in occult practices. She convinces Marshall they are the two witnesses of Revelation 11. With mixed theology of Christianity, astrology, science fiction and new age mysticism, Marshall and Bonnie began preaching their gospel to all who would hear their message. In the late 1970's the Heaven's Gate movement was launched by Marshall Applewhite and Bonnie Nettles. The core belief of this movement was aliens would come to rapture them and take them away in their UFO to the after-life. In this new existence they would become aliens themselves.

In 1985 Bonnie passed away, leaving Marshall to carry on the work. He told his followers Bonnie was not dead, but only shed her physical form. In meetings, Marshall would set an extra chair for Bonnie and would receive messages from her and relay them to his followers. Marshall made several alien rapture predictions that did not come true. Finally, Marshall hears from Bonnie again. She tells him all the members of Heaven's Gate must be as she is to achieve the blessed state. Afterwards, the alien rapture would occur.

Marshall shares this information with his followers and convinces them the aliens would not come to retrieve them unless they freed themselves of their physical bodies. Marshall explained the physical body was useless, the aliens needed the soul. Marshall went on to say the aliens would one day give them a prophetic sign from heaven to let him and his followers know that he was speaking the truth.

In early 1996, Marshall relocated his community to a rented mansion in Rancho Santa Fe. In the fall of 1996, Marshall is looking through his telescope and discovers the prophetic sign in the heavens. He knew the extra-terrestrials would come in their spaceship in the form of a comet called Hale-Bopp. On March 26, 1997, a former member visiting the mansion discovered the dead bodies of all 39 members of Heaven's Gate.

Jim Jones – Was a loner growing up. Around the age of sixteen Jones began preaching against racism. In 1955 Jones established the Peoples Temple of the Disciples of Christ. In the mid 1960's Jones and about 150 followers relocated to northern California.

In the next several years the racially mixed congregation swelled to about 450 in membership. Jones quickly created the religious teaching that all a person's earnings must be laid at the apostle's feet. People would give their entire paychecks or sell their home to become a part of this growing religious movement.

To achieve complete control over his members, Jones enforced rules of celibacy. He forbade secret conversations between any two people. If people did not obey his every command, he would inflict a beating with the lash. Jones commanded all members of the Peoples Temple of the Disciples of Christ to call him dad. It was rumored that Jones was a sex offender, sex abuser, drug addict and con-artist.

In 1977 Jones proclaims he is a prophet, and commands total loyalty from all his followers. He gives the congregation Kool-Aid. After everyone drinks, Jones tells them they have just drunk poison, and they would be dead very soon. After several gasps and worries the congregation became silent accepting their fate. Jones then says the Kool-Aid was not poisoned, and that he was just testing their faith and loyalty to him. Jones said everyone passed the test.

As the Peoples Temple of the Disciples of Christ grew, rumors and accusations by ex-members reached the Press. In 1977 Jones decided it was time to go. He commanded all his followers to move to his compound in Jonestown, Guyana. When members arrived, Jones confiscated their passports and money. There were no phones, internet, and no way to contact the outside world. Jones now had total control over his flock.

In 1978 calls from concerned family members flooded the office of Congressman Leo Ryan. Jones is alerted that Congressman Ryan and a small delegation would be paying him a visit. Jones preps all his members on how they should respond once the delegation arrives. When the Congressman arrives things seem to go well. Later someone slipped one of Ryan's Aides a 'Help Me!' note. When Congressman Ryan confronted Jones, he claimed the note was all a lie. Jones felt Congressman Ryan and his delegation should leave.

The next day Congressman Ryan, his delegation, and a hand-full of defectors were confronted at the airstrip. Bullets rang out killing four and injuring others. Congressman Ryan would lose his life on this day. Jones knew that it was no turning back. He would force his flock to drink the poisoned Kool-Aid or shoot them. The kids drank the Kool-Aid first, loyal members drank the Kool-Aid second, and those that tried to escape were shot; others committed suicide. When it was all over, around 900 people were dead, and only 15 escaped. Jones took the easy way out by putting a bullet in his head.

"Little children, it is the last time: and as ye have heard that antichrist shall come, even now are there many antichrists; whereby we know that it is the last time." – I John 2:18

Many prominent Christian leaders spoke on behalf of God in favor of President Trump being re-elected. Trump lost the election.

Trust and believe the United States Presidential Election was the last thing on God's mind. God has other pressing matters to attend to. Teaching, preaching, or prophesying on God's behalf is a serious matter. In the Old Testament falsely prophesying in God's name would bring that individual a death sentence.

Today false prophecies are spewed as if God's Word is a game. It is not a game! Jones and others is why First John Chapter 4:1 tells us not to believe every teacher or preacher, but to compare their message against what the Bible says. To do this, one must study the Bible for accurate comparison. It is the only way to be sure.

Just because a man or a woman is preaching from the pulpit, it does not mean they know what they are talking about (First Timothy 1:7). Frankly speaking, they may not know God at all. Demons are not just stationed in the pits of hell; they are also stationed in the pulpits. Here are some warning signs that I have picked up over the years to identify a false teacher of God's word –

- God gave me a new revelation
- If the prophecy does not come true
- A minister that constantly sees visions
- God gave me another dream last night
- Always puts him or herself on a pedestal
- Teachers that constantly add and take away from scripture
- A minister that constantly speaks in tongues without an interpreter
- I feel, I believe, this is what I think, this could possibly mean, Jesus said this but…
- If the minister speaks out of both sides of his/her mouth. Preaching one thing, but doing another
- When a teacher constantly reassures that he or she is a prophet, or some great leader called by God.

False teachers exist because of their pride. These are simply set in their ways. You cannot tell false teachers anything, suggest anything or teach them anything because they are God's chosen and you are not. You will know when their doctrine is suspect when they use these phrases:

- I believe what this is saying is…
- This is the only reasonable explanation because…
- Many people believe as I do…

- It must happen this way because…
- That is just symbolic

"…Take heed that no man deceive you. For many shall come in my name, saying, I am Christ; and shall deceive many." – Saint Matthew 24:4-5

- Come in my name, means people will represent Christ
- Saying I am Christ, means people will replace Christ
- Shall deceive many, means people will lead many away from Christ

Jesus is not saying that many people will say they are Jesus; though some make that claim. Jesus is saying in these last days many false teachers of the Bible will come saying they represent Jesus, but will deceive many. The mantra is: You do not have to listen to Jesus anymore, because Jesus speaks through me. I have a special relationship with Jesus. And what I have to say is particularly important.

These capture the hearts and minds with the word of God, but twist, manipulate, and change the word of God to suit their own agenda, thus leading people away from Christ. False teachers set themselves up as being equal with Jesus and mediate as a go-between Church folk and God. They become your god, but give you the illusion that you are following Christ. They create another gospel as a go between as though more alternatives are available. Jesus made it very clear there are only two masters; God or the things of this world (idols). You can only serve one or the other (Saint Matthew 6:24), but false teachers say you can have your cake and eat it too. In other words you can make your own rules and serve God too. That is why false doctrine is so appealing.

God is perfect, is He not? God's Word is perfect, is it not? Jesus told us to be perfect even as the Father is perfect. So why are these false teachers twisting God's perfect Word? They set themselves up as demigods to manipulate and control their congregation at their will. The God of the Bible gives us free will to accept or reject him. False teachers think everyone should obey them but the God of the Bible gives you choice to obey or reject him. False teachers set themselves on a pedestal, but Jesus was humble. The God of the Bible was falsely accused, mocked, spit on, abused, hated, and finally killed. These false teachers are confusing the God of the Bible with the god of this world.

Christians are fooled time and again by these Charlatans who come in the name of Jesus, but will eventually lead them onto the road of destruction with their doctrine of devils. I should know. At one point in my life a minster of the devil had me thoroughly convinced I was serving God until I had a negative near death experience. In his love and mercy, Jesus gave me a second chance.

"Enter ye in at the strait gate: for wide is the gate, and broad is the way, that leadeth to destruction (Hell), and many there be which go in there at: because strait is the gate, and narrow is the way, which leadeth unto life (heaven) and few there be that find it. Beware of false prophets, which come to you in sheep's clothing, but inwardly they are ravening wolves..."
– Saint Matthew 7:13-15

When Satan tempted Jesus in the wilderness, he was not using scare tactics or blackmail. Satan was using scriptures to attack Jesus. Let me say that again! Satan was using scriptures to attack Jesus! The devil manipulated and twisted scriptures to try to convince Jesus to follow his own path. The devil was trying to convince Jesus that he could be the King now, overthrow the Romans now, and take the nation of Israel to glory now. And the best part of the deal was Jesus would not have to suffer the cross of Calvary. What a deal! This is the prosperity gospel: You can have it all, now! All these feel good gospels convince many to follow their own gospel of gratification, and have made many believers soft as cupcakes. Christians must be led by the Holy Spirit. The doctrine of devils did not fool Jesus, but it is fooling many Christians today. Satan will allow a person to have all the religion they want, as long as they are not being led by the Holy Spirit. Obedience to the Holy Spirit is the key to pleasing God.

If Jesus himself came to me with new scriptures, I will have a problem with this false *Jesus*. There are no new revelations, no new scriptures; no new way of seeing God's word. Those who teach with error, whether knowingly or not, are false teachers. I am not talking about a minor error here or there. I am referring to major errors like the Deity of Christ, the Power of the Holy Ghost, living under the law, and – **all these others false teachings going on in churches today**. **Any message skewing fundamental doctrine that lay the foundation of the Church is a false message!**

"But though we, or an angel from heaven, preach any other gospel unto you than that which we have preached unto you, let him be accursed." –
Galatians 1:8

When the Bible instructs us to let no man deceive you by any means, God literally wants us to trust only in him. In other words, trust no man, woman, boy, girl, pastor, teacher, television program, news report, corporation, government, etc. before you trust in God. Surprisingly, a majority of Christians appeal to fallacy of irrelevant authority whose ideology is rooted in ones' belief that an authoritative figure must be correct because he or she holds a position of authority. Many Christians mistakenly leave scripture interpretation up to teachers simply because they may have a title in front of their name. Christians who follow false teachers make gods out of these men and women. My Bible taught me to let God be true and let every man be a liar.

40

Many church folks are led astray easily because they choose not to study the Word of God for themselves. Some choose to be ignorant of God's Word on purpose thinking ignorance will be their excuse on Judgment Day. God's knowledge and wisdom is there for the taking. Ignorance is a choice. Ignorance will not excuse you now, on Judgment Day, or forever.

"My people are destroyed for lack of knowledge: because thou hast rejected knowledge..." – Hosea 4:6

Nowadays many people want others to think for them. Blind followers follow blind leaders. Blind followers will read a clear Bible verse that contradicts a false teacher, yet they will still believe in that false teacher. The First Commandment states, *"Thou shalt have no other gods before me!"* Why would you put your eternal soul into someone else's hands? Good luck with that! God gave you the ability to reason: so reason! Pray for spiritual discernment and use your critical thinking skills because your soul may depend on it. Stop drinking the Kool-Aid. Pray directly to Jesus and ask Him for His understanding. Jesus told us if we ask, we will receive. I can hardly balance my checkbook and can barely navigate my life. How am I going to navigate eternity? I need the Holy Spirit to lead me, guide me, and teach me how to please God. If Jesus is not happy, I am not happy!

The only way to understand the Bible is to study for you! And do not only study; study to show yourself approved to God. Stop depending on a person to dictate the Bible to you. Stop depending on mere men and women who make themselves out to be gods. Step out on **faith** and ask the Holy Spirit for wisdom and understanding. Please do not misunderstand what I am saying. All pastors are not bad. Just be careful who you submit yourself to.

"Know ye not, that to whom ye yield yourselves servants to obey, his servants ye are to whom ye obey; whether of sin unto death, or of obedience unto righteousness?" – Romans 6:16

Many listen to the words of Jesus, but do not fully comprehend the words of Jesus (Saint Matthew 13:13). We think we understand, but we do not. The Holy Spirit taught me how to listen to Jesus. I am going to tell you what the Holy Spirit taught me. Many years ago a commercial aired on television. This financial investment guy called E.F. Hutton was seated in a restaurant eating lunch. His friend asked him an investment question. Suddenly the entire restaurant went so silent you could hear a pin drop. The crowded restaurant wanted to hear what E.F. Hutton had to say. They desired to hear the wisdom, importance, and value of his understanding. In the same way that is how we need to listen to the words of Jesus. When Jesus speaks, stop what you are doing, sit down, be quiet, and listen (Saint John 2:1-11)!

We must hang on every single word uttered from the lips of Jesus Christ (Saint Luke 9:35). Man shall not live by bread alone, but by every word that proceeded out of the mouth of Jesus Christ (Saint Matthew 4:4).

"His mother (Mary) saith unto the servants, whatsoever he saith unto you, do it." – Saint John 2:5

When the disciples asked Jesus about end time events the first thing Jesus said is to take heed that no man deceive you. Deception is all around us; in religion, music, television programs, and universities. We are inundated with deception on every side. Even our modern day appliances have built in spy technology. Do you think when you power off your computer the government cannot access your computer files? Do you think that software updates on your computer, cell phone or electronic pad are actually software updates? Hmm?

Do you think deception is only on the outside walls of the Church? Some preaching and teaching the Word of God are twisting many to their will. Devils love religion because it is easy to control and manipulate Christians. The words in the Bible are important, but more so, it is the message contained within the words that matter. If you are not getting the correct message from a teacher, you must be able to discern it.

"But strong meat belongeth to them that are of full age, even those who by reason of use have their senses exercised to discern both good and evil." – Hebrew 5:14

A perfect example of religion versus faith is the account of Cain and Abel in Genesis Chapter four. Both Cain and his brother Abel brought a sacrifice before the Lord. Abel brought the firstlings of his flock, which the Lord accepted. Cain brought an offering to God that was not acceptable. More than likely it was not Cain's best nor was it the correct sacrifice. Both Cain and Abel lived a life of religious activity, but Cain was serving God his way.

I know of a religious couple that claims they know God. They study, read, and preach. They even have a weekly radio program on the internet. Their messages have many errors. The Holy Spirit has advised them to be humble, stop preaching, and to retrain. Instead of humbling themselves and taking biblical correction, they conjured up several excuses to justify their behavior. On Judgment Day many Christians will go before Christ and offer up a myriad of excuses. The only excuse you will have to get into heaven is what Jesus did on the cross and your obedience to Him.

Unfortunately, this couple refuses to listen because they have not submitted to the righteousness of God. They preach their own gospel. Instead of following the Holy Spirit they want the Holy Spirit to follow them. Obviously, **Second Timothy 3:16** do not apply to them. They think because they know about the scriptures it will put them in good graces with God. This religious couple speaks highly of Jesus, but do not obey Jesus. All their religious activities are lawlessness.

"And the Father himself, which hath sent me, hath borne witness of me. Ye have neither heard his voice at any time, nor seen his shape. And ye have not his word abiding in you: for whom he hath sent, him ye believe not. Search the Scriptures; for in them ye think ye have eternal life: and they are they which testify of me. And ye will not come to me, that ye might have life." – Saint John 5:37-40

It is good to have knowledge of the Bible, but the Bible says, *"Above all, get understanding."* Knowledge is the biblical map. What good is a map if you do not understand how to read it? It is not enough to read, study, and know the Bible. One must make it applicable to their life. Knowledge of God is one thing. Obedience to God is another.

Just because a person attends church every Sunday does not impress God. A person can know every single scripture in the Bible and not impress God. A person can pray twenty-four hours a day seven days a week and still not impress God. Some think they are in God's will because they do religious acts. Church folks are embracing this lie from the devil. These types of Christian's reality are based on their own perception, and they recreate God in their own image. People that worship God in religiosity do so by their own strength, power, and understanding because they are blinded by this very lie.

"Not everyone that saith unto me, Lord, Lord, shall enter into the kingdom of heaven; but he that doeth the will of my Father which is in heaven." – Saint Matthew 7:21

I have heard teachers make up their own doctrine that rhyme and sound like I am at a Christian comedy club. Did Jesus ever use colloquial rhymes? I was listening to an audio broadcast of a sermon. The teacher said God is holy and should be reverenced at all times. A few minutes later his cell phone rang. Another teacher took over, but I could still hear him talking on his cell phone in the background. If God is holy, he should shut off his cell phone before teaching God's word?

I have heard ridiculous theology with catch phrases that have nothing to do with sound doctrine. I heard another teacher say Jesus is the sin trapper. I find that nowhere in the Bible.

43

I did find **First John 1:7**, that tells us Jesus is the sin cleanser. I heard one teacher say that Gog is Abaddon, and Abaddon is the king of the locusts. He went on to say the king of the locusts is the demonic spirit and leader of the angels of the Abyss (Bottomless Pit).

Gog is also the leader of the fallen angels. Gog is also the Antichrist, and he has many names. Gog is also a Nephilim creature that will come out of the Abyss to lead the army of locusts to attack the nation of Israel. #*Whatthewhosaidwhatsid?* #What? #What?

Nothing this teacher said was confirmed or accompanied by any scripture. He kept jumping to Greek and Hebrew pronunciations. He kept using fancy words to impress his congregation. After he said Gog like thirty times I was almost convinced. This teacher went on to say many unscriptural things that were ridiculous. I was speechless and dumb-founded beyond perpetuity.

Teaching and preaching sound doctrine is not difficult. Just stick to the script. If the Bible states it, then you can teach it. If the Bible does not state it, then do not teach it. God is not complicated. We make things complicated when we do our own thing. Just because they are preaching from the Bible, they think it is okay to make up stuff. It is not okay! Where is the fear of God?

The devil's greatest strategy against Christian teachers is to have them believe they are in God's will simply because they are doing religious things. With a little false doctrine here and there over the years, some start to believe that their religious works please God. Many make the mistake of Cain, who had a form of godliness (religion), but denied the power of truth. Over the years some Christians become lax in their walk with God and begin to feel as though they can take their own liberties. These skew onto the road of religious works of the flesh and remake the Bible into a god that best suit their selfish desires. Church, the Bible and God become their own little project.

The Word of God is not a toy to be played with. The Word of God is a sharp two-edged sword. If you do not handle this sharp sword properly you may injure yourself. You just cannot make stuff up because it sounds goods. What you say must be doctrinally sound. When you manipulate the Word of God, it becomes the doctrine of devils. Doing religious acts is one thing. Serving God is another.

Instead of these teachers being proud of their religious achievements they should be eating a seven course meal of humility. False teachers' words will have the right sound, the right lighting, and the right stage. However, if their lifestyle and what they are saying does not align with God's word, then run away as fast as you can; if you do not you will commit spiritual suicide.

If God is not your supreme authoritative truth, you have already broken the First and Second Commandment. Works wrought by faith is the key to God's heart, not religious human righteousness. Many Christians will be sincere about their convictions, but many will be sincerely wrong. Do it God's way or do not do it at all! Serving God is not a ritual, it is a relationship.

God shall not, will not, and cannot allow partial obedience into heaven. Either believe all God's word or believe none of it. No man can serve two masters. Either you will hate the one and love the other. You cannot find and lose your religion when it suits your mood or agenda. You cannot be wishy-washy in your walk with God and unstable in your faith.

Are you being led by the Spirit of Understanding or by the understanding of someone else? Sitting under a person's teaching is only half the equation. The other half is confirming the teaching. Listening to the correct voice will save you much heartache and may make the difference between life and death. In today's world with so much deception you cannot take any chances. I know what has been taught. I know what has been accepted, but what does the Bible say? What the Bible says and obeying what the Bible says will determine your entrance into heaven. He or she that obeys their Organization, Church, Elder, pastor, father, mother, sister, brother, boyfriend, or girlfriend more than Jesus is not worthy of Jesus.

"He that loveth father or mother more than me is not worthy of me: and he that loveth son or daughter me than me is not worthy of me." – Saint Matthew 10:37

Jesus said, *"My sheep hear my voice, and I know them, and they follow me." – Saint John 10:27.*

Sadly, regardless of Saint John 10:27, people will still listen to the voice of their father, sister, friend or pastor before they would ever listen to God. When the blind lead the blind both will fall into the ditch (Hell). We have taken judgment and hell and replaced it with watered down sermons as not to hurt someone's feelings. If you knew what Hell is like, your fragile feelings would disappear instantly. Most people are not going to Hell because they have a hatred for God, but rather these follow the doctrines of men. I am not telling you not to listen to your father, sister, friend, or your pastor. I am telling you if you listen to your father, sister, friend, or your pastor before you listen to God; you are setting yourself up for a bad situation on Judgment Day. Whoever you listen to, their actions, motives, lifestyle and counsel must be in sync with the word of God. You should always confirm what is being taught by a person who shepherds your soul.

Are you a sheep of Christ or are you a sheep of your pastor? Are you hearing and following the voice of Jesus? Or, are you hearing and following the voice of your pastor, elder, father, mother, sister, girlfriend, or boyfriend? Whose voice are you listening to (Romans 8:14)? Doing ministerial works are good, but it is not intimacy with God. Some Christians think religion is a relationship with God. Religion is a form of godliness. A form of godliness cannot save you. People do not fully comprehend who God is, and some Christians treat God and the Bible as though they are an after-thought. The Bible tells us to test the spirits to see what kind of spirit it is. We test the spirits by the Word of God. If you do not study the Bible for yourself, how can you test the spirit(s)? When you study the scriptures for yourself, you will be able to identify false doctrine. Christians that blindly follow their teachers have swallowed the blue pill of the Matrix.

The Matrix was a science fiction movie released in 1999 where 99% percent of Earth's population lived inside and was controlled by a powerful computer system called the Matrix. The people were actually living in stasis pods unconscious to the real world, but conscious in a computer simulated dream world. A leader named Morpheus who lived in the real world would rescue people from the Matrix and give them a choice between a red pill and a blue pill. Those who stretched out on faith and took the red pill were delivered from this system of control. Those who opted to take the blue pill remained a slave to the Matrix for the rest of their natural lives.

Our world has its' own matrix too, but it is not science fiction. Our matrix is a spiritual prison for your soul. It is a prison you cannot feel, touch, see, taste or smell. It cannot be perceived by our sensory perception, yet it is ubiquitous. It has its' own ideas, ways, theories, thought patterns and truth wrapped up in the one world religion known as 'Me'ism'. In our matrix you are spoon-fed the gospel of comfort, the gospel of gin and juice and the gospel of rest; be merry and take thine ease. We are in a war for our very souls and the devil is out for blood. When have you ever seen soldiers in a war rest, be merry or take their ease?

Our matrix has full control over how we think, what we wear, what we eat, how to eat, who to have sex with, and what to have sex with. The world thinks they are free, but they are not free. The world thinks they are in control of their lives, but they are not. Lucifer has set many traps to ensnare us the moment we are born. Our world is in bondage and its' inhabitants do not even realize it. It is not the physical that is in bondage, it is the spiritual that is in bondage.

From the day we are born into this fallen world we are born in sin separated from God. Like that mouse that gets stuck on the sticky trap, humans get stuck in situations and circumstances. The mouse does not realize that it is already dead.

People that have not accepted Jesus Christ as their personal savior are walking zombies. They are already dead; they just do not realize it. This world, this construct is a virtual prison, and we are on death row. Capital punishment awaits us upon physical death. Lucifer is the god of this world, and this world system Babylon is his matrix. Lucifer's matrix is an illusion. The blood of Jesus Christ is your only way to escape the sticky trap.

Regardless of what the Bible says, Christian and non-Christian alike are still swallowing the blue pill and believing what they want to believe. To all those that follow these false teachings I urge you to go into the Bible to look at these teachings a little deeper yourself. Take the red pill so God can remove the veil from off your mind.

The **'Falling Away'** not only refers to apostasy within the church. In a broader sense it speaks of mankind's lack of the fear and respect for the Living God. Many antichrists are in the pulpits today telling you how special, how great, how majestic you are, because you are God's child. They tell you things that make you feel good. They never explain you are a low down rotten filthy yellow belly sinner saved by grace. When you come to the conclusion how ugly and wretched your sin nature is on the inside, and how holy and righteous God is, you will reverence God in a new light.

True Christians see themselves broken before God, knowing their works cannot get them entrance into heaven, but rather through Christ's atonement for their sins. These will examine the ugly deeds, thoughts, and motives of their heart, and will repent before God. A true Christian understands the sin nature resides within even after they have accepted the gospel. Because our sin nature has a voracious appetite for disobedience it is not always easy to live these things. You must fight and struggle against your sin nature to follow the Spirit of Truth. In the struggle we grow and mature in Christ. We will thank and worship the Lord for giving us power to become a Child of God.

Religious Christians will ignore their ugly deeds, thoughts, and motives of their heart. These will vehemently produce religious activities to the point of deceiving themselves into thinking their good deeds out-weigh their bad deeds. These will constantly remind themselves they are a Child of God, with no real confirmation. In these last days, those who have swallowed the lies and teachings from false teachers will take God's gift of grace for granted. These types of Christians will pick, choose, and violate God's word by convincing themselves that Christ's atonement covers continuous disobedience. It does not. If I am describing you, you need to ask yourself, "Am I a real Christian?"

"For if we sin willfully after that we have received the knowledge of the truth, there remaineth no more sacrifice for sins." – Hebrew 10:26

A religious Christian is a complacent Christian. If you have been attending church for years and there has been no spiritual growth, you may not be a Christian at all. On the Day of Judgment many Christians will be as the Laodicean Church.

"And unto the angel of the church of the Laodiceans write, these thing saith the Amen, the faithful and true witness, the beginning of the creation; I know thy works, that thou are neither cold nor hot: I would thou wast cold or hot. So then because thou art lukewarm, and neither cold nor hot, I will spew thee out of my mouth. Because thou sayest, I am rich, and increased with goods, and have need of nothing; and knowest not that thou art wretched, and miserable, and poor, and blind, and naked." – Revelation 3:14-17

The gospel is not supposed to make you feel good; it is supposed to convict you of sin. Conviction does not feel good. Truth does not feel good. Truth reveals how ugly we are and exposes the sin in us. God told us man must know the good and the evil. It is not enough to know the good about yourself; you must also know the evil. If you do not know there is anything wrong with you, how can you fix the problem?

Examining oneself destroys pride, arrogance, and hypocrisy. We must not be stiff-necked, but always seek and surrender to the will of God. Contrary to what carnal Christians believe, there is only **ONE WILL** in heaven. Every day I monitor my thoughts, attitude and motives against First Corinthians 13:1-11, Proverbs 6:16-19, Second Timothy 3:1-5, Romans 8:8, and Galatians 5:19-21, 22-23.

The thoughts that come into your mind will either be your thoughts, God's thoughts, or the devil's thoughts. Any thoughts entering your mind or doctrine you listen to must be measured up against the Word of God. Ask God for discernment, because the devil is no one, but the devil can potentially be anyone; even you!

"... And Peter took him, and began to rebuke him. But when he had turned about and looked on his disciples, he rebuked Peter, saying, Get thee behind me, Satan: for thou savorest not the things that be of God, but the things that be of men." – Saint Mark 8:32-33

"Jesus answered, he it is, to whom I shall give a sop, when I have dipped it. And when he had dipped the sop, he gave it to Judas Iscariot, the son of Simon. And after the sop Satan entered into him..." – Saint John 13:26-27

Unclean spirits have traded their thoughts for my thoughts many times. Do not think you are so high and mighty Satan cannot fool you.

He can easily out-think us even on his weakest day, playing on our naïveté, hubris, and ignorance. The enemy's most powerful weapon against the human psyche is the Jedi mind-trick. To be spiritual is not enough. Examine yourself daily to see if you are in the faith. I have gone to God on several occasions asking forgiveness.

"This I say then, walk in the Spirit, and ye shall not fulfill the lust of the flesh." – Galatians 5:16

"For as many as are led by the Spirit of God, they are the sons of God." – Romans 8:14

God is not so much concerned with your works, but what motives are behind your actions. Christianity is not about religion. It never was. Christianity is about who you are, what you are and your purpose in the family of God. Christianity is about pleasing God in total love for, and obedience to him. Obedience is when, how, who, what and where God says to do it. It is not what you know; it is not what you pray; it is not what you do; it is not what you say; but rather will you reverence the Son and obey. Obedience, love, and respect are interchangeable. Do we ever stop and ask Jesus what he thinks? What color does Jesus like? Does Jesus prefer sandals over sneakers? What is Jesus' favorite food? Can you see where I am going with this? We are just one tiny drop or water in a vast ocean. Brothers and sisters in Christ: It is not about you! It is about God. God poured all his reckless love into Jesus not only to save you from the Burning Hell and the Eternal Lake of Fire, but to love you in a relationship forever without end; without time.

God is a being with feelings and emotions. He wants to be loved and respected just as we do. As with any relationship you need to spend intimate time with God. Through intimacy you get to know the very thoughts, intentions, and inner most feelings about God. How can you get to know God if you do not spend time with Him? How can you get to know God if you never open your Bible and study it for yourself? God wants to make love to you. When you make love to your mate do you invite everyone to see it? No, it is just you and your mate alone with the doors shut. The only thought in your mind is how you can please your mate. You want to connect on an emotional, mental, and spiritual level. It is not about the physical contact; it is about the person. This is what God wants from us.

My late wife and I had an intimate relationship like this. I would start her sentences and she would finish mine. It was as though we knew what the other was thinking. We had an unbreakable bond. Can you imagine finishing the sentences of God? The one being that created everything and everyone.

The one being that knows all, sees all, and is all powerful. The one being that is Omni-benevolent wants you to be his child. God wants an intimate personal relationship with **you**.

"But his delight is in the law of the Lord; and in his law doth he meditate day and night." – Psalm 1:2

Meditation is concentration and intense focus on God. Shut off your television, shut off your cell phone and block out everything that would hinder your intimate time with Jesus Christ. Sit still before the Lord to ponder, think intensely on, and ask for His understanding. Your walk with God is an on-going process. Your relationship with God will grow throughout eternity and far exceed any religious sacrifices. I feel like a little kid in a candy store because God has taught me many things in my personal relationship with Jesus. Intimate and personal time with Christ will:

- Strengthen your faith
- Increase your awareness of God
- Give you joy in your spirit
- Correct preconceived notions
- Filter out error from truth

The Omnipotent, Omniscient, Omnipresent, and Sovereign wants to commune with us. But we would rather listen to and follow a human being that can neither put us in a heaven or hell. Intimacy is a privilege God has allotted mankind. Everything Lucifer cannot earn God has freely given to mankind. On Judgment Day of the sheep and the goats, the goats will say they were sincere about their faith. The Lord will reply, *"Your faith was in a man, in a woman, in a religion, in a building, in a Sabbath day, in a motivational speaker, and not me. For my word teaches, let God be true and every man a liar. Depart from me, I never knew you."*

'**Knew**' speaks of intimacy i.e.; and Adam **knew** Eve his wife, and she conceived and bare Cain.

In conclusion

It is a given that 77% percent of humanity is on its' way to Hell. The other 23% percent represent Christians. Out of this 23% percent, more than 66% percent will not make it into heaven. Out of every hundred, only about ten people will make it into heaven.

Everything God has done from the beginning of time up to this very moment has been about you. When is it going to be about God? A person who is truly saved can conclude true Christianity is to hate what their flesh loves and love what their flesh hates. We must hate evil and love good; hate lies and love truth; hate the flesh and love the Spirit; hate the selfish nature and love Christ's nature; hate that which God hates and love that which God loves. You follow the Holy Spirit where he leads because you want to please God. You obey the commandments of Jesus because you want to please God. You love without bias because you want to please God. I owe Jesus my life, my love, and my loyalty in perpetuity. Enoch understood the meaning of true Christianity.

"By faith Enoch was translated that he should not see death; and was not found, because God had translated him: for before his translation he had this testimony, that he pleased God." – Hebrews 11:5

All-encompassing fear and reverence must be present whenever God's word is being preached. God is not some fictional invisible character in La-La Land. God will hold teachers accountable to the highest standard. I suggest if you do not know what you are talking about, then go sit down somewhere. But I already know you will not humble yourself because your pride will not let you. Never assume you have earned heaven. Never under estimate the cunning of the dark side. We must always be sober, alert and vigilant. Never let your guard down. As long as we are on this planet, we are not safe. We are only safe when we hear these words: WELL DONE! THOU GOOD AND FAITHFUL SERVANT!

If you are not taking your walk with Christ seriously, you may want to start working out your salvation with fear and trembling. Many are called to heaven, but only a few will actually make it into heaven.

- You call me the Wine, but Drink me not.
- You call me Lord, but Reverence me not.
- You call me the Vine, but Cling to me not.
- When I condemn you to Hell, Blame me not!

"For many are called, but few chosen." – Saint Matthew 22:14

Rightly Dividing the Word of Truth

The Bible is not a charades game. Neither is it a guessing game. To know what is in the Bible you must read the Bible. To understand the Bible you must study the Bible. When I study the Bible I see equations, formulas, and numbers. In my personal studies I have come to realize the Bible is mathematical. To understand or solve an equation you must have the correct variables. Let's say (? + ? = 4). Both question marks are called variables, which are part of an equation. You can apply this technique when studying the Bible. In this example 4 equals the Rapture. The question is, *"How do we arrive at 4?"* To get the 'how', we search the scriptures for the variables. The problem with error in scripture is some teachers of God's word are making up their own math. They add their own variables and arrive at the wrong conclusions. The Bible's variables are 2+2 = 4. Opinionated or preconceived notions tell you 3+3 = 4. If you have preconceived notions you are not doing the math correctly. Parroting theological jargon perpetuates **bad theology**. It is like the blind leading the blind. Being a Christian is not blindly following a teacher. Contrary to popular belief, faith is not blind. These opinionated or preconceived notions are the reason for so many misinterpretations of the Book of Revelation.

How many different teachings and explanations are on the internet about the end times? I would say thousands. There is so much confusion in Revelation's timeline because many teachers are not putting in the work to interpret the Book of Revelation correctly. Doing the math is of the upmost importance. Without math we would not be able to tell time, build homes, cars, or buildings. Without math you would not be able to search your favorite websites. Our DNA is mathematical. Everything that God created is predicated on math.

Another thing I noticed while studying the Bible is, like algebra, you must work out the equation once you get the correct variables. For example, 4x=16. We would then have to solve for x. In other words, 4 times what number will give you 16? The answer is four (x=4); 4×4=16. The Bible gives us all the variables we need to properly divide the word of truth. The problem with some is they hop on the anecdotal bandwagon without checking things out, and these false doctrines are pounded into our heads constantly. These try to fit a car key into a house lock. It just does not work, but they try to make it work. To make it work they use several scriptures and hours to make a simple point. Hearsay teachers try to make the Book of Revelation fit their theology, when it should be the other way around. Most of what is being taught about the Book of Revelation from many is parroted theology. I have heard teachings on the final prophetic seven years include all Seven Seals, the Rapture, the Wrath of God, and even Jesus Christ's Second Coming. Cool, just throw everything into the prophetic blender and let us make ourselves a prophetic daiquiri.

We trust in traditions of men that pound the belief into our head that Jesus died on a Friday. That is why we commemorate the crucifixion on Good Friday. Jewish days start at sundown around 6pm. Night-time begins at 9pm. One day and night is 6pm to 6pm. If you do the math and count backwards three days and three nights from Jesus' Sunday morning resurrection to his crucifixion; Jesus died on a Wednesday. Most scholars date the death of Jesus between 26 AD and 34 AD. According to intercontinentalcog.org, Jesus died on Passover Wednesday, 31 AD. At first, I was skeptical until I did the math.

Died	–	–	–	Resurrection
Passover	○	○	○	○
Wednesday	Thursday	Friday	Saturday	Sunday
○	○	○	○	○
Btw 3pm - 6pm	6am to	6am to	6am to	6am
Buried		DAY ONE	DAY TWO	DAY THREE
Btw 6pm - 9pm	NIGHT ONE	NIGHT TWO	NIGHT THREE	

When preaching God's word one must be on-point. God's variables are there! You just need to know where to find them. Get the right variables, do the math, and you will get the right answers. Math will always work itself out.

When you study the Book of Revelation will realize you must interpret from seven perspectives. When you apply these seven perspectives with the Spirit of Understanding, the Book of the Revelation of Jesus Christ will become quite clear. These seven perspectives are:

- Biblical
- Political
- Historical
- Mathematical
- Current Events
- Cultural (Jewish)
- Unbiased with critical thinking

"Study to show thyself approved unto God, a workman that needeth not to be ashamed, rightly dividing the word of truth." – 2 Timothy 2:15

Dividing is division, and division is mathematical. The Bible is dynamic, and it has tenses. We must be aware of those tenses. If we are not, we may mistake this for that and that for this. We must rightly divide between the past, present, or future tenses. Here is just one example.

53

*"And there was war in heaven: Michael and his angels fought against the dragon; and the dragon fought and his angels, and prevailed not; neither **was** their place found any more in heaven." – Revelation 12:7-8.*

*"And the great dragon **was** cast out, **that old serpent**, called the Devil, and Satan, which deceiveth the whole world: he was cast out into the earth, and his angles were cast out with him." – Revelation 12:9*

'**Was**' is a Greek key word meaning an event that took place in the distant past. This Greek form is being used in an aorist tense (past tense). This is not a future event as some teach. This event occurred a long time ago.

*"And he (Jesus) said unto them, I **beheld** Satan as lightning fall from heaven." – Saint Luke 10:18*

'**Beheld**' is another Greek key word used in the imperfect tense (past tense). Imperfect tenses are linear actions that have transpired in the past. Saint Luke 10:18 occurred more than 1,800 years ago.

*"...now is come salvation, and strength, and the kingdom of our God, and the power of his Christ; for the accuser of our brethren **is cast down**, which accused them before our God day and night." – Revelation 12:10*

In the original Greek, '**Is cast down**' is also being used in the past tense. Salvation came at the cross when Jesus said, *"It is finished."* Jesus is our lawyer who mediates on our behalf. Now we have an advocate with the Father. Lucifer can no longer hold the power of Death over us because Christ now holds the Keys of Death and Hell in his right-hand. Lucifer can no longer accuse us of anything because he was kicked out of heaven long ago. Lucifer is no longer allowed to come before God's throne. However, he can impose legalities over us if we are not in the will of God. Satan means one who stands against to falsely accuse. In the Book of Job the devil went before the throne of God and was accusing Job of all sorts of things (Job 1:6-12).

I have heard it preached the devil will be kicked out of heaven right before the great tribulation period and he will have seven years to jam us all up. *"...Woe to the inhabitants of the earth and of the sea! For the devil is come down unto you, having great wrath, because he knoweth that he hath but a short time." – Revelation 12:12.* We already know the great tribulation period will only last for 3½ years, so we can disregard this flawed theology. From God's point of view one thousand years on earth is only one day (2 Peter 3:8). The Bible refers to the devil as 'That Old Serpent'. Old, in human terms would be around seventy years of age. Even if we gave the devil the benefit of the doubt and equate one year on earth to one day in heaven, in humans years that would make the devil 25,568 thousand years old (365.25 days × 70 years).

Lucifer the rebellious, who challenged the God of all creation, must have been around for quite some time. If Lucifer is as old as I think he is, 2,000 thousand years is a short amount of time. Lucifer could possibly be tens of thousands, or maybe hundreds of thousands of years old. Two thousand years for humans may be a long time, but a being that may be more than 25,000 thousand years old, two thousand years is a short time. I can barely pay off my car note in seven years. Besides, we do not know how old Lucifer was at the time of his rebellion. We judge time from our aspect of relativity. Human beings think like human beings, and not like God. God's thoughts are not our thoughts, neither his ways our ways.

Jesus told us the last days would be just like the days of Noah when the entire earth was filled with violence. People are walking around ignoring God and consequences, because the world hates God. We see all these feel good commercials where everyone is happy and smiling. Everyone on this planet is not happy and smiling. It is bad out there! Look around you! Earth has become a cesspool of demonic activity. Lucifer and his angels are here and have been for quite some time. Do you **not** see it!

Not only is the world violent and haters of God, but they also want to erase the very existence of God from their lives. Today people are just going about with their daily routine, and they have no clue the world is going to end very soon. Satan and his angels have us so preoccupied with our games and toys, so many of us are not aware of Jesus' warnings in the Book of Revelation. This is how intelligent the forces of evil are. I have to give credit where credit is due. Lucifer is a force to be reckoned with. He has blinded the wicked and deceived many believers. Look at all the apostasy in the Church today.

The devil does not mind if you feel good after Church service. Just as long as that pastor's teachings does not draw you closer to God, knock yourself out with all the feel good euphoric religion you want. The devil loves it! Have you seen the YouTube videos where pastors are dancing on a pulpit of money? People are coming up from the congregation in a wild frenzy throwing money on the altar of God. WOW!!! – God's Holy Temple is not a Strip Club!

"But there were false prophets also among the people, even as there shall be false teachers among you, who privily shall bring in damnable heresies, even denying the Lord that bought them, and bring upon themselves swift destruction." – 2 Peter 2:1

"And many shall follow their pernicious ways, by reason of whom the way of truth shall be evil spoken of. And through covetousness shall they with feign words make merchandise of you..." – 2 Peter 2:2-3

The devil knows most humans are creatures of habit and gullibility. Most of the false teachings I hear today are rumor. One teacher heard it from somewhere and so on and so forth without anyone ever checking it out because it sounded good. In my early years as a Christian I made the same mistake listening to teachers without checking it out for myself. I heard one preacher say, *"This is what Jesus said, but he really didn't mean that so let me explain to you what Jesus really meant."* The congregation gave thunderous applause, but do not realize they are like lambs being led to the slaughter.

When you twist the Word of God you are calling God a liar. All these feel good non-biblical teachings push success, prosperity, and earthly wealth. When you die none of that is going with you. By God's definition the world is essentially dead. Why would anyone hold on to death? The Bible I read tells me true success is an intimate relationship with Jesus Christ. The spiritual works in the same way as the natural. When your diet consists of bad foods your physical body suffers. When your spiritual diet consists of bad foods your spiritual body suffers. False religion and false doctrine may smell good, look good and taste good, but it is not good for you. All these feel good sermons are full of empty calories. ! Understanding God's Word is the only remedy that will break this spell of deception and open your eyes to see reality for what it is. A Christian should ask him or herself these questions after Church service…

- Did I learn anything?
- Did my faith increase?
- Did my knowledge increase?
- Did my understating increase?

I have heard enough of the prosperity gospel, holy laughter, and itching ears; enough of the speak it and claim it doctrine, sowing a seed, and being slain in the spirit! I have heard enough of ask God for anything and he will give it to you! Enough with the *"I can have my cake and eat it too gospel."* Enough! Enough! Enough! None of these teaching are in the Bible. As I matter of fact, this is not your best life now.

"Set your affection on things above, not on things on the earth." –
Colossians 3:2

God is not here to please us at our whim. God is not here to give us everything we want. God does not come to attention when we summon him. God is not your secretary! God is not your banker! God is not your magic genie! God is the Omnipotent; Omniscient; Omnipresent; The Sovereign!

The Four Most Common Mistakes Some Teachers Make

#1 – An analogy is mistaken as literal

*"And being in agony he prayed more earnestly: and his sweat was **as it were** great drops of blood falling down to the ground." – Saint Luke 22:44*

Hematidrosis is a condition which blood vessels that feed the sweat glands rupture, causing a person to sweat blood. Jesus' sweat was **'as it were'** great drops of blood, not blood.

'As it were' is an analogy used to make a comparison between two things, but it is not the same thing. If Jesus sweated blood, the scripture would read like this... *"Jesus, being in agony, prayed more earnestly: and **Jesus' sweat became great drops of blood** falling down to the ground."*

This scripture has nothing to do with blood; it is referring to sweat. In other words Jesus was sweating so profusely, his sweat was just dripping down his face onto the ground. When you see the word **'as'** in the Bible it is usually making an analogy. There are other words or phrases used in prepositional form similar to the word **'as'**.

- For example - **Similar to, Like unto, Likened to, As if it were**

In the Book of Revelation many analogies and phrases are being thrown around. These are the subtleties we must recognize. We look at the big things, but the small things are also equally important.

#2 – Words are being omitted from scripture

I have heard many preachers say, **"Money is the root of all evil."**

*"For the **love** of money is the root of all evil..." – I Timothy 6:10*

When you take away 'po' from police, you get lice. It works the same way biblically. When you subtract or omit one word from the Bible, it may change the entire meaning of that portion of scripture. God gives us dire warning not to do such things.

"And if any man shall take away from the words of the book of this prophecy, God shall take away his part out of the book of life, and out of the holy city, and from the things which are written in this book." – Revelation 22:19

#3 – Words are being added to scripture

*"Then the devil taketh him up into the holy city, and setteth him on a pinnacle of the temple, and saith unto him, if thou be the Son of God, cast thyself down: for it is written, He shall give his angels charge concerning thee: and in their hands they shall bear thee up, **lest at any time** thou dash thy foot against a stone." – Saint Matthew 4:5-6*

*"For he shall give his angels charge over thee, to keep thee in all thy ways. They shall bear thee up in their hands, **lest thou dash thy foot against a stone**." – Psalm 91:11-12*

Did you see that subtle maneuver by Satan? Psalm 91:12 never stated, *"lest at any time thou dash thy foot against a stone."* The true saying is, *"lest thou dash thy foot against a stone."* Satan intentionally misquoted scripture in the hope that Jesus would throw himself down to his death. Angels will not bear us up **at any time** because angels cannot interfere with our will. If you decide to jump off a skyscraper with the assurance that your guardian angel will bear you up, good luck with that.

Whether it is ones' pride, self-deception, or ignorance, false prophets and false teachers twist the scriptures to suit their agenda just like their father the devil. When you add to and subtract from God's Word you are altering what God said. To alter God's Word is false doctrine. God is Holy and 100% percent complete. If you alter God's Word by 99% or 25% or 1% or ½%, you have just created false doctrine. Doctrines of devils are adulterated scriptures. Do not add to or subtract from God's Word. Just stick to the script.

#4 – An entire sermon is built on one scripture & hearsay

Have you ever heard a teacher draw many scriptures from all over the Bible to explain one scripture? If this happens the person is unsure about his or her theology. I believe they do this to convince themselves that what they are saying is true. If it takes more than ten minutes and multiple passages from all over the Bible to explain one biblical point, then that theological interpretation is probably wrong.

I saw a YouTube video of a teacher spend nearly one hour explaining why the Rapture must occur before the great tribulation period. When he finished, his chalkboard looked like spaghetti works. In his mind all his scriptures, ideas and thoughts convinced him that he was absolutely correct, but the Bible stated otherwise. Jesus said, *"When ye therefore shall see the abomination of desolation spoken of by Daniel the prophet...* (Saint Matthew 24:15), he was referencing Daniel 9:27. The desolation begins 3½ years later after Antichrist's makes his covenant with the nations of the world.

58

It is during this 3½ years or 1,260 days Antichrist will make war against the Jews and Christians. For Jews it will be the desolation period. For Christians it will be the great tribulation period.

"Immediately after the tribulation of those days shall the sun be darkened, and the moon shall not give her light, and the stars shall fall from heaven, and the powers of the heavens shall be shaken: and then shall appear the sign of the Son of man in heaven: and then shall all the tribes of the earth mourn, and they shall see the Son of man coming in the clouds of heaven with power and great glory" – Saint Matthew 24:29-30

Many confuse the above scriptures as Christ's Second Coming. This event is not the second coming. This event is the Rapture. As you can clearly see from scripture the Rapture occurs after the Abomination of Desolation. Thus: *immediately after the tribulation of those days*. What tribulation? – Abomination or Great Tribulation. What days? – The days of Antichrist. But how do we know this event is the Rapture? We know because Jesus tells us in verse 31.

"And he shall send his angels with a great sound of a trumpet, and they shall gather together his elect from the four winds, from one end of heaven to the other." – Saint Matthew 24:31

The Bible is not deep. It is simple, precise, and to the point. False teachers without biblical understanding make his word complicated. Some of them even seem as though they are in competition with one another. This is not competition; it is about glorifying the God of heaven. I understand that no one person knows everything, but taking a scripture or subject and running with it is something else. Truth be told, I assume many things when reading and studying the Bible. However, if your ideas and thoughts do not line up with scripture you must toss it in the trash instead of trying to make it fit your theology.

When you take a small portion of scripture and create an enormous theory around it, I will definitely have a problem with it. I do not care how many titles you have in front of your name. I do not care how many certificates you have on your wall. I do not care how many mega churches you have established. I do not care if you have been studying the Bible for one hundred years. If you say or preach anything contrary to the King James 1611 Bible, then expect a heartfelt rebuttal from me. Here is another example of parroting theological jargon.

"And it came to pass, when men began to multiply on the face of the earth, and daughters were born unto them, that the sons of God saw the daughters of men that they were fair, and they took them wives of all which they chose...There were giants in the earth in those days; and also after that, when the sons of God came in unto the daughters of men, and

they bare children to them, the same became mighty men which were of old men renown." – Genesis 6:1-4

The first thing I hear is the angels that rebelled against God and followed the devil, left their first estate, and came down to earth and had sexual relations with human females. These females birthed hybrid babies that grew to become great giants called Nephilim. Am I reading the same Bible? My Bible says the angels that rebelled and came down from heaven were bound in chains of darkness.

"And the angels which kept not their first estate, but left their own habitation, he hath reserved in everlasting chains under darkness unto the judgment of the great day." – Jude 1:6

"For if God spared not the angels that sinned, but cast them down to hell, and delivered them into chains of darkness, to be reserved unto judgment..." – 2 Peter 2:4

The darkness of which the Bible speaks is hidden places inside the earth. If you are bound in prison with chains, how then are you able to run carefree and have willy-nilly sexual relations with women? Do you understand where I am going with all of this? The angels that left heaven and descended down to earth were locked up in prison until the judgment of the great day. To what judgment and what great day is the Bible referring? Krisis, in the Greek means final judgment or the Wrath of God. These beings will make their appearance at the end of the world, and it will not be to experience sexual relations with women.

A one hour show aired on television on this subject. How do you get a one hour program based off four scriptures? I will tell you how: by concocting fables and science fiction that directly contradicts the Bible. Read Genesis 6:4 again. As a matter of fact, read Genesis 6:4 a million times.

Not once does it say, *"Angels came in unto the daughters of men."* and had sexual relations with females? It says sons of Gods. Angels are not created in the image of God, but Sons of God are. Sons of God are not angels and angels are not Sons of God. Through Adam mankind is a special class of creation, fashioned in the image and likeness of Almighty God. Mankind is unique. Whether before the 'Fall' or after the 'Fall', all Sons of God came through the lineage of Adam, because Adam was created as God's first son.

"...which was the son of Seth, which was the son of Adam, which was the son of God." – Saint Luke 3:23-38

The dichotomy between angels and Sons of God are vastly different because it is different classifications of creation. If angels came down from heaven the scripture would read like this:

60

*"And it came to pass, when men began to multiply on the face of the earth, and daughters were born unto them, that the **angels** of God saw the daughters of men that they were fair, and they took them wives of all which they chose…"*

*"There were giants in the earth in those days; and also after that, when **angels** of God came in unto the daughters of men, and they bare children to them, the same became mighty men which were of old men renown."*

As you can see these two scriptures appear nowhere in the Bible. Even if angels wanted to, they cannot have sexual relations with one another, let alone with human beings. Angels have the ability to manifest in physical form, but they still need permission from God to do so. When they do manifest in physical form, they still have no gender even appearing as male or female. There is masculine and feminine in heaven, but no gender. There will be no gender in heaven, as there will be no need for procreation. Procreation is not necessary in heaven because there is no death.

But just for the sake of argument I am going to entertain this nonsense. Let us say God allowed this act. On the one-hand God would allow angels to have intersexual relations with a lower-class species. But, on the other hand will not allow human beings to have intersexual relations with lower species, such as dogs, cats, or horses. Hmm? Sounds like a double standard to me. If I cannot explain something in the Bible, I will just say I do not know. I will not make something up because it sounds spectacular.

"Beware lest any man spoil you through philosophy and vain deceit, after the tradition of men, after the rudiments of the world…" – Colossians 2:8

If fallen angels came down and had sexual relations with women, the Bible would have said it. The devil is the author of confusion, not God. God says what He means and means what He says. When the Bible says Sons of God, then it is Sons of God. Stop adding all this stuff to God's word. It is mind boggling to even think Christians would believe fallen angels came out of heaven and had sexual relations with women, and God just stood by and did nothing. Some Christians believe this nonsense because it has been pounded into their heads over and over and over until it becomes a widely accepted belief even-though the Bible contradicts it. Jesus already told us angels cannot have sexual relations because God did not create them with genetic material, gender, or procreation ability. When people preach non-biblical things such as these it dismantles God's Sovereignty.

As we speak, there are trillions of rebellious angels on earth. If these angels can impregnate women, why are there no Nephilim giants walking the earth today?

61

If you believe a spirit can have sex with a woman and get her pregnant then you are teetering on blasphemy making angels, demons and Satan equal with God. Only God can place himself inside the womb of a woman, and He only did it once never to be repeated. Ever! – Saint Luke 1:26-38

God did not only create sex for pleasure; He created sex in our species for the purpose of procreation. God stated you should only have sex inside of marriage. When you die you take your masculinity or femininity with you into heaven, but not your gender. Angels are already in heaven. How can angels have sex if they have no gender? When teachers introduce their ideas, views, thoughts, opinions, feelings, emotions, and their mannerisms, they have just tainted the word of God with their lawlessness. These people just, **ruin the ride**. I am not one to debate because I think it is a waste of time, but I had to explain this because we read the Bible, but at times we do not understand the Bible.

"...Ye do err, not knowing the Scriptures, nor the power of God. For in the resurrection they neither marry, nor are given in marriage, but are as the angels of God in heaven." – Saint Matthew 22:29-30

Now that we know this teaching is in error, let me give you my exegesis of Genesis Chapter 6:1-4, as I rightly divide the word of truth. When God created Eve and brought her to Adam it represented the first marriage. God instituted marriage for the purpose of family, procreation, and pleasure. God commanded Adam and Eve to have a great deal of sex; to have babies and to multiply and fill the earth with their kind, and subdue it.

"And God blessed them, and God said unto them, be fruitful, and multiply, and replenish the earth, and subdue it..." – Genesis 1:28

When God gave the command for Adam and Eve to get busy doing that thang, it was before 'The Fall'. Adam and Eve may have lived thousands of years before they were tempted by the devil. That would mean before recorded history a *Pre-Fall Era* existed before the corruption of mankind. If this were the case, Eve would have birthed children before 'The Fall'. Thus, the Sons of God (Eve's male sons born before the fall) saw the daughters of men (Eve's female daughters born after the fall).

This would make more sense to me rather than fallen angel spirits having the power of the infinite God to impregnate women. I know what you are thinking. Adam and Eve's children were having sexual relations with each other. Make no mistake about where we all come from. We all come from Adam and Eve. Technically we are all brothers and sisters. I know your next question is, *"What happened to the Sons of God?"*

62

That is an easy puzzle to solve. Let us say Adam and Eve never sinned. There would be no death. The earth would eventually become full of people. To keep the earth's populous balanced people would have to be removed from off this planet. Since death would not exist, the only other way would be translation. We clearly see in scripture that translation overrides death. Enoch walked with and pleased God, so God removed Enoch from planet earth before he died. Enoch made the transition from earth to heaven without dying.

"By faith Enoch was translated that he should not see death; and was not found, because God had translated him: for before his translation he had this testimony, that he pleased God." – Hebrews 11:5

After 'The Fall', death was written into our genetic code, which altered our DNA. Attrition of population before 'The Fall' would be translation. Attrition of population after 'The Fall' is death. Adam's sons born before 'The Fall' would not be subject to death because they were not born in sin and shaped in iniquity. They would eventually reach an age of maturity and transition from earth to heaven just as Enoch was. As some of these super beings waited on their age of maturity, they mated with the fallen women. Even-though these sons of Adam were not in a fallen state, they still had gender because they were human.

Due to the fact our DNA was altered, the genetic code of the 'Sons of God' and the genetic code of fallen humans were non-equivalent. When the 'Sons of God' saw the 'Daughters of Men' and had sexual relations with them, their babies grew up to become famous giants called Nephilim. The Nephilim race became very famous due to their great size, strength, and uncanny abilities. Nephilim were more than likely famous for hunting dinosaurs. Yes, in the Book of Job dinosaurs roamed the earth alongside mankind. Land dinosaurs were called behemoths and water dinosaurs were called leviathans (Job 40:15-18 & 41:1). Another name the Bible gives for dinosaurs is dragons (Job 41:18-21 & Psalm 74:13-14).

After Adam and Eve sinned, God told Eve he would greatly multiply her conception in sorrow (Genesis 3:16). For God to greatly multiply her conception, Eve would have already known what conception was. Inference implies at some point in the past before 'The Fall', Eve conceived children. If Eve never birthed any children, why would God bother to tell Eve about child birth being painful? God was telling Eve from that day forward she would travail in child birth. I could write a book on the first eleven chapters of Genesis alone. Genesis is filled with much information we miss so many things in the first three chapters alone. For instance:

- In Genesis 1:2, earth did not have a rotation

- In Genesis 1:3, when God spoke (let there be Light), he was referring to the Pre-incarnate Christ who is the brightness of God's glory. God did not call forth the sun and moon until Genesis 1:14-16

- In Genesis 1:4-5, God created the 24 hour day rotation of nighttime and daytime. The 24 hour day was the first thing God created. Everything else God created afterward was predicated on the 24 hour rotation of the Earth. These two verses alone dismantle the ridiculous theory of evolution.

- In Genesis 1:5-31, God created everything in six days, and he rested on the seventh day. But if you noticed the evenings and the mornings completed the days. The evening is 6pm and the morning is 6am. God does not work in the dark; he works in the light. God's activity was during the day from the morning (6am) to the evening (6pm). That is only 12 hours a day for 6 days, which is 72 hours. Technically, God created everything in three days.

This whole Nephilim theory sounds good on paper until you apply common sense and read the scriptures for yourself. When you add common sense, non-sensical theology makes no sense. If the devil can remove your common sense, you will begin to believe anything. He has been using this tactic on human beings for over 6,000 years. The devil has been studying human behavior for thousands of years. He knows Christians better than they know themselves. Even I am not immune. That is why I had to approach the Book of Revelation from a different perspective than what is commonly taught in most Christian churches.

When your foundation is sure your spirit will be able to discern any false doctrine the moment you hear it or when it rears its ugly head. If your foundation is not sure you will not be able to recognize false doctrine that will eventually lead to your spiritual demise. The truth is the only thing that will give you understanding. All scripture is given by inspiration of the Holy Ghost, and the Holy Ghost testifies Jesus Christ.

From beginning to end, the Bible is all about God's redemptive plan of mercy and grace through Jesus our Lord. If you are reading a Bible that does not confirm these points of truth, then you are reading the wrong Bible. This is Truth:

- Jesus is God's only **begotten** son

- Jesus was born of a **virgin**

- God, the **Word** was manifested in **human flesh**

- Jesus fulfilled the prophetic scriptures regarding **Messiah**

- Jesus died on a cross for the **sins of the world**

- Jesus resurrected in a **fleshly body**

"For there are three that bear record in heaven the Father, the Word, and the Holy Ghost: and these three are one." – I John 5:7

When I say, *"Let's do the math."*, it also means to confirm what a teacher is preaching. If any teacher tells you 800 × 800 = 16,000, just do not believe them; do the math. Many Christians just believe what teachers or preachers tell them without researching and doing the math. When you do the math, the answer is 640,000. It is also important to have the proper Bible. How are you going to confirm anything if you do not have the right Bible?

American Standard Version	1901	Verse 7 is missing	FAIL
Contemporary English Version	1995	In fact, there are three who tell about	FAIL
English Standard Version	2001	Verse 7 is missing	FAIL
Good News Translation	1966	There are three witnesses	FAIL
International Standard Version	2011	Pass the 1st test	PASS
The Living Bible	1971	Verse 7 is missing	FAIL
New English Translation	2006	For there are three that testify	FAIL
New International Version	1973	For there are three that testify	FAIL
New King James Version	1982	Pass the 1st test	PASS
New Living Translation	1996	So we have these three witnesses	FAIL
New World - Jehovah Witness	1960	For there are three witness bearers	FAIL
New American Standard Bible	1971	For there are three that testify	FAIL

First John 5:7 is based on the Masoretic/Dead Sea Scroll text that dates back to about 400 BC. The Masoretic text confirms the authority and Deity of Christ, who is the author and finisher of our faith. This is why it is very important to have the correct Bible.

BISHOPS BIBLE	MASORETIC TEXT	YEAR 1568
COVERDALE BIBLE	MASORETIC TEXT	YEAR 1535
GENEVA BIBLE	MASORETIC TEXT	YEAR 1560
GREAT BIBLE	MASORETIC TEXT	YEAR 1539
KING JAMES BIBLE	MASORETIC TEXT	YEAR 1611

The Masoretic text is the authoritative text of the Jewish religion, and the Dead Sea Scrolls are virtually identical. They only differ in the use of some consonants. The Codex Sinaiticus or New Testament dates back to the late 4th C.E. Would you rather have a Bible written in the 16th century that agrees with the Dead Sea Scrolls? Or, would you rather have a Bible written in the 20th century that does not agree with the Dead Sea Scrolls? Would you base your eternal future on a Bible published in the 20th century, or a Bible printed in the 17th Century whose writings agree with original text dating back to the 4th Century AD? Are you using the correct map to locate the treasure? Only two Bibles passed the test, but let us dig a little deeper.

(NKJV) – "In this was manifested the love of God toward us, because that God sent his _only begotten Son_ into the world, that we might live through him." – I John 4:9

(ISV) – "This is how God's love was revealed among us: God sent his _uniquely existing Son_ into the world so that we might live through him." – I John 4:9

ISV   INTERNATIONAL STANDARD VERSION - 2011   FAIL

NKJV   NEW KING JAMES VERSION - 1982   PASS

The only Bible that stayed true to the Deity of Christ was the New King James version and those written in the 16th Century. This is why I only use the KJV 1611. In my opinion other translated versions either add or take away from the Word of God. They make these changes because it makes the Bible easier to read. However, when they make these changes, important fundamental teachings may get lost in translation.

66

I am not advocating you drop all other translations of the Bible, nor am I saying making these slight changes are demonically inspired. You should use more than one Bible during your studies, because it will definitely help you. What I am saying is your primary reading and studies should be based out of the KJV 1611, with any other translation as an auxiliary. Even though the KJV 1611 version is not as smooth as we would like it to be, it agrees with the Dead Sea Scrolls.

The problem is not the King James Bible; it is these false teachers and false prophets manipulating the Word of God for their own means. The underlying message here is false doctrine is powerful enough to kill you. We must not lean to the left or right when studying the Bible. Do not veer off the long skinny road to heaven. The Word of God must be in a straight line, and that starts with having the right Bible. Jesus is the treasure chest, and the King James 1611 Bible is the map. Eternal life is like a 77 Karat diamond in a treasure chest full of gold, silver, pearls, and precious stones. Do not let anyone cause you to have your name blotted out of the Lamb's Book of Life.

Mistakes, assumptions, conclusions, theories, and preconceived ideas are due to unscriptural indoctrinated seeds planted over the years. This is why you must have the proper Bible. In addition to reading the Bible you must meditate, pray, and ask Jesus to give you clear understanding of the Bible. Jesus will enlighten you.

I have explained the issue of false doctrine: now let us solve the problem. One day I purchased the **Hebrew-Greek Key Study Bible** (KJV 1611) by AMG Publishers. It was the best investment I made in my entire life. This Bible is amazing. It has key words in the text numerically coded to Strong's Exhaustive Concordance of the Bible.

It has New Testament grammatical helps, concordance, lexical aids, exegetical notes, center-column references, Strong's dictionaries, an 8 page color Bible atlas, pronunciation of Hebrew and Greek consonants and vowels, footnotes, Greek dictionary, abbreviations. It also has modernization of archaic English spelling and vocabulary. I know it is a mouth full, but these tools are what you will need to rightly divide the word of truth. After purchasing this Bible and using all the aids I realized I was overwhelmingly misinterpreting quite a few scriptures. One's study and teaching must be rooted in the original thought of the text, not just the text itself. Is the mood sarcasm? Is the mood rhetorical? Is the mood light-hearted? Is the mood that of endearment? Is the mood that of wrath?

Because the word of truth is not being broken down to its' bare essentials, non-sensical notions and parroting theological jargon prevails. Eventually this leads to misinterpretation of sound doctrine. Every nuance, word and paragraph is a piece of the puzzle.

You fit those pieces together to get the big picture. You cannot take one piece and build your theology around it. This is the biggest problem I see today with biblical exegesis. And what makes matters worse is everyone has an opinion; everyone wants to be a prophet. Some say they are pastors and they are not. Some say they are prophets and they are not. Some say they are Christians and they are not. All these people want **their prophetic voice** to be heard, but instead of putting in the work they parrot bad theology on YouTube. This problem is systemic within the Church.

To understand the Bible you must break scriptures down to their bare essentials. In most Christian churches this is not being done. Let me give you some advice. When you study the Book of Revelation you must start with a clean slate. Whatever you have learned or been taught over the years, forget about it. If you do not, your preconceived notions will get in your way.

I was making many errors in my studies, because I was not equipped with the right tools. Now you will have all the tools you need to break down every word, thought, and attitude the scriptures are relaying to you. After you purchase the **Hebrew-Greek Key Study Bible** by AMG Publishers, you will not need any other translated version of the Bible, because you will be able to translate it yourself. Your understanding of the Bible will increase exponentially because your studies will be built on the original articulation of the Hebrew and Greek. When we understand the nuances, then and only then, can we rightly divide the word of truth. To purchase this amazing Bible go to rapture2061.org and click the link in the top right corner.

"...be a good minister of Jesus Christ, nourished up in the words of faith and of good doctrine, whereunto thou hast attained." – I Timothy 4:6

Chapter Four
1st and 2nd Seal

The White Horse

"And I saw when the Lamb opened one of the seals, and I heard, as it were the noise of thunder, one of the four beasts saying, come and see. And I saw, and behold a white horse: and he that sat on him had a bow; and a crown was given unto him: and he went forth conquering, and to conquer." – Revelation 6:1-2

It thundered when Jesus opened the First Seal. One of the beasts asked John to come and see. John saw someone sitting on a white horse. He had a bow and a crown. He went forth to conquer and continued conquering.

I have heard it said the person sitting on the White Horse is the Antichrist of Revelation 13:1. This theory is based off three verses (Revelation 19:11-13) where Jesus is riding a white horse. The white horse in Revelation 19:11 is a literal horse in a physical sense with a literal rider, and Jesus is specifically mentioned as being the rider.

Some teach Antichrist will bring war, famine, pestilence, and death. The Red Horseman of the Apocalypse (war) follows the White Horseman. Look around you; war, famine, pestilence, and death are already here. It is bad now, but these end-times are going to get worse, much worse. Even-though things are bad now we are not to that point yet. When the entire world comes under great distress, Antichrist will make his appearance. In the Book of Daniel Chapter 9:27, it states when Antichrist comes into power he will usher in a seven year peace armistice, not war. Antichrist will only fight two wars after he rises to power. The first war will be against the Christians and Jews (Revelation 12:17). The second war will be at the Battle of Armageddon (Revelation 16:13-16).

Revelation 6:2 tells us the White Horseman went forth conquering, and to conquer. When you conquer you take by force. But Revelation 13:1 introduces the Beast that rose from the sea of humanity. This beast is symbolic of Antichrist. According to Revelation 13:2, Antichrist does not go forth conquering and to conquer by force. Apropos, power is given to him by Satan.

"...and the dragon gave him his power, and his seat, and great authority." – Revelation 13:2

"...and power was given him over all kindreds, and tongues, and nations." – Revelation 13:7

The widely accepted mistaken beliefs by some imply Antichrist and the White Horseman of the Apocalypse are one in the same. The White Horseman rides out to conquer humanity. Antichrist (Beast) is given power over humanity. By understanding their dichotomy, both are not one in the same. I know it sounds good on paper, but the Bible never implied the one sitting on the White Horse in Revelation 6:2 is a man, let alone human. The Bible never states nor suggests the White Horseman is the Antichrist. None of the Four Horsemen of the Apocalypse are in no way shape or form, human beings. The Holy Spirit is a He, yet the Holy Spirit is neither a man nor human. One must understand that 'he', is being used in masculine form.

We use terms like Mother Nature, Mother Earth, or Hurricane Katrina; yet nature and earth is not a woman, and a hurricane is not female. You cannot equate corporeal and non-corporeal as being the same. It is like saying an apple and a pear are the same because they are both fruit. You cannot equate symbolism and literalism. You must separate them. The Four Horsemen of the Apocalypse are symbolic, angelic in nature, but their actions are literal. They work as a team, and are pulling all the strings in the background. They are the cause and effect. The White Horseman's job is to deceive and turn our attention away from the truth of Jesus Christ.

"And every spirit that confesseth not that Jesus Christ is come in the flesh is not of God: and this is that spirit of antichrist, whereof ye have heard that it should come; and even now already is it in the world." – I John 4:3

Rider on the White Horse

"And I saw, and behold a white horse: and he that sat on him had a bow; and a crown was given unto him: and he went forth conquering, and to conquer." – Revelation 6:2

So, the question is, *"What is the rider on the White Horse conquering?"* Let me give you an example. I walk into a store and put a gun to the head of the cashier and say, *"Give me all your money now!"* Instinctively the cashier empties the cashier's drawer of all the money without any hesitation. Afterwards I tie up the cashier and locked him in the backroom of the store. The cashier did not know there were no bullets in my gun. Did I subdue the cashier with brute force? No, I subdued the cashier on a psychological level. Notice the rider on the White Horse had a bow, but no arrows. In our day and age that represents a gun with no bullets. A bow with no arrows denotes a psychological weapon, yet the rider on the White Horse continues to conquer. The White Horseman's power is emotional, psychological, and mental manipulation on a subconscious level. He conditions, modifies, conforms, and alters human thinking and reasoning of those he holds captive at his will. If evil has your mind, it already has your soul.

The White Horseman wears the crown because he is the most powerful of the group and the forerunner for Antichrist. The forerunner for Antichrist is the *Spirit of Deception*. The White Horseman is the **'Programmer'**. He is responsible for the 'Falling Away' of Christians and non-Christians alike.

- The bow with no arrows is a subliminal or psychological weapon
- The crown signifies leadership
- Conquering and to conquer means ongoing (generation to generation)

The White Horseman knows that human beings perpetuate learned behaviors. A perfect example would be the grandmother, mother, daughter, and granddaughter stuck in the welfare system. Those, whose minds have been programmed, become dependent and unable to think beyond their programming. This programming also occurs in the Church over the spectrum of many religious groups. The person becomes stuck in a loop, repeating the same things over and over expecting different results. If you are dependent on anything or anyone other than God, you will never see what God needs you to see. The White Horseman of the Apocalypse blinds those that reject the Gospel of Jesus Christ. Even those who say they are Christians.

Nowadays the masses seemed swayed as if they are under a spell. People do not think anymore. They allow social-media, music, movies, fake news, television, false prophets, and false teachers do all the thinking for them. Two of the White Horseman's greatest weapons are intangibility and anonymity. Those under his spell cannot see they are brainwashed. With the world under a spell, it will be much easier for Antichrist to control the masses when he comes into power. The devil knows us better than we know ourselves. Like sheep, humans have no direction. If a crowd of sheep starts to walk in a certain direction other sheep will follow, then others. This is the mentality humans share with sheep. People just go with the program. Just because everyone is saying it or doing it, people think it is ok. *"A lie doesn't become truth and wrong doesn't become right just because it's accepted by the majority."* People, who continually make bad choices for what they say, do, and think in this world will give account to God in the next. People that do such things do not realize they are storing up wrath for the Day of Judgment.

The White Horseman is synonymous with an angel of light, and He is the 1st Seal. He will come masked as truth, when in all actuality it will be deception on a global scale. This is why the horse is white. He comes as light, when in fact he is darkness. He presents himself as good, when in fact he is evil. He fools the mind into thinking it is right, when it is wrong. He convinces people to take good for evil and evil for good. The White Horseman's power is to control you without you realizing you are being controlled. That is his greatest weapon.

Observe how some believe any preaching that comes from the pulpit no matter how irrational the teaching. When **unsound** doctrine is repetitiously repeated Christians believe it because many other Christians believe it. The mentality of the world is the same. Nowadays Christians seem more concerned with signs and wonders than sound doctrine. As a young adult I succumb to false doctrine and false prophets, because I was unskilled in God's word. Deep down inside I felt there was something wrong, but I could not zero in on it. I felt it easier to leave it up to my spiritual leaders. I did not recognize the signs of being bewitched. If you have an inkling of doubt, check it out. I am currently writing a book titled, *"The Bible and the Spiritual Realm"*, which I write about that episode in my life. You will find this book remarkably interesting.

The first Four Seals are four specific agendas the Dark Forces has set into motion already. All Four Horsemen are powerful entities working together behind the scenes to push the world into the New World Order. Antichrist will not make his appearance until the period Jesus called 'Beginning of sorrows', in which the entire world will be experiencing great difficulties. This will occur between the 4th and 5th Seal. How can the 1st Seal (White Horseman) be the Antichrist if all Four Horsemen of the Apocalypse are preparing the way for Antichrist?

The true identities of the Four Horsemen are four powerful demonic princes with many billions of foot soldiers under their command. These beings exist just outside the range of the five senses. Their foot soldiers enter our realm through the mind of human beings. Spiritual warfare begins in the mind. If you accept the White Horseman's programming your mind become a doorway. The mindgate is their doorway (portal) to our world. They enter your mind by what you hear, feel, and see. They can also enter the mind through sexual fornication, music, drugs, and other sinful pleasures. You must be extremely careful what you watch, what you listen to, and whom you listen to.

Angelic beings are ministering spirits. They have the ability to project thoughts into our mind. You must be careful how you react to your thoughts because they may not be your thoughts. As Christians we must discern God's thoughts and the Devil's thoughts from our thoughts. When demonic persuasion enters the mind, we can either choose to reject or accept those thoughts. If you allow these seducing spirits to control your thinking they will blind you from the Truth of Jesus Christ.

The White Horseman is the puppet master of all those who reject the truth of Jesus Christ. That is why it is so hard for people to accept the simple message of the gospel. That is why it is so hard for carnal Christians to accept sound doctrine. If you are not rooted and grounded in God's word evil spirits will try to open as many doors as possible.

The more doors they open the more demons will cohabitate and hide inside your mind, and the more evil entities will enter our dimension through that individual. That is why some people are so wicked. These spirits will live vicariously through a person without that person ever realizing it. Once they get in, they will plant seeds of conflict, lust, fornication, greed, rebellion, false doctrine, propaganda, drama, etc. This is the reason each passing generation is getting worse and worse. You may in fact be talking to a serial killer, sociopath, psychopath (demon) and not even realize it.

"When the unclean spirit is gone out of a man, he walketh through dry places, seeking rest, and findeth none. Then he saith, I will return into my house from whence I came out; and when he is come, he findeth it empty, swept, and garnished. Then goeth he, and taketh with himself seven other spirits more wicked than himself, and they enter in and dwell there: and the last state of that man is worse than the first. Even so shall it be also unto this wicked generation." – Saint Matthew 12:43-45

The White Horseman also blind susceptible Christians to God's will. This rider will conquer the hearts and minds of humanity, squeezing out God. This powerful entity is an influencing force on the entire world, attacking the moral psychology of human beings moving us further and further away from God and closer and closer to our wants and desires. As iniquity abounds common sense is lost, and morality will spiral down into a godless state of mind without that individual ever realizing it or wanting to admit it.

The White Horseman of the Apocalypse will work his magic over time, just like the fable frog being boiled alive. This is what conquering and to conquer means. Put a frog into boiling hot water and it will jump right out. Put a frog into lukewarm water and slowly boil the water. The frog does not notice the change or that it is in danger and eventually it will be cooked to death over a period of time.

People Nowadays

Technology, computers, music, television, and the media are altering the minds of most to accept whatever is handed to them. I would say corporations and the rich are running our lives and raising our kids. Instead of thanking God, we thank the gods of this world. We watch television reality shows where drama, backstabbers, and slanderers program our children to hate authority. Eventually they show little appreciation for the love and protection their parents give them.

If you look at society today you can see the changes. The mindset is I do what I want to do, when I want to do it, how I want to do it, and in what position I want to do it in. Some sin with impunity and make excuses for their behavior as though that will absolve them of their sin.

Lastly, there is no fear or respect of God. When I think about the mindset of our culture these come to mind: There are no consequences for my actions. I am entitled. I have rights. I am invincible. I am special. Just do it. I deserve respect. My needs come first. I am better than you. You are beneath me. I want it all and I want it now!

The White Horseman tricks people into thinking they can wrap themselves in their own cocoon of reality. These have accepted the lie their thoughts and intentions shape their reality, and everyone and everything revolves around them. People I come in contact with from day to day seemed focused on their wants, desires, and are oblivious to everything and everyone around them. They actually think they are the center of the universe. Nothing matters except what they want. They do what seems and feels right in their own eyes, and they do not want boundaries, because they love lawlessness. A lawless person is a dangerous person. Many walk around in the vanity of their own mind thinking they are right when they are wrong. When you point out their error, instead of taking constructive criticism they become angry.

It may be advice on the simplest thing like do not cross the street on a red light. In their mind no one tells them what to do. How dare you tell a person the truth! Some people seem almost mildly sadistic in their behaviors as if causing drama to someone's life is some kind of game. These exhibit sociopathic attributes as if the rules do not apply to them. When you say good morning to a stranger where I live, most look at you like you are crazy or ignore you all together. In this present day culture, I am experiencing what seems like respect for ones' neighbor goes right out of the window. I do not know if it is sensory overload, but people carry an 'I can care less' attitude. The only time they show urgency is when they want something, and are normally reckless trying to obtain it. Today it is even unsafe to keep your doors unlocked.

It is a mystery to me when you love with all your heart, and the more you give of yourself the less your partner treats you like a human being. Kids have the best things in life, but they curse and disrespect their parents. People hate you just because you have a difference in skin color. People never think about how the decisions they make today can affect them or others tomorrow. Today's attitude is tunnel vision on steroids. Everybody's opinion matters except God's. We never ask God what He thinks we should do with our lives. We live carefree until something negative happens, then we blame God.

People are self-absorbed, having great desires for their own pleasures. They boast of their abilities while looking down on others that may not have obtained up to their status. They are rash and they perform actions out of instinct instead of logic and common sense.

The compromise of Christianity is rampant, and the anti-god mentality is a way of life for many unbelievers. People are narcissistic, sadistic, impious, sociopathic, violent, foolhardy, conceited, and self-serving as if it is their inalienable right to have their desires met. They love themselves more than the God that created them. Most people do what they want, and think it is okay. Well... it is not okay!

This last generation is self-serving and arrogant. Many walk around in their pride, vanity, and arrogance not knowing whether they are coming or going. Some act as if nothing can hurt them. The White Horseman convinces people to accept there is nothing wrong with suppressing the truth in unrighteousness, and these become nose-blind to consequences. If a majority of these people were mindful of consequences this world would be a better place to live in. Because there is no fear of God this feat can be accomplished easily. The scariest thing today is people think it is nothing wrong with their immoral behaviors. Antichrist will be accepted because the attitude of mankind will already be conditioned to accept him with open arms. When the Beast comes into power, he will blaspheme the God of heaven and the world will love and worship this guy. What mindset will our culture be in when the name of God is blasphemed with thunderous applause?

With each passing generation the rider on the White Horseman will gain a tighter stranglehold on the minds of men. The main objective is for us to accept that there are no moral absolutes, that we shape reality into what we think and feel, and that our truth is the only truth that matters. If you believe this it becomes easier to believe there is no God in heaven. If there is no God in heaven to be accountable to, there are no consequences. If there are no consequences, then there is no judgment after we die. If there is no judgment after we die, there is no afterlife. If there is no afterlife, then this life is all there is, and I am going to live it to the fullest by saying and doing what feels good to me.

Many people believe this or believe if they do meet God after they die a loving God will not send them to Hell. People always make themselves out to be the victim. They say if God is all loving He would not send anyone to Hell. They are absolutely correct, so I will explain it this way. A student is a repeat absentee, never wants to learn, does not do homework or his assignments, but blames the teacher when he is held back. The teacher did not flunk him. The student flunked himself. Contrary to what some think, God does not condemn you. You condemn yourself if you reject the truth of the gospel. God do not send people to Hell; they send themselves. The student was given a choice. God also gives you a choice.

The world wants to play God and make up our own rules as they go along. When people allow deception to enter their heart they rationalize the end justifies the means. Normally, humans want what they cannot have. The more we cannot have it the more we want it. When they want to obtain something or someone they fall into the trap of the enemy. The devil plays this weakness against us time and again. Those that refuse to see the error of their ways will continue down a path of deception where they will start believing in their own lies. These will dig a spiritual grave so deep they may not recover.

There is a myriad of tactics the enemy uses. If the devil can control your day to day thinking without you ever realizing it, then he has accomplished his purpose in your life. Control a person's heart and you will control how they think. Some people actually think it is their thoughts when in fact you can tell who is really controlling that individual by examining their actions. I am sure you can see all the psychological problems people are experiencing today. Because we reject God, he has no choice but to let us have free will to choose evil. Accepting evil ruins the mind.

"And even as they did not like to retain God in their knowledge, God gave them over to a reprobate mind, to do those things which are not convenient; being filled with all unrighteousness, fornication, and wickedness..." – Romans 1:28-32

"This evil people, which refuse to hear my words, which walk in the imagination of their heart, and walk after other gods, to serve them, and to worship them, shall even be as this girdle, which is good for nothing." – Jeremiah 13:10

Attacks from the White Horseman are meant to push a person away from God into coping methods like alcohol, drugs, sex, and other things. Jesus knows the psychological attacks of the enemy can do more damage than physical attacks, because the mind is very fragile. The devil's attacks are constant day in and day out. The White Horseman of the Apocalypse attacks your emotions and psyche. The White Horseman of the Apocalypse is extremely powerful!

Anyone of these disorders **may** be psychological consequences for sinful actions and **may** apply to a person that has been turned over to the White Horseman because they have rejected the word of truth. Some mental, emotional, and psychological disorders can be direct assaults from the White Horseman. However, this is not true in every case as people are born with or develop certain disorders over a period of time. The only solution is God's word. There is psychological, emotional, and spiritual healing in Jesus. He will touch your mind and heal you from the inside out. But Jesus cannot do that if you do not come to Him with an open heart. Jesus wants to give rest to your spirit, mind, body, and soul.

"Come unto me, all ye that labor and are heavy laden, and I will give you rest." – Saint Matthew 11:28

Not only is the White Horseman of the Apocalypse draining the life out of some, but he is also responsible for many social changes in the last sixty years. In 1962 the Supreme Court ruled that prayer in public schools is unconstitutional because it infringed on another person's belief creating an atmosphere of communal group peer pressure and forced orthodoxy. Back in those days when prayer in public schools was a normal activity to start the school day, the Almighty God was acknowledged for his blessings and goodness. These truths were instilled in children and teenagers, but have long since been lost.

On November 17, 1980, Stone v. Graham, it was ruled the Ten Commandments that hung on the walls of public schools was unconstitutional. On June 27, 2005, McCreary v. ACLU of Kentucky, it was decided by the Supreme Court the Ten Commandments displayed at the McCreary County and Pulaski County Courthouse was unconstitutional. It ruled on the grounds that it violated Separation of Church and State. As we fast-forward to our times, we can see the dramatic changes in our youth since the Ten Commandments and prayer have been removed from public schools.

So, let us regress for a moment and think back. Since prayer was removed from public schools, have we seen a decline in family values and family community? Since television became popular in American homes, have we seen a decline in family values and family community? Since the Ten Commandments have been removed from off the walls of our judicial system, have we seen a decline in family values and family community? As you can see every time a change was made in our laws that defy the laws of God, America's morality has gotten worse.

The White Horseman of the Apocalypse is very patient; making changes in small increments like the fable frog. Many do not notice because these toys and luxuries have drawn our attention away from God. God is yelling danger! But society is more concerned about what is on their cell phones than what is in the Bible. Since television made its' appearance to the masses in the 1960s, we have seen our society move further and further away from God's moral absolutes. Society does not want to retain God in their train of thinking. I believe technology, television, music, and the media play a major role in lulling the mind into a state of complacency. The art of common sense and critical thinking no longer exists. People operate with uncommon sense and they do not have to think anymore because technology does all the thinking for them. Have you ever noticed when people stare into their cell phone they almost seem hypnotized?

The cultural shift is conditioning the way we perceive and think. The world is swayed at the whim of the Prince of the Power of the air by constant propaganda from television shows, movies, music, and the media. Propaganda wants to control what, how, and when you think. It is the greatest tool of mass manipulation. Today many fall under its' spell. Like sheep, many are being led to the slaughter because they follow the masses out of habit and do not think for themselves. In small increments the things of this world increase while the things of God will decrease. It is for this reason God must judge mankind.

"And for this cause God shall send them strong delusion, that they should believe a lie: That they all might be damned who believe not the truth, but had pleasure in unrighteousness." – 2 Thessalonians 2:11-12

With some I cannot distinguish whether they are Christian or not. Societal attitudes have changed so severely that I can barely watch television shows nowadays. Every time I turn on the television all I see is witchcraft, demonology, sex, perverseness, ungodly dramas, demigods, and rebellion; and these are the kid shows. If these shows were on television sixty years ago there would have been societal uproar. Television is not for your entertainment. It is a tool for psychological manipulation and propaganda. Most of the television programs, movies, and the music we listen to are indoctrination tools directly from Satan. Music, television and technology are the Pied Piper of the 21st Century.

Why do you think they are called television programs? They are called programs because they program you to act a certain way, think a certain way, and respond a certain way. Ask yourself; have we become more of a godly nation or more of a godless nation in the last sixty years? The 'Conditioning' has been taking place right before our eyes over the last several generations. It has been hiding in plain sight and will progressively worsen to a rapid decline. These are the primary psychological tools of the White Horseman:

- Repetition
- Propaganda (Persuasion over the masses)
- False Doctrine
- Subliminal messages
- Information overload
- Cultural Peer-Pressure

Nowadays some Christians will not accept sound doctrine or godly counsel, but will look at good as though it is evil and evil as though it is good. People act as if they do not know right from left or left from right. People know what is right, but they choose to ignore their conscience.

Our government created politically correct phrases to legalize sin and destroy our inalienable rights. Do not let them confuse you with politically correct phrases like *"This is the new normal or social distancing."* The new normal is prophecy unfolding right before your eyes. If you cannot see it, **'The Illusion'** already has you.

"Woe unto them that call evil good, and good evil; that put darkness for light, and light for darkness; that put bitter for sweet, and sweet for bitter." – Isaiah 5:20

We are born in sin and shaped in iniquity. We are born in a world set up against us. We are born into a world that hates God. It is only natural for us to violate God's moral laws because the heart of mankind is desperately wicked. We are born spiritually separated from God in a spiritual prison. Earth is the Devil's holding cell, and we are on death row awaiting capital punishment. All these people walking around that have not accepted Jesus Christ as their personal savior have already been sentenced to death, and they do not even realize it. These people think they are alive, but they are dead men walking.

"He that believeth on him is not condemned: but he that believeth not is condemned already, because he hath not believed in the name of the only begotten Son of God." – Saint John 3:18

We live in a world that no longer makes sense. It was not this way sixty years ago. Back then kids and teenagers had respect for their elders, but today a teenager will cuss an elderly person without hesitation. Now do not get me wrong, there are some good kids out there, but where I live it seems like most of our youth have little respect for authority. In today's world, these types of people are not open to resolution. They cannot be bargained with, reasoned with, and they do not have pity or remorse, respect, or fear. It sends chills down my spine to see self-righteous arrogance from what seems like the majority from the younger generations. Sometimes after coming home from work, I just fall on my knees and pray. If it is this bad now, what will it be like in the next twenty years?

I do not fully comprehend why people love this world and the things in it. This existence is a dim fading light. None of this stuff is going with you. Your possessions, status, fame, and achievements are not going with you when you die. The only thing that matters in the hereafter is what kind of relationship you had with Jesus. Your only entry into heaven is Jesus. Your only hope is Jesus. Only the things done for Jesus Christ will last forever. This life is but a speck in eternity.

"If ye be risen with Christ, seek those things which are above, where Christ sitteth on the right hand of God. Set your affection on things above, not on things on the earth." – Colossians 3:1-2

The signs are lighting up like a Christmas tree. With everything happening in the world today people think it is normal. Things are not normal. If you notice, things are becoming undone. That is why we must aggressively compare scripture against what we hear, whether from your father, mother, sister, brother, friend, or pastor. You must pick up your Bible and study it for yourself to aggressively compare scripture against deception. You must meditate and spend time with God. God will give you the Spirit of Understanding, discernment and wisdom if you ask Him. Ask and you will receive. Knock and God will open his door to you. Jesus scolded the religious leaders in his day for this same reason.

"...When it is evening, ye say, it will be fair weather: for the sky is red. And in the morning, it will be foul weather today: for the sky is red and lowering. O ye hypocrites, ye can discern the face of the sky; but can ye not discern the signs of the times." – Saint Matthew 16:2-3

The only way to escape Hell fire is Jesus. If you do not have Jesus; may God have mercy on your soul. Jesus came to pardon and to forgive our sins. His death on the cross gives us the opportunity to be set free from our spiritual chains. Put your faith in, and trust in Jesus.

Jesus will give you a new way to live and grant you eternal life. Jesus will write a new law on your heart. Trust that Jesus is who he says he is: God in human form. Trust in, believe in, and live for Him; for he is the **Door to Heaven**.

- Admit you fall short of God's glory
- Ask God to give you a repentant heart
- Ask God to let his will be done in your life
- Accept Jesus as your personal savior
- Ask God to forgive you of all your sins
- Ask Jesus to come live inside your heart and mind
- Love God with all your heart, mind, strength, and soul
- Treat others the way you would like to be treated
- Start reading the King James Bible starting with Saint John
- Pray and talk to God – He will hear you
- Go: live what you read

The Red Horse

"And when he had opened the second seal, I heard the second beast say, Come and see. And there went out another horse that was red: and power was given to him that sat thereon to take peace from the earth, and that

80

they should kill one another: and there was given unto him a great sword."
– Revelation 6:3-4

The Family Court System

In 1969, the Governor of California signed No Fault Divorce into law. Since then, the divorce rate increased significantly in the United States. Today the divorce rate exceeds more than fifty percent. It only takes about fifty dollars and ten minutes to get married, but years to get a divorce. Getting a divorce in America can be very costly. More money passes through Family Court than the Justice system. A close personal friend of mine named Mac got trapped in the sticky web of Family and Divorce Court.

Mac was a hard worker and always provided for his wife and kids. Mac had a good paying job and his wife was a home-maker. He paid all the bills and gave her an allowance each week. Mac is a person who lived within his means. His wife on the other hand wanted the best things in life handed to her. It is nothing wrong with wanting nice things, but she wanted him to work two jobs to fulfill her selfish desires.

Mac confided in me and asked me what he should do. He told me his wife was never happy, it was always something wrong, and she was always full of drama. He loved working a straight forty hours, because it gave him more time with his kids. I told him that family and his kids are the most important things on this planet. In the end Mac refused to sacrifice a relationship with his two young boys to work two jobs. Some things are more important than money.

Mac confronted his wife on the issue and told her if she wanted more money, she would have to earn it herself. Instead of his wife applying for a part-time job, she sued for child support and spousal support. Two months later Mac's wife moved out of the area to go live with her father. She said she was not happy, and she was taking the two boys with her. After several months Mac became so lonely and lovesick; he made the 24 hour trip by bus to visit his wife and kids. Mac's father-in-law allowed him to visit because he did not want the family to be separated.

Along the way traveling from Philadelphia to Arizona, Mac thought about reuniting with his wife and kids to bring them home. His father-in-law let him stay for a week to hash things out. During that time, he told his wife that he loved and missed her, and they should work it out. After he returned home, his wife and kids came back a month later. They had a long talk and decided they should work out their martial issues. Initially for the first several months' things seemed to be going well. But my friend would soon see he was wrong.

81

His wife went back to her original ways and demanded that Mac give her the extravagant lifestyle every husband should give his wife. By this time, my friend was already working two jobs to make ends-meet because he was still paying child support. Mac was so busy working two jobs, he trusted his wife to pay all the bills on time from his bank account. He was making good money, but she continued spending it behind his back.

The more Mac tried to please his wife, the worse the atmosphere became. His wife wanted him to obey her every command, and wanted to be in charge of everything, but had no idea of how to navigate. As time went on Mac realized the bills were not being paid on time. Mac refused to let his wife take away his manhood. He told her that she must get a job and stop spending money recklessly. Mac had enough of her selfish ways and finally put his foot down.

Surprisingly, his wife goes and finds a full-time job with excellent benefits and good pay. However, the money from their joint account was still being drained. She refused to put her paychecks in their joint account. Instead she opened a separate individual account. Mac became infuriated, so he took his name off the joint account and moved what was left of the money to a new account in his name. He told his wife that he needed to get the finances back on track and that he would be in charge of paying the bills for now on. His wife became angry and revealed to him that when she was living out of state, she committed adultery with another man. Mac was angry, but he forgave her. Mac was just trying to keep his family together because he grew up in a broken home. After all, the guy was in another state, so he overlooked her transgression.

Over the next several months hostility became the daily normal between Mac and his wife. Mind you, his wife was a so-called lover of Jesus Christ. In the past they went to church every Sunday and Bible study every Wednesday. She used to always tell her kids she loved God. Mac would reply, *"How can you love God whom you have not seen, and don't love me, who you see every day?"* Mac's wife would get furious and storm out of the room.

After years of abuse by his wife, Mac finally gave up and told her that she does not love him, and they should go their separate ways. He told her he would move into the basement for several months until they amicably work out the details. Mind you, Mac's wife never cancelled the child and spousal support. After spending a week in the basement, he received divorce papers in the mail indicating he was being sued in court for a divorce. His wife stopped speaking to him altogether.

Every Sunday morning before dragging the kids to church Mac's wife would listen to televangelists while shouting out hallelujahs and amen(s). As she walked by Mac on her way to church, she did acknowledge his presence. One Sunday morning she was out running errands. Mac had to go to his church, so he took the boys with him that morning. A couple of hours later in the middle of the preacher's sermon; his wife showed up and angrily drags the boys from the congregation.

Three years pass by with the same treatment. For three years Mac lived in the basement. For three years Mac was dragged in and out of court nearly every other month for spousal support, child support, and divorce hearings. For three years while living under the same roof, Mac was a stranger in his own home. It was all about money, power, and control. His wife did not love God, she loved herself. After three years Mac had enough of her games, so he decided he was going to go upstairs in his room, lie in his bed and watch his television. When he entered the room, his wife was puzzled.

When Mac laid down on his bed his wife tried to push him off. When that did not work, she tried to kick him off the bed. When that did not work, she called the local authorities and told the operator Mac assaulted her. When the police officers arrived, they placed Mac under arrest without reading him his Miranda Rights. They never told him he was under arrest. They just took him down to the police station and processed him. Mac spent almost two days in jail.

Eventually Mac went before a judge via monitor. The judge asked the arresting police officer if there were any signs of abuse on Mac's wife. The police officer responded, "No." The judge then asked the police officer if there were signs in the house of any type of struggle. The officer responded, "No." The judge then released Mac on his own recognizance. He was released around 4 a.m. in the morning, and was scheduled to appear in court at 9 am for a protection order filed against him. Exhausted and frustrated, he walked about two miles to his home.

When he entered the home his oldest son who was now 14 years old at that time gave him a big hug. He did not understand why his father was being treated so unfairly. He and his younger brother came into the room that night and they saw their mother assaulting their father. Mac's 14-year-old son Bob decided to be a witness on his father's behalf. Mac and Bob went down to Family Court. Mac hid Bob in the men's room. As Mac waited, his wife showed up with a sinister smirk on her face. She entered the courtroom first to tell her side of the story.

At that moment Bob was retrieved from the bathroom. After ten minutes or so, Mac gets called into the courtroom. The judge asked if he assaulted his wife. He told the judge the only person assaulted was him. Mac's wife then tells the judge Mac punched her, kicked her, and slapped her. She told the judge both of her sons were there, and they saw the whole thing. Mac told the judge that both boys were there. As a matter of fact, his oldest son Bob is in the waiting room, and he has come to testify of what actually took place.

The demeanor on Mac's wife face immediately went from a sinister smirk to bewilderment like a deer caught in headlights. Mac's wife started to explain how he did not assault her, that she was exaggerating, and so forth. The judge asked Mac if he had anywhere to go. Mac responded, "No." and told the judge how he was living in his basement for several years, and that he and his wife should have been divorced long ago. The judge dismissed the case and ordered that he be confined to the basement to avoid any further arguments. Even-though Mac beat the Order of Protection, he still had to appear in criminal court to face the charges of assault. Mac sought legal representation which cost him $1,000.00.

Soon after, Bob and his mother got into a bitter argument. Mac went upstairs to break it up. Once again Mac's wife called the local authorities and told the operator that she was being assaulted by her husband. When the policer officers arrived that day Mac had just gotten off work and he was dressed in his work uniform. The police officer knocking on the door was the same one that arrested Mac the first time. The officer recognized Mac. When he arrested Mac the first time, Mac obeyed his every command with, 'Yes sir' or 'No sir', and was compliant. The officer then turns to Mac's wife and said, *"If you call us again, the next person to be arrested will be you!"* – #Hallelujah! God had enough of her foolishness!

From this point on Bob became public enemy #2. Bob received the same treatment as Mac, only worse. His mother treated his younger brother like royalty and treated Bob like dirt. Bob learned at an early age that standing up for the truth can cost you dearly. Bob and his mother would always have heated verbal arguments almost daily. She would tell Bob the Bible tells children to obey their parents. When Bob replied, *"Parents provoke not your children."* She would become angry and storm out of the room. Mac was so proud of his oldest son even-though he was being persecuted for standing up for the truth.

Several weeks later after coming home from work Mac opened his front door only to discover the entire home was empty. The washing machine, refrigerator, beds, dressers, clothes, televisions, pictures, and whatever was not bolted down was gone. Mac was paying child/spousal support and did not even know where his kids were. Even-though Bob and his mother did not get along, she took him because she was getting child support for him.

Mac loved his two boys. His two boys were his pride and joy. That is what kept him going and his wife knew it. Again, Mac was summoned to court for custody and visitation rights. At this point Mac was so frustrated and bewildered with the injustice being served he did not know what to do.

Little did Mac know things would become worse! When he went before a judge to plead his case for 50/50 custody, the judge shows little mercy, ordering he can only have one hour a week visitation rights.

During the divorce proceedings the lawyer of Mac's wife made accusations against him that were bold face lies. He accused Mac of being a bad parent and a wife abuser among other things. Mac's wife and her lawyer knew they were committing perjury. After another mediation hearing Mac lost, his wife's lawyer shook hands with the mediator and invited him to lunch.

Mac told me his wife came from a broken home. Something happened in her past that caused her pain. Mac did everything he could to help her, but she began taking her hurt and pain out on him. Her refusal to forgive what some other guy did to her and her refusal to obey God costs her a great blessing. If you do not forgive you run the risk of being broken forever on the inside. After twenty long years of marriage there was nothing left. Mac lost his home, his parental rights, and his funds decreased significantly. After ten long years in Divorce court Mac's wife finally signed the divorce papers. When all was said and done, Mac's paperwork stood around seven inches thick. I felt bad for my best friend.

The United States Constitution states that in court you have a right to a trial by jury to ascertain the circumstances. This should apply to Family Court. Unfortunately, Family Court does not uphold your rights under the Constitution of the United States because the system of Family Court is a system of equity, not law. Because there is no jury of peers, interpretation of a situation is now open to a peer of judges under a corrupt and unfair system. We pay many taxes, yet have no representation. We pay many taxes, yet we are denied the right to a jury of peers. Who gave judges the authority to tell you how many hours you can spend with **your kids**? Courts of Equity were instituted to mediate on behalf of the best interest of the child. As you can see it has had the exact opposite effect, as children are ripped away from mothers or fathers.

There should not be any long drawn-out mediations and court order appearances. Both parents had the child together. In most cases both parents should have 50/50 rights to their child. Debt and income should be split 50/50 right down the middle. These judges and lawyers have forced their will on us with impunity. They make themselves out to be gods and have openly made merchandise of the family.

When or if you go through the system, you will need a lawyer. Of course, it will cost you. It may cost you a little, it may cost you a lot, but it is going to cost you. The first objective the Family and Divorce Courts do is to determine how much money you have. What is your yearly income? Do you have any stocks and bonds? Do you have a 401K? Do you have gold or silver?

How many cars do you have? How many houses do you own? How much money in your bank account? Do you have a Trust Fund? Where are your secret jewels hidden? Do you have money hidden under your mattress or in your underwear? Do you have any gold teeth? Why do you think they want to know about your money? Because they are getting ready to bleed you dry.

To make money lawyers file frivolous motions to consume it. There are hundreds of family code laws that no common person could literally interpret them all. They make these laws to confuse the average citizen to force the aid of an attorney. And as you already know, it may cost you a little, it may cost you a lot, but it is going to cost you. The more laws that go on the books, the more complex Family and Divorce Court becomes, the more families they destroy.

If you go into any court without an attorney, the judges will view you as an irritating annoyance. This forces you to find and scrape up the money that you do not have to get an attorney. The lawyers on either side file the initial paperwork and try to incite both couples to win at all costs. Opposing lawyers collude to add fuel to the fire. The bigger the fire the bigger they line their greedy pockets.

The more accusations made by the other party, the more the opposing team must respond. The more accusations: more paperwork. More paperwork: the more you are billed. The more you are billed: the more they make. Both couples are played against one another as the family suffers. Little do they know it is only a win for the lawyers and the System, as the family structure is ripped a part.

In my opinion Family Courts, Divorce Courts, and Criminal Courts are very unfair. Why is it that you can only get enough justice as you can afford? I will tell you why. It is the double-standard policy of law. One side of this policy favors the rich and powerful, while the other side of this policy dishonors the masses. All these laws were created to generate money for these systems. Never-mind about the pain and heartache it has caused. Never-mind about the families they have broken up. Never-mind about the kids they have destroyed. For this, God will sorely judge every last single corrupt cop, lawyer, and judge. May God, have mercy on their souls. If you are not a corrupt cop, lawyer, or judge, then you have nothing to worry about.

In Scandinavia only 2% percent of custody cases go before a Family Court Judge. In Scandinavian Family Court, the plaintiff must pay the legal fees of the person whom they are suing. This eliminates people lying and abusing the system for financial gain or revenge. The Scandinavia Family Court system prevents fighting over custody, money, the destruction of the family, and lawyer greed.

Child support is limited to a fixed monthly amount based on the basic needs of each child, not the lifestyle of the child. This amount is fixed regardless of who has less or more custody of the child. This eliminates children as pawns. In Scandinavian Family Court there are no custody evaluators, expert witnesses, or outrageous court costs. Usually, custody with each parent is split 50/50. This eliminates drawn out court cases. And did I mention the elimination of lawyer greed? Oh yeah! I DID!

Scandinavia's Family Court is equitable and fair across the board. It welcomes healing instead of generational trauma. The United States Family Courts should migrate from its' broken system to a Scandinavian system that works. Why is this not being done as we speak? My guess is there is no money in it. If we had a fair system like the Scandinavians, people would not lose their relationship with their children, lose all their funds, have their credit destroyed, would not have to file bankruptcy, be thrown in Debtors' prison, or possibly lose their homes.

Family and Divorce Court were instituted to protect the children, but the devil has corrupted the system by paying off greedy lawyers and judges. The Red Horseman of the Apocalypse has been destroying families and creating anger within the last several generations. The first hour of my workday tends to set the course of my day. In the same way unclean spirits target kids at a young age to set the course of their lives. The devil is very strategic. As a majority, I find the younger generations as a whole to be detached from reality. They lack interpersonal relationship skills that affect how they treat one another. I also see a lack of empathy as the rules do not seem to apply to them. They are angry and they do not know why. Instinctual affection comes through strong family structure and values. As a result of this brokenness, love for ones' fellow neighbor decreases. As more families become broken, more hurt, more pain, and more rejection is translated to the children.

The Criminal Justice System

ibid, Prison Policy.org

On January 31, 1865, slavery was ruled unconstitutional ratified by the 13th Amendment. This sounds great except for a small embedded clause which states, *"Except as a punishment for crime whereof the party shall have been duly convicted..."* Those incarcerated over the years are basically slaves of the State. Notice the 13th Amendment says, 'Duly Convicted'. It is the same modus operandi of slavery, wearing a different mask. (**ibid, 13_Documentary**)

"The United States of American is 4% of the world's population, yet it jails 25% of the prison population." That is 450% percent higher than the rest of the

world. 1 out of 4 world inmates are imprisoned in the land of the free and home of the brave; the land where you are innocent until proven guilty.

In 1970, the incarceration rate in the United States was 200,000. In 1982 the incarceration rate jumped to 300,000. In 1984 under the Reagan Administration, the Sentencing Reform Act was signed into legislation. In one year, the incarceration rate jumped 16.67% percentto 350,000 by 1985.

In 1986 under the Reagan Administration, the Anti-Drug Abuse Act was signed into legislation. The *"Just say no to drugs."* campaign seemed like a good idea at the time. However, they failed to tell us they would be throwing people into prison and locking them up for years for seemingly petty crimes. Within the next decade the incarceration rate jumped nearly 100% percent from 350,000 to 700,000. By the year 2007 the incarceration rate was round 800,000.

By 2020, the incarceration rate was 2.3 million. That is an increase of 288% percent within thirteen years. Between the mid-1980s and the Millennium, huge chunks of fathers disappeared into the prison system. The 1980s was the beginning of mass incarceration, or should I say mass slavery.

My nephew went to the store to buy a soda. A young male accused him of being with a group of boys that robbed him. Even before my nephew got to the store the cops were already on the scene. My nephew walked right pass the cops into the store to buy his soda, came out of the store, and they arrested him on the spot. Who robs a person, then comes right back to the scene of the crime to buy a soda? All the cops had to do is ask the store owner if he saw my nephew commit a crime or check the outdoor security cameras. My nephew's bail was set at $5,000 dollars just for buying a soda. They put multiple charges on my nephew so he would take a plea deal to a crime he did not commit. The total trumped up charges totaled fifteen. By the way, my brother had to pay another five thousand for a lawyer, who did absolutely nothing. My nephew was forced to make a plea deal to avoid jail time. My nephew now has a record.

Once those handcuffs are place on you, you are guilty until proven innocent and you will be promptly escorted to jail to be processed. But do not worry; you can get out if you pay money. If you cannot bail out, you will sit in jail for two years until your trial comes up. Or maybe God, I mean the District Attorney will make a deal with you. Admit to the crime and the State will give probation, or 3-5 years with time off for good behavior. If you do not admit to the crime after spending two years in prison, you can take your chances and be found guilty. A friend of mine was thrown in jail for owing a thousand dollars in child support due to an income change in his employment. Sometimes you do not have to do anything wrong to be arrested.

For the last several decades harsh mandatory sentences for non-violent crimes, low level offenses and misdemeanors have been separating patriarchs (fathers-protectors-providers-heroes) from their families. *"Seventy-four percent of people held in local jails in the United States are not convicted of any crime. And 26.5% of people held in federal prison in the United States have not been convicted of any crime. Over 555,000 people are locked up in the local jail system that haven't been duly convicted or sentenced."*

The Federal Prison System includes the US Marshall Service, Bureau of Prisons, I.C.E., and the Office of Refugee Resettlement. There are people sitting in jail right now that have not been convicted of anything. The system set bails so high the poor cannot afford to post bail. If you have not been duly convicted of a misdemeanor crime why do you have to pay bail money? I thought you are innocent until proven guilty. Are you telling me some civil servants do not lie, cheat, or plant evidence? Do not tell me otherwise, because I have been there.

There are innocent people sitting in jail right now because they were framed, identified falsely of a crime, or simply too poor to make bail. To add insult to injury, after a person is released from serving prison time it is hard to find employment. In many cases a person is branded a felon for the rest of his or her natural life. Is that justice? Once a person has paid their debt to society their record should be immediately expunged for low level non-violent crimes and their inalienable rights should be fully restored.

Prison should only be for hardcore offenders, sex offenders and murderers. There are many other ways to reform first time offenders without locking them up, especially if it is for a minor crime. Initial options to reform should be boot camp, house arrest, probation, fines and restitution, community service, mental health treatment, drug rehab, or anger management. When fathers are prosecuted and sent to jail for minor offenses families are destroyed and broken. In the early 1980s Ronald Reagan allotted millions of dollars for prison and jail facilities. The Clinton Administration carried that torch into the 21st Century.

There have been promises and big talk made in the past for prison reform, but it was just talk. Now twenty years later we still hear voices from some of our leaders on prison reform. To date, nothing extreme has been done to turn the tide. Why? Just ask O.J. Simpson. O.J. Simpson's defense team cost him $50,000 a day during his criminal trial. Some people have hired lawyers at $600/hour. Mass incarceration is good for business; and there is no reforming big business. Vendors of these prisons also profit by providing their services. Everything from jeans to guidance systems to sports uniforms, and many other items are being produced or assembled through prison labor. This thing is so big it has taken on a life of its' own.

This monster is too big to stop because everyone in the chain of gain from corporations to the legislators to the wardens to the little man, are part of this system.

Is the Criminal Justice System about justice or big business? Is the Criminal Justice System about justice or prison labor? Privatized prisons are more than a seven billion dollar a year industry. The United States spends about eighty billion dollars a year on incarceration. That is your hard-earned tax money at work. Do you know you can become a potential stockholder in companies that build private prisons? Buy some stock, sit back and relax as the prison system earns you money. People stuck in the Criminal Justice System are essentially livestock. I am not going to even talk about prisons for profits giving campaign contributions to push their agendas. If you do not understand politics is a rich man's game, **'The Illusion'** already has you.

The Latino and African American races suffer a great deal more punishment for the same crimes. The absence of the patriarch highly increases the odds of the family structure being torn apart. Only a real man can teach his son how to be a real man. Far too many strong black women are taking both roles of patriarch and matriarch, because one out of nine fathers is locked up in prison. *"One in three African Americans will have some interaction with the Criminal Justice System during their lifetime. Nearly six million kids are impacted by parental incarceration."*

When you disrupt the family, you disrupt the community. When I was growing up it took a village to raise a child. That type of communal support does not exist anymore. Today we are seeing the repercussions. Generations of leadership has been stripped out since the Reagan and Clinton Administration. How is locking up people for low level offenses and destroying communities a war on drugs? Locking up entire communities will not solve the problem as you can see. Going to the source of the problem will stop the problem. Stop the supply and you will stop the drugs and those using it. This hardcore agenda by the Reagan Administration was not a war on drugs; it was a war on the family. The African American and Latino communities were hit the hardest. The numbers show this beyond a reasonable doubt. Numbers do not lie.

Similar to Family Court, those persons who make the laws prosper from those laws at the expense of the common people. Laws were made for us, but those who are placed into a position of power, heavily abuse that power. If you decide to walk around with your eyes wide open, you will see the impact over the last several generations. Was the Criminal Justice System designed fairly or designed to destroy families? Does the Criminal Justice System hold you innocent until you are proven guilty, or it is the other way around?

Is the Criminal Justice System big business or is it about equality among all colors? Does the Criminal Justice System favor the rich or the poor? Hmm? When I looked at the condition of our society over the past several generations, I have seen a division of families, peoples, and nations where no love, hypocrisy, hate, and criticism abound. Peace, respect, and brotherly love have dissipated over the last several generations. These are strategies of the enemy of your soul.

"For we wrestle not against flesh and blood, but against principalities, against powers, against the rulers of the darkness of this world, against spiritual wickedness in high places." – Ephesians 6:12

What about these generations of kids growing up without a father? Can you imagine the trauma that carries over from generation to generation? I came from a broken home due to my parents' divorce and I grew up angry because my dad was out of the picture for several years of my life. My anger was ignited by hurt, pain, rejection, fueled by the bitterness of life. If you allow it, anger will dictate how you perceive life. Something vital was missing in me. That something is the glue of honor, love, integrity, and morals that holds the family together. Without this glue, core family values fall apart. That glue is the father.

For many of these kids growing up, life just is not fair. God instituted marriage and family. Why do you think the devil wants to tear families apart? Back in the day you went to church as a family; ate at the dinner table as a family; talked and reasoned as a family. How many children of broken and dysfunctional families get the gospel every Sunday? The devil knows the absence of leadership creates instability within the family structure. With no stability and boundaries kids are prone to make many mistakes. Some act out in school, experience behavioral problems or depressive symptoms which can affect them for a lifetime and spill over to the next generation. At the very worst, the family will become dysfunctional.

If you look around you can see we are on our way to an anarchic society. Part of the process of healing is to ask God to help you to forgive. Believe it or not forgiving people is the road to healing. If you have an unforgiving spirit, you are only damaging your relationship with God and others in the long run. As God has forgiven you of your trespasses, you too must forgive others that trespass against you.

"For if ye forgive men their trespasses, your heavenly Father will also forgive you: but if ye forgive not men their trespasses, neither will your Father forgive your trespasses." – Saint Matthew 6:14-15

Unfortunately, we are living in the last days. Instead of forgiving past hurts, people hurt by other people, tend to hurt other people.

Divorce and Family Court, and the Criminal Justice System among others have strategically destroyed the love of many. The devil knows if he can unravel family structure, he can unravel society. His red knight (Red Horseman) has been destroying families and creating anger over the last several generations. Over the generations the hurt gets deeper and deeper, and anger grows stronger and stronger. The end result is bitterness and resentment against God and everyone around them. As the family structure deteriorates, anger and an unforgiving spirit become more prevalent in our society and around the world.

This plague of modern-day slavery has destroyed many fathers, many mothers, many children, and many households. Many of the municipal, state, and governmental systems setup supposedly to protect the family has in a real sense damaged the family at its' core. Children that come from these types of homes carry emotional and psychological trauma from incompleteness of loss. The irony is what affects one affects all. Things that affect the family affect society. Those things that affect society affect the world. We are all connected regardless of race, creed, or color. These systems in place seem to cause more problems than they solve.

Many of our systems were established with the best intentions, but systemic greed pervades withal. These laws and systems create contention, because they are inherently flawed, due to one-sided injustice towards the masses. Absolute control over the masses corrupts those who make themselves out to be gods. Can you feel the noose being tightened around your neck? Our due process, civil liberties, First Amendments rights, and privacy have diminished significantly over the last sixty years. This means we are moving towards a One World Government.

From a biblical viewpoint humans are inherently evil with the capacity for good deeds (Saint Matthew 7:11). At some level contention is systemic within us all. It is not just world war, but war within. The Red Horseman of the Apocalypse has created an atmosphere of war within the heart of mankind. In other words, the world is essentially at war, because we are at war with one another. It is world war on a continuous basis because we do not love one another. The world we live in is defiant, selfish, and unforgiving. We are subjected to a system of laws that cater to the rich and powerful. The Red Horseman has been assigned for the purpose of destroying the love that binds all humanity together. This includes the sanctity of marriage and family. The destruction of the family and devastation of children globally has created a response of hostility and apathy. It will get worst with each passing generation, because contention is the seed of all wars.

"And because iniquity shall abound, the love of many shall wax cold." – Saint Matthew 24:12

Chapter Five
3rd and 4th Seal

The Black Horse

"And when he had opened the third seal, I heard the third beast say, Come and see. And I beheld, and lo a black horse; and he that sat on him had a pair of balances in his hand. And I heard a voice in the midst of the four beasts say, a measure of wheat for a penny, and three measures of barley for a penny; and see thou hurt not the oil and the wine." – Revelation 6:5-6

In the early 1900s farmers made up 25% percent of the United States workforce. The turn of the 20th century brought a convergence of technologies. Through automation, farming began to decrease making way to modernized society. Refrigeration, air conditioning, elevators, washing machines, telephone, antibiotics, the sewage system, silent movies, aircraft, radio, the assembly line, mechanized farming equipment, combustible engines, instant camera, and the jukebox were new emerging technologies. The electrical grid changed life and truly transformed the lives of many. The technologies we take for granted today was cutting edge technology back then. As luxuries became necessities Americans began to experience an era of prosperity and innovation. With this new era came the stock market.

The Dow Jones Industrial Average was created in 1896 and the stock market was mainly traded by the rich and wealthy. By the 1920s Wall Street became popular for the average individual. Around this time banks opened up a new opportunity for the average American to sample a piece of the economic pie. What made Wall Street popular was another innovation known as 'Buy now, Pay later'. Today we call it consumer credit. The ideology then was to live in the moment, enjoy life, take thine ease and be merry. Buy now pay later became very popular. When credit was extended it gave the average person purchasing power to attain a better quality of living as well as the ability to engage in the stock market.

Ordinary people saw the stock market as a place to get rich quickly, grow their investments, and ultimately live a life of luxury. The average nobody could become rich through stock investments. Ticker tapes showing the results of the stock market began showing up everywhere. They were on cruise ships, railroad stations, trains, and beauty parlors. Trading firms would literally be set up daily to broker trades. The exchange of money and non-secured credit was flowing like milk and honey.

It was an age of prosperity for the working class, and it seemed it would never end. More and more people began to invest in the stock market. Many deemed it as a new kind of wealth. The money was there for the taking. It was like getting free money. Everyone was singing the song of prosperity and there was a sense of confidence all the way up to, and including the presidency. In the mid-1920s, investing in the stock market became so popular it was deemed respectable and reliable to do so. Those that did not invest for one reason or another were deemed foolish and irresponsible because monetary gains were like taking candy from a baby. Brokers were in the best possible position, earning a generous commission on each trade.

The selections of stocks were plentiful. There were real estate stocks, pharmaceutical stocks, utility stocks, transportation stocks, retail stocks, mining stocks, electronic stocks, entertainment stocks, food company stocks, industrial stocks, oil stocks, and energy stocks. Between the years 1924-1929, the stock market quadrupled its earnings. The stock market seemed so prosperous and sustainable, more and more Americans jumped on the Wall Street bandwagon. Even the shoeshine boy to the housewife would invest in this new and exciting phenomenon. Wall Street was the talk of the town and the number one topic on everyone's lips. Wall Street was viewed as an institution that could not fail.

Wall Street dazzled the minds of Americans and consumer borrowing became excessive. People came out in droves to invest in the stock market. Millions of Americans wanted a piece of the Wall Street pie. Out of 120 million Americans, one in three spun the roulette wheel on the stock market. By 1929 over forty million Americans invested over two billion dollars in the stock market. Such an increase over a period of about six years seemed uncanny. As Wall Street grew bigger and bigger, there was little governing laws to regulate its' practices. Unfortunately, by the year 1929 the stock market was not based on its' real value. The Stock Market was ridiculously over inflated and based on speculative value.

The rich and wealthy, who had insider information, was manipulating the stocks. The rich and wealthy would buy up enormous amounts of stocks, driving up its' values, only to be the first ones to cash out with enormous profits. Middle to lower class individuals experienced great losses when the price of those stocks plummeted. The novice investor was unaware the stock market was a virtual gambling casino rigged by those who controlled it. People who invested their life savings lost in the end. Wall Street was one big Ponzi scheme.

What was troubling back in those days is no one asked, *"What would happen if the stock market crashed?"* The belief was the stock market would not and could not crash.

Brokers, speculators, Wall Street experts, and even the POTUS assured the American people the stock market was on the up and up. It seemed that either no one cared, or no one had enough sense to know that eventually all good things are not meant to last.

There were a few economists that warned stock companies were highly over-valued and eventually consequences would arise. These economists also warned that credit margin was a bad idea because it grossly over inflated the stock market. People, politicians, and bankers simply ignored the danger signs. The higher the stock market rose, the more these economists shouted "Danger!" Because the Dow Jones index quadrupled within a five-year period, the Stock Market would eventually correct itself.

Because consumer credit was so available by brokerage firms through the banking system, people invested in the stock market through margin. Margin is an investment made with borrowed money. For instance, if you purchased $100 dollars of stock you would use $75 dollars of margin and $25 dollars of your own money. A person could invest in several ways. One of those ways was to speculate whether a stock would rise or fall. If you bet against a stock, you would make a profit, but if that stock did not fall in your favor, you would take a loss. This Wall Street gambling frenzy with borrowed credit created enormous credit risk as people were investing in trust companies. The problem was these trust companies were borrowing money from the banks and using margin to play the stock market themselves. As long as speculation worked in one's favor everything was good, but if the projection did not work in one's favor, how would the money be paid back? No one thought about the consequences. There are always consequences. Nothing, not even the stock market would continue in an upward trend.

On October 24, 1929, the stock market crashed. The speculative financial bubble finally burst. This day was known as 'Black Thursday'. It was like a domino effect that grasped panic-stricken shareholders putting them in disillusionment. People began to walk around like mindless zombies in utter disbelief. Investors were stupefied and confused, which led to all out panic, communal anxiety, and emotional ruin. When the stock market finally bottomed out its' estimated losses were about eighty percent totaling a loss of about twenty-five billion dollars. All the margin lending could not be repaid to the banks. This caused the banks to fail. This led to a financial crisis, which closed many banks.

Back then bank insurance (FDIC) did not exist. When the bank failed and shut down, all your money in the bank went with it. When banks began shutting down people rushed to withdraw their money causing a run on the banks. By 1933 over four thousand banks shut their doors.

Because there was no money there was no consumer lending, which led to no consumer spending and a sluggish economy. No buying power led to a downward motion in the economy. Businesses imposed compulsory layoffs, which eventually led to the collapse of many businesses. Factories closed down, stores boarded up, and businesses went bankrupt. This domino effect further plunged the American economy into a downward spiral. Since the stock market crash of October 1929, the economy went from bad to worse leading to the Great Depression of the 1930s. Fear, strife and turmoil began to multiply exponentially as the Great Depression lingered on.

When large masses of people began losing their jobs, confidence in the economy hit an all-time low. Other sectors like the steel industry, the housing market, and agriculture felt the effects too. Unemployment hit an all-time high of about twenty-five percent. Back then there was no unemployment compensation or financial safety net to assist people when unemployment visited their homes. The steel industry loss ninety percent of its production and had to lay off most of its workers. Those that kept their jobs had reduced hours and salary.

Agriculture was hit the hardest. Farmers were affected more than anyone. Wheat went down in value and the prices farmers would generally charge for produce went down significantly. Farmers literally could not make a profit to keep their farms, let alone make ends meet. There were tons and tons of food and produce that was unmarketable. Because their produce was not marketable some farmers would destroy their crops instead of giving the food away to feed the hungry. Subsequently, many farmers were evicted because they could not meet their mortgage payments and their farms auctioned off. This led to a mass migration of farmers looking for work to feed their families. Many became day laborers or migrant workers. Those who managed to hang on to their farms and were not affected as much, grew their own produce, and lived off their livestock. Everyone felt the plight to some degree or another except for the rich and wealthy.

The housing market was hit heavily, and many homeowners defaulted on their mortgage payments, which in turn caused turmoil in the housing market. Families were evicted and forced to live on the streets. Because the welfare system did not exist back then, Americans began to rely on bread lines and soup kitchens to eke out a meager existence to survive through these trying times. Many had to travel for miles just to get a bowl of soup and piece of bread. As the Great Depression lingered on, more families became dependent on charitable organizations to feed them. A charity known as the ACSF (Associated Charities of San Francisco) would deliver boxes of food every week.

Poverty became so bad people began to rummage through garbage looking for any morsel of food because the bread lines and soup kitchens became overloaded. People wore raggedy clothing full of holes and wrapped their feet with newspaper and cardboard, because they did not have shoes. The homeless population increased and relocated to rural areas. Families built makeshift shacks out of rolls of housing material to cover the outside of the home to survive the cold winters. These makeshift huts were usually temporary as the unemployed would eventually migrate to look for food and employment.

Hobos, a term used for the homeless, would ride railroad trains from station to station hoping to find a home where they could ask the homeowner for something to eat and drink. Girls that went to school only had one or two dresses in their wardrobe. Boys only had one pair of pants and one pair of shoes if they were lucky. Children would play baseball with rocks and sticks. In some areas of the country blackberry trees were plentiful. Blackberry pie was cheap and easy to make. Mothers would use a little lard, sugar, eggs, and flour to bake children a tasty treat. Sometimes blackberry pie was the only thing for breakfast, lunch and dinner.

When the American economy took a steep plunge, people rushed to liquidate their assets for pennies on the dollars. Thousands of dazed and confused investors gathered at Wall Street looking for answers. Back then the POTUS, Herbert Clark Hoover did nothing to restore confidence of panic-stricken Americans, but contrariwise offered false assurances that never came to fruition. Credibility in Washington D.C. was loss as many loss hope. There were many demonstrations and picket lines calling for the government to solve the economic crisis.

The irony was, even amid the Great Depression the warehouses were full of clothes, and car dealerships were full of automobiles and trucks. Caviar, Shrimp, lobster, and filet mignon was still available. Confectionery treats and tons of food were still available. Homes and apartments were empty while people slept on the streets. Back in those days a coke, hamburger and fries cost about 15¢, but people could not even afford that luxury.

It was the cynicism of greed that led millions of Americans into the plight of homelessness, poverty, and unemployment. The desperate would take any job no matter how menial to feed themselves or their families, going so far as to sell apples on the street. Families that migrated to the west and east got lucky. There were jobs available in the San Joaquin Valley working in the cement plants, while in the east; logging jobs paid about seven dollars a day cutting cord wood.

The POTUS, Herbert Hoover did little to turn around the economic woes. He spoke many wonderful words, but in reality, did little to swell the economic crisis.

Americans lost all hope in President Hoover and wondered what messiah would come and rescue them. On July 2, 1932, the D.N.C. nominated Franklin Delano Roosevelt to run for the next presidency. In November 1932 Franklin Delano Roosevelt was elected the 32nd president of the United States. His slogan was 'A New Deal' for the American people. FDRs Administration created fifteen new laws that would go into effect to create new jobs, boost crop prices, improve the Tennessee Valley, prevent home foreclosures, insured bank deposits, and stabilize the economy. Unlike the previous administration, FDR felt the federal government needed to take on a greater responsibility to kick start the economy. Roosevelt understood that restarting the economy was based on psychological faith in the system. Putting people back to work was the main objective. FDR presented himself in a way that showed the American people that Congress cared and would do everything in its power to restore the economy.

FDR promised to regulate the financial system, create a healthy currency, and provide economic and social aid. His first task was to start over. Through a new and exciting technology called radio, FDR would use this venue to inform the American people of his progress. FDR's presidential radio addresses would come to be known as 'Fireside Chats'.

Aided by his cabinet, AKA 'The Brain Trust', FDR quickly put all his generals to work to directly launch an assault on the economic crisis. The first order of business was to clean up Wall Street and to correct the banking system. In the year 1932, Glass–Steagall legislation was enacted to separate commercial banking from investment banking. This would prevent securities firms and investment banks from taking deposits from ordinary people. This was one of the main reasons that caused Wall Street to crash.

EBRA – *Emergency Banking Relief Act of 1933*: Gave the government the power to regulate and control the banking system and allocated funds to failing banks. FDR closed all the banks temporarily, but assured the American people that when the banks reopened, they would be reliable, and their money would be safe.

FDIC – *Federal Deposit Insurance Corporation* was created by Congress to preserve stability and public confidence in the nation's financial system by insuring deposits.

SEC – *Securities & Exchange Commission* was created in 1934 to protect investors. Wall Street would be cleaned up by implementing new regulations against stock manipulation, insider trading, and fraud.

GRA – *Gold Reserve Act of 1934*: Outlawed the possession of privately owned gold and any held gold certificates. Executive Order #6102 made it illegal to buy, own, trade or sell gold. If you owned gold you would have to sell it to the United Stated Treasury. The price of gold would be fixed against the American dollar and was readjusted from about $20 dollars a troy ounce to about $35 dollars a troy ounce. FDR's Administration felt the GRA was needed to protect the currency system. That same year FDR fixed the gold standard, deflating the American dollar to about 71% percent of its' actual value. That 29% of capital was used to jumpstart the economy.

FERA – *Federal Emergency Relief Administration*: Allocated $500 million dollars in aid to soup kitchens, nursery schools and job creation in 1933. Its' main purpose was to make funds available for the destitute. FERA was eventually divided into two programs; the WPA or *Works Progress Administration*, and what we know today as the *Social Security Administration*.

CCC – *Civilian Conservation Corp*: Put 250,000 men to work in the summer of June 1933. With a job title of gardener/volunteer firefighter, these individuals made $30 per month planting, preventing soil erosion, and combating forest fires.

NIRA – *National Industry Recover Act*: Created jobs to build roads and bridges, outlawed child labor, increased wages, and improved working conditions. Eventually the NIRA branched off into the (PWA) *Public Works Administration* and the *National Recovery Administration.*

AAA – *Agricultural Adjustment Administration*: Assisted in raising crop prices by reducing crop production. This is basic supply and demand. Aid was given to help with mortgage payments and modernized farming equipment through the *Farm Mortgage Refinancing Act of 1934.*

TVA – *Tennessee Valley Authority*: Created jobs in the Dam industry which created hydro-electric power (power grid) to service rural areas in the south. The FDR Administration instituted many other programs also.

- CWA = *Civil Works Act*
- FSA = *Farm Security Act*
- FSA = *Federal Securities Act*
- FLSA = *Fair Labor Standards Act*
- Wagner Act = *National Labor Board*

To enact these programs the laws had to be changed. New Deal legislation did jumpstart the economy. However, it took about seven years for the economy to finally turn around.

When World War II began, many more jobs were created to build ships, tanks, automobiles, sew uniforms and create all materials needed to fight the war in Europe. This surge in economic growth unofficially ended the Great Depression.

It was almost one hundred years ago FDR fixed the gold standard. The attrition of our buying power actually began on August 15, 1971, when the Nixon Administration completely came off the gold standard, thus deflating the American dollar well below its' actual value. The currency of a country is supposed to be based on a monetary system backed by gold. Since the 1970's our economy has been based on a FIAT system.

FIAT money has no intrinsic value. The money you have in your bank account, wallet or purse may as well be monopoly money. The intrinsic value of paper money is not worth the paper it is printed on. Paper money is a promissory note. It is the government's promise to make good on that promissory note. If you really knew how much your dollar bill is worth based on a gold standard it would give you the heebie-jeebies. When the South lost the Civil War confederate money became as useless as monopoly money. Your money has a time limit on it as well.

The Euro and the Pound Sterling also operate on a FIAT system. Other nations have followed suit making FIAT currency the normalcy. When I was a teenager a candy bar costs 25¢. Today a candy bar may costs a dollar or more. That is an increase of four hundred percent. Back in the 1930s a new home cost between $4000 to $6000 dollars. Nowadays, based on where you live, an average new home can costs upward of $200,000 dollars or more. No longer on a gold standard, the governments of the world dictate how much money is worth. The global economy is like a pair of designer jeans. Put a famous name on a $10 dollar pair of jeans, and instantly that pair of jeans cost $200 dollars. However, those same jeans still have a value of $10 dollars.

As of 2020, unpaid student debt was a whopping 1.7 trillion dollars. National Debt reached 27 trillion dollars and Global Debt is expected to reach 277–281 trillion dollars by the end of 2020. When President Hoover repatriated funds from Germany during Europe's recession it only affected a few countries, but today everyone is riding in the same ship. When the United States crash, all other countries will crash. When all other countries crash; the United States will crash. When the ship goes down, we all go down together. We are all connected to the global stock market. When the economy of the United States crashes, it will not be stagflation, inflation, or a recession, but an economic global collapse. It will be a repeat of the 1930s Great Depression on a global scale. The Second Great Depression of the 2030s will make the Great Depression of the 1930s look like a picnic.

Since then, many of the regulations FDR imposed on Wall Street were deemed to be outdated and have slowly and quietly been dismantled putting our economy at risk once again. In 1999, President Bill Clinton passed the *Gramm-Leach-Bliley Act,* which repealed portions of the Glass-Steagall Act that loosened housing regulations. This made it possible for banks to lend money in low-income neighborhoods to people on fixed incomes.

Remember the housing crisis of 2008? Because of reduced bank regulations via the Clinton Administration, banks could contract mortgage loans to virtually anyone. Banks were giving home loans to consumers with low incomes, no assets, or no collateral. These loans were known as sub-prime mortgage loans. These types of loans were granted to millions of individuals with poor credit scores. These sub-prime mortgage loans were packaged as neat little financial securities and sold to investors on the stock market with brokers making a commission on every trade. Had these investors known these securities were worthless irredeemable I.O.U.s, they would never have bought them. An I.O.U. is only good if it is paid back.

The problem was created from the very beginning due to easy lending of adjustable mortgage loans. The lending institutions knew fully well if interest rates went up then mortgage rates would go up leaving the mortgagee in a financial bind. There were also dubious practices like teaser rates and higher rates for minorities with hidden terms in the contract only a lawyer could decipher. International banks were investing in these financial securities from London to Paris to Dubai to Iceland and beyond with little to no government regulations.

Banks all over the world began to buy and sell these dubious types of financial securities. When interest rates shot up on these adjustable mortgage loans, the rates also increased the mortgage payment that many could not afford, causing massive foreclosures. In 2007 the housing crisis began to show cracks in its armor which eventually led to the housing crisis of 2008. By 2008, over one million homeowners experienced foreclosure. People were put out on the streets. Some slept in their cars, others moved into shelters, and sadly there were others that committed suicide. By the end of 2008, the housing crisis had spread to other parts of the world. Around 1 trillion dollars of securities were invested in failing sub-prime mortgages and the housing crisis began to affect the global market. The international housing market began to panic as other world banks worried if they too would fail.

About 37%–43% of purchases are credit driven. The Feds realized if there is no lending there is no economic continuity, and therefore no economic momentum. The economies of the world are built on the circulation of money. It is not money, but rather the flow of money that keeps the global economy going.

A.I.G. was one of the largest insurance companies that needed a bailout. The five major banks would also need a bailout. If A.I.G. and the banks failed it would have spelled economic disaster. The government needed to pump money into the financial system to allow continuity and momentum to save us from another great depression. The government would use taxpayer money (FIAT or I.O.U. or Debt $$$) to buy assets owned by these failing entities. The federal government stepped in to bail out A.I.G., Bear Stearns, Fannie Mae, Freddie Mac, and other financial institutions with a whopping 700 billion dollar package. Not only did the banks get those homes that went into foreclosure, but they also received a bailout courtesy of the United States Federal Government. So, the banks made out twice. After the government bailed out the banks you would be surprised at the net-worth of these institutions today. The fifteen largest banks assets total almost 14 trillion dollars.

When Europeans and Asian banks began to fail their governments had no choice but to follow America's strategy to bail out the banking system to save their economy. The global community was saved by this strategy; but for how long? The global housing crisis began affecting other sectors of the economy and spilled over into the auto industry. In 2008 about 80 billion dollars in taxpayer's money was used to bailout the automotive industry.

These stock market crashes are not the only two our economy has encountered. The stock market crashed on Black Monday October 19, 1987. March 10, 2000, the Dot-Com bubble burst. May 6, 2010, Wall Street experienced a flash crash, dropping the DJIA 1,000 points. Every time the Feds carry out a government bailout, we move closer and closer to a crescendo of utter economic collapse.

Because the problem is systemic, more and more FIAT money is being pumped into the global economy. Every time the government introduces money into the economy it creates inflation. It is like robbing Peter to pay Paul. The government has robbed Peter so many times over; Paul will never be paid back. Each time the government swoops in to save the day the rich and powerful take their cut right off the top and leave us little folks with the crumbs. When new money finds its' way down the economic pyramid, our wages may increase, but things cost more. Trickledown economics is so ridiculous it is laughable at best. As the rich get richer, the middle class becomes poorer and poorer, and the economic bubble grows ever so larger.

The banking system is universal, and links the economy of America with the economies of the world. 97% percent of the money in the economy today is created by banks through loans and printed money. This means only about 3% percent to 7% percent of your money is real. Money is 'Borrow Now, Pay Later' money. Does this phrase ring a bell?

It is just like the scenario of the 1920s when the banks were lending credit and margin. FIAT money is negative money, not positive money because it is not backed by gold or for that matter any collateral. What if the loan is never paid back? One-hundred years later we have fallen back into the same sticky trap.

Greed is systemic within our laws which favor mega corporations, the rich and the powerful. Make no mistake and believe me when I say the POTUS is not running things. America is the greatest nation on this planet, yet poverty, food insecurity, and malnutrition are among us. The cynicism of greed serves the needs of the few instead of distributing wealth fairly. Our entire economic system is one inequitable vicious cycle. In an age of plenty why are some children in America going to bed hungry? The system is rigged against us.

Fast food restaurants take in thousands of dollars every hour, but pay their employees pennies to survive. It is just not right. The FIAT system is profit driven and will eventually run our economy into the ground. The global economy is an illusion, and it is one of the world's greatest Ponzi schemes ever. This game of charades will one day play itself out. We have already dug an economic hole so deep on the day of reckoning and balancing the books; the consequences will be most severe.

"And when he had opened the third seal, I heard the third beast say, Come and see. And I beheld, and lo a black horse; and he that sat on him had a pair of balances in his hand." – Revelation 6:5

The pair of balances in the Black Horseman's hand is symbolic of the global economic system. If we balance the global economic scale today there is not enough gold in the world to cover the amount of World Debt. Money is hopelessly hilariously ridiculously inflated, and it has been for quite some time. The governments of the world cannot keep creating money out of thin air.

In 2020, when *COVID-19* appeared the stock market plunged. This demonstrates how fragile our economy really is. The United States Government initially set aside a two trillion-dollar *COVID-19* stimulus package; with more stimulus packages to follow. Where is this money coming from? Realistically they will create it out of thin air, which will add to the enormous amount of debt that we already have on the back end.

Why do you think they call it the National Debt? They call it national debt because it is debt. The government already knows this debt will never be paid back nor reconcile itself. Very soon we will come to the end of our monetary rope. There will come a day when lowering interest rates will not work, a government bailout will not work, a stimulus package will be ineffective, and adjusting the cost of living will be fruitless.

The next time a catastrophic event occurs no plan will be enough to bail us out. Bailouts treat the symptoms but do not solve the problems. We are only delaying the pain for a later date. The economy is an adaptive system which no one can foresee. There are billions of people making billions of choices that can affect the stock market on any given day. People make decisions on emotions like fear, hope, or joy. Different nations of the world have their own way of doing things that contribute to global dysfunction. The left hand does not know what the right hand is doing, and the right hand does not know what the left hand is doing. When the old ways of solving the systemic problem will not work, there must be a better and equitable way to eradicate the cynicism of greed embedded in our laws.

What we are currently experiencing in our economy is a desert mirage. The water in the well dried up with the last Government bailout which occurred during the Obama Administration. FIAT money only carries a life span of about twenty seven years. If you believe this and you do the math you will know that we do not have much time left. The year 2008+27 years would put us at the year 2035. When the clock tolls twelve the only thing with purchasing power will be gold and silver. Even then the government can re-enact Executive Order #6102.

Leaders all over the world and the so-called experts are saying the economy is robust, the economy is strong, the economy is doing well, but they know fully well what is going to happen. To trust in our leaders, media and so-called positive economists is to trust in fools. It is not whether we will crash, but when we will crash. When government shut downs and raising the national ceiling debt becomes the normal, you will know the global economic collapse is imminent. The storm will come! On that day people will be paralyzed by disbelief, stunned with incredulity, emotionally destroyed, and financially ruined. On that day your savings, checking, stocks, bonds, and such will experience a significant decrease in purchasing power. Banks will fail and Automated Teller Machines will go offline. When this happens say goodbye to your: 401K, SSI, pension plan, ROTH IRA, social-security checks, saving and checking account, stocks, bonds, etc.

"For when they shall say, Peace and safety; then sudden destruction cometh upon them, as travail upon a woman with child; and they shall not escape." – I Thessalonians 5:3

The United States Federal Government and other governments of the world know fully well **Judgment Day Is Inevitable!** If nothing is going to happen why has the government been building underground bunkers since the 1960s? Why are the extraordinarily rich and powerful investing millions of dollars in underground shelters with food, water, heat, air conditioning and all the luxuries that will house them for a decade? Doomsday preppers are not crazy.

In this one particular case I agree with our government not to tell the American people because it would cause a national wave of pandemonium. For now, the governments of the world must act as if everything is hunky dory just to keep up with appearances of a healthy economy. I do not know what is going to cause the global economic collapse, but surely the Black Horseman of the Apocalypse is coming. I am not even going to say hope for the best. I am telling you to prepare for the worst. If you do not see what I am seeing, **'The Illusion'** already has you.

When global famine make its' appearance, the American dollar will then reflect its' true value, which will be a loss of over ninety percent of purchasing power. Banks, postal services, distribution services, supply chains, malls, supermarkets, pharmacies, stores, and exports will begin to shut down.

"And I heard a voice in the midst of the four beasts say, A measure of wheat for a penny, and three measures of barley for a penny..." – Revelation 6:6

- 1 Measure (Choinix) of wheat = 5 Cups
- 3 Measures (Choinix) of barley = 12 Cups

Contrary to what you may believe supermarkets and stores do not grow their own food. Deliveries stock their shelves on a daily basis. When Distribution comes to a screeching halt, supply and demand will kick in, and food prices will soar between 1,000% – 2,000% percent. Food prices will be ten to twenty times higher.

During the Second Great Depression when your one dollar bill will be worth about 5¢, it will take a full days' wages to buy a measure of wheat and three measures of barley just to eke out a meager living. In Saint Matthew 20:1-9, Jesus spoke about the day workers who were contracted by the owner to work a 12-hour day for a penny wages. Today a loaf of bread cost about $2.50 and a can of soup cost about $1.60 totaling $4.10. In the near future minimum wage in Pennsylvania will be $16 per hour. $16 × 8 Hours = $128, and $77 dollars after taxes. During the Second Great Depression that loaf of bread will cost about $40 dollars, and a large can of soup will cost around $25 dollars.

"Wheat for a penny and barley for a penny."

Wheat is used to make bread and barley is used to make soup. ***Revelation 6:6*** is a metaphor for the bread lines and soup kitchens. Imagine standing in line all day for a bowl of soup and a slice of bread, only to hear that rations for that day are exhausted. When a loaf of bread and can of soup cost about a full days' wages, this will mark another dark period for the history books.

Employers will not make payroll and the unemployment rate will skyrocket. Consumer spending will decrease dramatically. Businesses will close down. People lucky enough to keep their employment during these harsh times will be working to eat just to survive. There may come a time an employee paycheck may be based off food and water rations, not money. When these days come, food and water will be the most valuable commodities.

Contrary to what you may think your debt is not going to disappear. How will you pay your mortgage, utility bills, car note, and other cost of living expenses? How will gasoline prices be affected? How will the healthcare system, dental and prescription plans be affected? Money and purchasing power essentially controls every sphere of our lives. Without the flow of the global economy our world is going to fall apart. When the global economic system falls apart people will fall apart.

In the 1930s, people were more civilized than unruly. Today people are more unruly than civilized. A lawless person is a reckless person. A reckless person is a dangerous person. People do not even know how to act when the traffic light goes out at an intersection. When all the stop lights go out at an intersection many drivers become lawless and reckless. How lawless do you think people will be when the global economy crashes? How do you think people will react when they lose their life's savings in one day? How do you think people will react when they cannot feed themselves or their family? How do you think people will react when they think it is the end of the world? Symbolically speaking, it is going to be the zombie apocalypse. During this period Jesus called the beginning of sorrows, it will be human eat human.

In 2013, the Venezuela economy suffered a crushing blow when its' GDP dropped 40% percent. By 2017, hyperinflation caused basic food shortages. Hunger, crime, and poverty increased dramatically. Now apply what happened in Venezuela on a global scale. The riots, looting, and anarchy will take place everywhere! The East St. Louis riot of 1917, Tulsa race riot of 1921, and Los Angeles riot of 1992 will be nothing compared to the loss of life, looting and destruction of property when that day comes.

The inner cities will become war zones. This will be the perfect time for gangs, murders, rapists, and the criminal elements to operate with total impunity. On that day people will be scattered like sheep without a shepherd. When everything comes crashing down, its' effect will be like a bad chemical mixture of napalm. You think Walmart is crowded now? Just wait and see how crowded Walmart will be on that day. It may come down to a period of time when a free for all frenzy will be reality where only the strong survives.

It is going to be a mad, mad, mad, mad world. Lawlessness will be like a powder-keg exploding from within, and civil unrest will be magnified on a global scale. During this period of lawlessness do what you need to protect yourself and your family. The Bible says he that lives by the sword shall die by the sword. The Bible does not say you cannot protect yourself. Now, I am not going to go out making any trouble. As a matter of fact, I am going to be home minding my own business. I am a Christian, but I am also a realist. I sleep with my Bible in my right hand and my 9mm in my left hand because you are not going to just take what I worked so hard for. If you come to my neck of the woods starting trouble, it is going to be a situation! I will go Old Testament up in your chocolate starfish if I must; and trust and believe this, I not going to lose any sleep over it. HEY, I'M JUST KEEPING IT REAL!

All I have to say is, **"Don't start nothing, and it won't be nothing!"** So, when these beasts coming knocking at your door to pillage your home, to kill your sons and rape your daughters you will not be able to say, "Jesus loves you." You try that and see what happens to you. Jesus said be wise as serpents and harmless as a doves (Saint Matthew 10:16). Jesus did not say you cannot defend your livelihood when your life is threatened. If it comes down to it force must be must met with force to protect your family.

"...the kingdom of heaven suffereth violence, and the violent take it by force." – Saint Matthew 11:12

The POTUS will institute Martial Law, but I do not think it will be enough to prevent Purge Day. Confidence in the governments of the world will be lost and society as we know it will end abruptly. It will be a time of the haves (10%) and the have-nots (90%). In those days soon to come it will leave many in the valley of decision to accept or reject Jesus Christ as their personal Savior. All will be tried by the beginning of sorrows. When people think it is the end of the world it will be global no holds barred chaos; but the end is not yet.

"And ye shall hear of wars and rumors of wars: see that ye be not troubled: for all these things must come to pass, but the end is not yet...All these are the beginning of sorrows." – Saint Matthew 24:6-8

In the past biblical famines were agricultural due to droughts and weather conditions. The Babylonian economy traded in agriculture and barter. The Medo-Persian economy traded gold, silver, slaves, materials, and livestock; mostly imported. The Greek economy traded craftsmanship, maritime commerce importing, and exporting goods and services. The Roman economy traded in commodities and was agricultural, but it was Rome that originally introduced the idea of using coined money to express prices and debt. The global economy is based off this idea.

"...and see thou hurt not the oil and the wine." – Revelation 6:6

Tons and tons of barges filled with shrimp, lobster, filet mignon, confectionery treats, caviar, water, wine, oils, diamonds, and merchandise will be available. The warehouses will be full of clothes and the car dealerships will still be full of trucks and automobiles. The problem will be 90% percent of people will not be able to afford these luxuries which are the finer things in life; symbolic of oil and wine. The Second Great Depression will not be an agricultural famine; it will be an economic famine. It will be the death of the dollar. Past civilizations have come and gone not because they were conquered but because they imploded. There is nothing new under the sun. What has happened then is happening now, and will happen again. Generally, at the height of hedonism, self-indulgence and hubris, God has announced judgment on nations. Today we live in a self-gratifying society of indulgence, pleasures, and decadence.

The very rich and powerful have been manipulating us for millennia. The system is against you, and it serves those in power that wield it; seemingly at their will. The Old World Order will soon be a forgotten memory. The New World Order is already here. You cannot see it, smell it, taste it, touch it, or sense it, yet it pervades every aspect of our lives. Every day we are bombarded with technology that seemingly programs us not to see what is right in front of our eyes. The New World Order is already setup in the shadows waiting for the old-world order to meet its' demise. Before you usher in the new, the old must be put to death.

The 'Powers That Be' – (Ephesians 6:12) can crash the global economy tomorrow if they wanted to. It would be foolhardy to do so because all of the pieces for the New World Order are not quite in place. There is one vital piece missing for the New World Order to truly be effective. Artificial Intelligence is the most crucial piece needed to insure the continued stability of the New World Order to control the populations of the earth. Presently Artificial Intelligence is in its' infancy, but in about ten to fifteen years Artificial Intelligence will have reached its' maturity. Maturity is to humans, as singularity is to Artificial Intelligence. It is rumored within the next fifteen years Artificial Intelligence will be of an equal level of intelligence as humans.

Credit cards came out in the 1950's. By the 1980's credit cards and debit cards became extremely popular. Today cashless transactions have predominately become the mode of buying and selling. Since *Y2K*, coins and paper money has dwindled significantly. This economic transition from cash to a cashless society is no fluke. The 'Powers that Be' know paper and coins will soon come to an end. When the wave of the Second Great Depression comes into fruition, paper money and coins will become useless.

This will force all nations of the world to go to a cashless currency. Because 75% percent of our transactions are plastic already, transitioning to a cashless society will be an easy one.

We are overdue for a global economic correction. I believe the Second Great Depression will be a centennial event, and it will occur sometime between the years of 2029–2035. When God pronounced a famine, it generally lasted three and one-half to seven years. I am preparing for three and one-half years because the Great Depression of 1929 lasted about three and one-half years. I estimate between the years 2030–2040, it is all going to come crashing down. This is not a prediction; it is only my opinion. If my estimate of 2030–2040 is correct, global solidarity of the New World Order will come to fruition sometime between the years 2040–2050. Since we have already rejected God as a global community, global oversight will be the only thing that will save us. In the 1930s it was called the 'New Deal'. In the 2040s it will be called the 'New World Order'.

During these times just before the global economic crash occurs, the stock market will seem to show favorable resilience to shocks. The Dow Jones will seem to be performing well. The unemployment rate will seem to be going down. Tech stocks will be looking great, and many stock prospects will seem positive. Everyone will be laughing, singing, and enjoying the fruits of the stock market as previously in the 1920s, until it all comes crashing down.

Open your eyes. The global economy is running on fumes. Our global economy as you know it is about to end. When global famine makes its debut, this should be a wakeup call for many to turn to Jesus. Unfortunately, it will be the god of this world and his false prophets many will turn to for answers. Behold, Jesus is knocking on the door of your heart. The world is so preoccupied they do not hear Jesus knocking. The **'System'** wants you to be distracted by your reality television shows, your sitcoms, your Soap operas, and your Super Bowls, while the 'Powers That Be' strategically move their pieces into position.

Sadly, people will not take heed to the Bible's warning. People are stuck in denial and do not want to believe we are literally living end-time events. This will be one main reason people will be ill-prepared. I have told you in advance what is coming. Now is the time to prepare. Tomorrow will be too late. Prepare yourself emotionally, spiritually, and psychologically for what is about to come.

The next question is, "How do you prepare?" Below I have made a list for myself, but you should always do your own research.

- **Protection/Defense** – Survival Manual, Dust Mask, Gas Mask, Protective Goggles, Mini Backup Survival Kit, 100% U.V. Shades, Pepper Spray, Stun Gun, Machete, Body Armor, Face Armor, Military Helmet, Swiss Army

109

Knife, Duct Tape. Sunscreen, Ropes & Cords, Automatic & Semi-Automatic Guns/Rifles, Multi-Tool for digging-chopping-cutting, Ammunition. Form a neighborhood militia; there is protection and power in numbers.

- **Navigation** – Compass, Maps, Binoculars, Night Vision Goggles.

- **Insulation** – Comfortable Weatherproof Boots, Poncho, Thermals, Thermal Jump Suit, Change of Clothing, Sleeping Bag, Space Blanket (To Retain Heat).

- **Illumination** – Candles, Crank Flashlight, Power Lantern, Crank or Solar Matches or Lighter, Solar Power Lights, Backup Generator, Equip Your Home with Solar Panels.

- **Fire Ignition** – Ferrocerium Rod, Matches or Lighter, Butane Lighter, Cup Fuel, Arc Plasma Lighter.

- **Kits** – First Aid, Sewing, Fishing, Cooking, Tool, Bee Sting, Surgical Suture. Your first aid kit should have assorted bandages, gauge, antibiotic ointment, prescription medications, tweezers, a small mirror, toenail clippers and burn dressing.

- **Hydration** – Find a natural spring source. Stack your supply of bottled water. Carry a canteen with you wherever you go. Gravity Water Filter. Water Purification Tablets. Home Water Filter, Portable Home Filter.

- **Shelter** – Waterproof Tent, Research ways to heat your home if your heating system goes out in the winter time. Research ways to cool your home if your electricity goes out in the summer season.

- **Communication** – Reflective Vest or Jacket, Crank Radio, Ham Radio, Flares, Whistle, Walkie-Talkies, (PLB) Personal Locator Beacon, Paper-Pen-Pencil, Rechargeable Batteries, Have a contact or meeting place with friends and/or family members. Form a Neighborhood militia; there is protection and power in numbers.

- **Health Aids** – Oregano Oil is antibacterial. Alcohol is a sanitizer. Peroxide is an antiseptic. You should have herbal items like **turmeric** powder which heals wounds and fight stress. **Garlic** boosts your immune system, **probiotic** and **aloe-Vera** for intestinal health, **honey** heals wounds and is an anti-fungal, **chicory root** reduces anxiety, **cinnamon bark oil** controls blood sugar levels, and **black-seed oil** reduces high blood pressure. You would do well to put mosquito spray on this list as well or look for ways to make natural mosquito repellant.

- **Hygiene** – Toothbrush, Floss, Rechargeable Razor, Lab Irrigation Bottle, Wipes, Rags, Towels, Toilet Paper, Coconut Oil, Soap (learn how to make your own soap). Learn how to make your own deodorant. Baking soda.

- **Foods – Survival Seeds** (5-year shelf life). Learn how to farm or find someone that does. **Survival Meats** (15–25-year shelf life). **Survival Fruits** (20-year shelf life). **Survival Veggies** (15–25-year shelf life). **Freeze Dried Eggs** (15–25-year shelf life). **Freeze Dried Milk** (15–25-year shelf life). Vacuum **Dry foods** like popcorn, rice, beans, pastas, barley, chickpeas, quinoa, lentils, and oats. Vacuum sealed foods should have a shelf life of 2-3 years. MREs.

- **Can goods** - like soup, fish, tomatoes, beans, red kidney beans, and coconut milk should have a shelf life of about 2 years depending on the product itself. Make sure you check the expiration dates. Also get **luxury items** like instant mash potatoes, non-dairy creamer, instant soups and noodles, instant oatmeal, herbs, spices, salt, and pepper. Do not forget the flour and cooking oil.

- **Vitamins, Spices, and Herbs** – Kallawalla, Sea Moss, Multi-Vitamin /Mineral, D3, Turmeric, Garlic Capsules, Probiotics, B-Complex, Flaxseed, Chia seeds, Coriander and other assorted spices.

- **Misc. Luxuries** – Ice Maker, Bread Maker, Hot Plate, Portable Solar Charger, Instant Coffee, Powdered Honey, Cash on hand, Gold & Silver Coins, Power Inverter (at least 400 Watts), Utensils (fork, spoon, knife, can opener), Battery Charging Bike, Gasoline Reserves. Make sure you put a gas lock on your car because people will siphon your gas. Equip your home with a Generac generator.

- **Misc.** – Move out of the city if you can. Pay off your debts if you can. And always have a plan B: Bug out bag, Bug out Location. Bug out Vehicle.

Jesus said these days would be the beginning of sorrows. The beginning of sorrows will be the days of global lawlessness. If Jesus said it, you better believe it is coming and take heed. Better to be prepared and not need it, than to not be prepared and not have it.

The Pale Horse

"And when he had opened the fourth seal, I heard the voice of the fourth beast say, come and see. And I looked, and behold a pale horse: and his name that sat on him was Death, and Hell followed with him..." –
Revelation 6:7-8

Pestilences, diseases, plagues, and epidemics are synonymous. These sprang from the first original sin on earth (Genesis 2:16-17). God instructed Adam not to eat from the Tree of the Knowledge of Good and Evil. If he ate from that tree, he would surely die.

Adam then instructed Eve not to eat from that tree, or she too would surely die. Along comes the devil to break up this happy family. Notice the devil did not go to Adam. He knew that Adam would see through his scheme, so he tempted Eve, knowing Eve was Adam's weakness. Let us see the devil's modus operandi in action.

"Now the serpent was more subtle than any beast of the field which the Lord God had made. And he said unto the woman, Yea, hath God said, ye shall not eat of every tree of the garden?" – Genesis 3:1

- **Translation:** Are you sure that is what God said or even meant when Adam told you not to eat from that tree? God did not tell you, Adam told you.

"And the woman said unto the serpent, we may eat of the fruit of the trees of the garden: But of the fruit of the tree which is in the midst of the garden, God hath said, ye shall not eat of it, neither shall ye touch it, lest ye die." – Genesis 3:2-3

- The first mistake Eve made was reasoning with the serpent.

"And the serpent said unto the woman, ye shall not surely die: For God doth know that in the day ye eat thereof, then your eyes shall be opened, and ye shall be as gods, knowing good and evil." – Genesis 3:4-5

- **Translation:** Are you sure that is what God meant? You will not die. God only said that because when you eat that fruit you and Adam will become wise as God himself.

"And when the woman saw that the tree was good for food, and that it was pleasant to the eyes, and a tree to be desired to make one wise, she took of the fruit thereof, and did eat, and gave also unto her husband with her; and he did eat." – Genesis 3:6

When the woman lusted for the fruit and justified why she should have the fruit, all common sense went right out of the window. Consequences did not matter. What Adam instructed Eve to do did not matter. The only thing that mattered in that moment was Eve's selfish desire.

Eve brought the fruit to Adam, and he also ate. Eventually Adam and Eve were driven out of the Garden of Eden. They had access to all the trees except one. Where is the common sense in that? To eat from one tree, they forfeited eating from all the other trees. When we want what we cannot have it seems to somehow magnify our lust on something or someone. The devil does not want us to think, he just wants us to do. When we think and reason about what God wants for us, we think about the consequences of our actions. When we do not think about the consequences, we do what is right in our own eyes.

The serpent outwitted Eve by convincing her that eating of the forbidden fruit was in her best interest. He is so intelligent he makes us think we are doing right when in fact we are doing wrong. He has many tools and use denial tactics against us. He puts doubts in the mind. When you begin to doubt God's words it leads to denial. When you begin to deny what you already know what God has specifically spoken, you are headed down a path of hurt, pain, and loss. The devil has been using this same strategy from day one. The sad part is it keeps working.

As a young child attending church I would often hear about the forbidden fruit. I would often hear many preachers say because Adam and Eve disobeyed God, human beings grow old and die. I think it is more to it than that. Before Adam and Eve consumed the forbidden fruit, they were immortal beings. After they ate the forbidden fruit Adam and Eve lost their immortality and all born afterwards.

Every single human being born after 'The Fall' is born in sin, shaped in iniquity, and spiritually separated from God. This is almost like the Butterfly Effect. One small act changed the entire destiny of mankind. This effect took place on a genetic level. Something in the fruit altered Adam and Eve's DNA. Humans became susceptible to a myriad of bacteria, micro-organisms, and viruses through their disobedience. It is a scientific fact that death is written into our genetic code. Since the unleashing of Pandora's Box in the Garden of Eden there have been numerous pestilences since. We will not concern ourselves with them, but rather let us turn our attention to today.

National Diabetes Statistics Report 2020

In 2018, about 34 million or 10% of people in the United States have some form of diabetes. This 10% does not include undiagnosed cases. With type I diabetes the body cannot make enough insulin. Insulin controls the body's blood sugar level (BSL). If your BSL is too high you may become hyperglycemic, possibly causing headaches, blurred vision, and severe medical conditions. If your BSL is too low, you may become hypoglycemic, possibly causing anxiety, fatigue, tremors, and other physical symptoms.

With type II diabetes the body becomes resistant to insulin. Eventually the body will stop producing insulin all together. Serious medical conditions like kidney or nerve damage, heart disease, or even a stroke can occur. More often than not people with type II diabetes must take insulin pills or injections for the rest of their lives to maintain a healthy lifestyle. A bad diet, high cholesterol, smoking or obesity could be some causes that play a role in developing type I or type II diabetes.

CDC and Prevention Data & Statistics: Obesity

In 2018, 42.4% or 137,150,000 million people in the United States were categorized as overweight and obese when compared to BMI (Body Mass Index). A little more than 10% percent or about thirteen million was under the age of eighteen years old. Physical inactivity and a poor diet seem the main causes of obesity and developing unnecessary weight. Many major health issues like stroke, depression, hypertension, or heart disease may occur if ones' obesity is not addressed. Seventy percent of Americans fall into the category of being obese and overweight.

CDC & Prevention Data & Statistics: Kidney Disease

In 2017, it was estimated that fifteen percent or thirty seven million adults in the United States have chronic kidney disease. Kidneys clean your blood by filtering out waste from your body. When your kidneys begin to fail, it triggers chronic kidney disease, which can lead to major health problems up to and including kidney failure. The end stage of kidney failure would require dialysis or a kidney transplant for survival.

CDC and Prevention Data & Statistics: COPD

Chronic Obstructive Pulmonary Disease obstructs airflow and causes lung problems and is related to emphysema and chronic bronchitis. If your infant(s) are exposed to mold for long periods they will develop chronic lower respiratory disease like asthma. Long exposure to secondhand smoke, air pollutants, and hazardous chemical environments may also play a role in developing COPD.

CDC and Prevention Data & Statistics: Colorectal Cancer

2016	2016	2020	2020
Diagnosed with Cancer	Died	Diagnosed with Cancer	Died
Breast - 245,299	41,487	Breast - 279,100	42,690
Lung - 218,229	148,869	Lung - 228,820	135,720
Prostate - 192,443	30,370	Prostate - 191,930	33,330
Colorectal - 141,270	52,286	Colorectal - 147,950	53,200
Bladder - 73,469	16,464	Bladder - 81,400	17,980
Non - Hodgkins - 68,639	20,268	Non - Hodgkins - 77,240	19,940

52,286 died of colorectal cancer, but there are other types of cancer that have also claimed the lives of many other people. **ibid, cancerstatisticscenter.cancer.org**

CDC and Prevention Data & Statistics: Arthritis

Based on the National Health Interview Survey between 2013-2015 diagnosed cases of Arthritis of 18 years and older was estimated at 23% or 55 million Americans. It is projected by the year 2040 this number will increase by 42% to 78 million.

CDC and Prevention Data & Statistics: Tuberculosis

Tuberculosis is caused by airborne bacterium that can attack any part of the human body, but primarily attacks the lungs. If you are coughing up phlegm mixed with blood or begin to experience chest pain, visit an emergency room immediately. If you experience a combination of symptoms of loss of appetite, night-sweat, fever, fatigue, and a cough lasting several weeks, please visit an emergency room.

People with a weakened immune system may be more susceptible to TB than others. TB can only be spread by a person with active TB who comes in close proximity of others. A medical doctor can take a skin or blood test to confirm infection. A person with strong immunity can become infected but not get sick. However, if a person acquires TB the bacteria will multiply in the body.

It is extremely difficult to get rid of TB. A cocktail of prescribed drugs would be required for at least six to nine months to treat TB. If not treated properly, TB may very well become antibiotic resistant.

"In the United States the prevalence of current cigarette smoking among adults has declined from 42% in 1965 to 18% in 2012." **ibid., ncbi.nlm.nih.gov-page 24**. When the Surgeon General reported smoking could cause health concerns many began to wise up. This positive report has declined TB from 49,000 reported cases in 1965 to 9,000 reported cases in 2018.

CDC and Prevention Data & Statistics: Cholesterol

The liver produces cholesterol, but too much can build up in your arteries and constrict or even block blood flow. Humans acquire additional cholesterol from meats, eggs, and diary. The CDC warns a person's eating patterns that include too much cholesterol may increase your risk of cardiovascular disease.

Lipoproteins carry cholesterol throughout your body. LDL or low-density lipoproteins are bad while HDL or high density lipoproteins are good. It is good to regularly get a checkup from your physician to see where your cholesterol levels are. Every six months I get a checkup. Some people are not aware they may have high cholesterol because there are usually no direct symptoms.

Overtime as plague builds in the arteries a person could develop high blood pressure, coronary artery disease, and or even a stroke.

CDC and Prevention Data & Statistics: HIV; AIDS

HIV became prominent in the early 1980s with the rise in illicit drug use of crack. HIV can also be transmitted through sexual contact with an infected person. Contaminated blood or organs can also infect a person. The human immunodeficiency virus severely compromises the immune system by destroying T-cells and white blood cells, making the body vulnerable to all sorts of diseases, bacteria, and viruses.

Ways to prevent getting HIV is to avoid promiscuous sexual practices. Even if you meet someone new in your life and you want to marry each other, go get tested first just to be sure. There should be no sex before marriage, but if you decide to go that route protect yourself and your partner by wearing a condom and go get yourselves tested just to be sure. Avoid dirty needles, kissing a person with bleeding gums, or eating after an infected person because the virus lives in saliva and blood. Every adult and young adult should regularly get tested for sexually transmitted diseases. HIV can affect anyone if the circumstances are right. We should never judge anyone with this virus because we do not know a person's story. As Christians we must never judge, but always love.

CDC and Prevention Data & Statistics: Viral Hepatitis

Hepatitis A-B-C-D-E attacks the liver. The liver filters the blood and detoxifies the body. Currently there is no vaccine for HCV, HDV, or HEV. Bacterium such as Campylobacter causes illnesses in 1.5 million nationwide every year. If the problem becomes severe, seek medical attention. Your physician will generally write you a prescription for an antibiotic to treat the problem.

Pandora's Box

"In 2013 official death certificates recorded 84,767 deaths from Alzheimer's Disease. The actual number of deaths to which Alzheimer's disease contributed is likely much larger than the numbers of deaths recorded on death certificates. In 2016, an estimated 700,000 Americans age 65 and older will die with Alzheimer's Disease due to complications." – **ibid, National Library of Medicine 2016/Alzheimer's Disease/Facts and Figures/PMID: 27570871/Abs.**

In 2017, 83,564 death certificate listed diabetes as the cause. **ibid, cdc.gov/pdfs/ data/statistics/ national-diabetes-statistic-report**

In 2017, heart disease claimed the lives of approximately 800,000 worldwide. **ibid, Interactive-Atlas of Heart Disease and stroke/nccd.cdc.gov/stats & ibid, https://USCS**

We have trillions of bacteria all around us. We encounter hundreds, maybe even thousands of viruses on a daily basis. The future concern that is being voiced in the medical community is antibiotic resistance. Overtime, bacteria within the body becomes smarter by mutating into super-bacteria, resistant to the original dosage of antibiotics. The future dilemma is if hyper-bacteria proliferate where does the medical and science community go from there? Personally, I avoid taking antibiotics at every turn because I know my immune system will compensate. Only in the direst situations will I consume antibiotics.

Several years ago, when my wife died, I hit rock bottom. I lost the will to live. I asked God to take me home, but he had other plans for me. I was eating one meal a day, and not taking any supplements. What I was eating had no nutritional value, and I stopped taking care of my health. Within two months my weight dropped from 185 pounds to 160 pounds. One day I went to work, and my co-worker told me I look like a crack-head. I did not care because I felt as though I had no purpose. Over time, Jesus healed my hurt, pain, and emotions. I did not realize then God had other plans for me to write this book. This book brought purpose back into my life.

Several months after I started writing this book my blood pressure began to spike to extremely high levels. My systolic and diastolic kept going up. I visited my family doctor several times within a month. My doctor kept telling me I was consuming too much sodium, and he kept prescribing various high blood pressure medications that did not work. My doctor never drew blood or ran any other test to see if he was wrong about his diagnosis. I kept telling my doctor my high blood pressure was not due to my diet.

He just kept telling me I had high blood pressure and told me to follow his dosage of HBP medicine, then whisked me out the door. I knew something else was causing my blood pressure to spike. A normal blood pressure reading is 120/80. At one point my blood pressure spiked to 180/120. I thought the enemy was trying to take me out so I could not bring this book to you, but I also concluded that I compromised my immune system, because I was not properly taking care of my health.

Every day I work with the public, and I encounter all types of people with all types of viruses and bacterium. I concluded that I must either have some type of viral or bacterial infection. I knew that if I trusted in the advice of my family doctor, I would have a stroke or lose my kidneys within the next several years.

I decided the only one who is going to take care of me, is me. I begin to research herbs that combat viral/bacterial infections, as well as minerals that help lower blood pressure. When I added magnesium to my diet my blood pressure decreased from 160/115 to 150/103.

117

After supplementing turmeric into my diet, my blood pressure decrease from 150/103 to 148/98. When I added garlic to my diet my blood pressure went down to 143/95. I am not a doctor, but in my opinion, if you have any herb in your apothecary, it must be garlic. I took garlic in the past, but never realized just how important garlic was. This supplementation worked for me.

During the next year I struggled with my blood pressure. I did not realize by compromising my immune system other disorders affected my blood pressure as well. I discovered I was anemic, and I had inflammation in my body, which contributed to my hypertension. My recent blood test results from my new doctor indicated high LDL and pre-diabetes. I cut out all the whites; white rice, white bread, white pasta, and rice noodles. I cut the honey in my tea and the creamer in my coffee.

A month later my blood test showed positive changes, but my blood pressure did not change. My blood pressure was at a standstill because I failed to realize my body and blood must be cleansed to reduce inflammation. I did more research and found some things that could help me. I needed to reset my body with a thirty day full cleanse. I began taking mullein and liquid chlorophyll for respiratory support. I needed to restore my oxygen levels. For my bowel cleansing I began taking yeast/fungal detox, para-cleanse and a proprietary blend called lower bowel stimulator. I began taking another proprietary blend called BP-X, which is good for cleansing the blood by assisting the liver, lymphatic system, and freeing the body of toxins. To address my high blood pressure I also took a proprietary blend called HS II. To access these amazing products go to rapture2061.org. Click herbs and vitamins.

During this two month regimen I ate mostly vegan with fruits, veggies, water, fish, and meatless products. Within three days I began to get more sleep and restful nights and I even lost a few pounds. My blood pressure dropped to 128/93. I was not as sluggish during the day and my vertigo all but disappeared. As it stands, about seventy percent of my diet is plant based and thirty percent pescatarian. A week later my blood pressure dropped to 120/89. I did notice when I consumed to much salt my blood pressure increased to 135/93.

I found the best diet for me. If I stay away from the salt and exercise regularly, I will be fine. As it stands now my blood pressure averages around 128/85. Within two months of going on a partial plant based diet my systolic dropped 22 points (mm Hg) and my diastolic dropped 13 points (mm Hg). I believe most of the credit goes to me eating organic Steel Cut oats every morning with sliced banana and one tablespoon of ground flaxseed.

I believe God created herbs in nature to heal us, but I also realized taking too many herbs can hurt you. I have learned you can do more harm than good when taking too many supplements, but I will take natural supplements over prescription drugs any day. The one thing I do not want is to be on high blood pressure medicine for the rest of my life, so I must be proactive in my personal lifestyle changes. Having said all this, you should never replace your doctor's recommendation. Again, if you decide to take an herbal supplement, please do your homework first. Check herbal dosages and how herbs may affect you, especially if you are taking prescription drugs. Do not believe everything you read online. Check reliable government websites, such as, nih.gov. And most importantly tell your doctor if you supplement with herbs.

There are many viruses trying to hurt us on a daily basis. Luckily God has given us the vaccine. The vaccine is your immune system. Do a full body cleanse at least twice a year and exercise at least three days a week. Cleaning your blood helps your kidneys, liver, and lymphatic system. Take vitamins and herbs that boost immunity. Incorporate antiviral, antibacterial, antimicrobial, and antifungal herbs into your diet. To boost your immunity, eliminate or minimize processed foods. Eat light and healthy, and drink at least 6cups of water a day. Your health is your life.

Exercising the external body is good, but you must also exercise the internal with proper nutrition and diet. What good is it to clean the outside of the cup when the inside is still dirty? Many people do not realize we have viruses, worms, and parasites that host in our body. If you live on this planet, you have some form of virus living inside of you. When a person is infected with a virus, antibodies are created and the virus goes latent.

Every now and then the virus will reactivate and cause minor or major symptoms depending on the strength of your immune system. If you have a good immune system, it will suppress the virus. As you approach old age, viruses will begin to mess with your systems. That is why I originally began supplementing my diet with garlic. Garlic is a natural antibiotic.

When *COVID-19* came onto the scene I was at the supermarket returning an item. The guy at the customer service desk acted like I was a walking disease when he handed me my money. I am not saying *COVID-19* is not real. My older brother was hospitalized with *COVID-19*. *COVID-19* is real, but some people are taking it too far.

I never get sick, but in January 2020 I got severely ill. My chest, throat and sinuses were full of mucous. For five days each night I added cayenne, garlic, and honey to my tea. I drank two cups a day. I also used a diffuser and I added ½ fresh squeezed lemon and 100% percent pure peppermint oil.

119

After five days I was back to my normal lovable self. More likely than not, I was infected with the *COVID-19* virus. My immune system developed antibodies against *COVID-19*. I know this because what I am about to tell you.

I was with my brother for about ten hours one day when he was feeling ill. We sat in my car for about five hours, because the clinic never scheduled his appointment. The next day my brother tested positive with the *COVID-19* virus. I scheduled a test two days later. My test was negative. Since then I have been to my brother's home several times. My father in law tested positive with the *COVID-19* virus. I visited and spent several hours at his home. That would explain why I did not test positive after spending significant time with my brother and father-in-law. My immunity is not 75% or 90% percent effective. It is 100% percent effective against *COVID-19*. I eat the right foods, exercise, drink plenty of water, supplement with herbal remedies and vitamins, and get at least 8 hours of sleep. Now that I have immunity, why do I need the *COVID-19* shot? If you are elderly and you have a weak immune system, by all means do what you think is right.

As far as numbers go, it is reported that *COVID-19* is now the number one leading cause of death in the United States as of May 2020. **ibid, cdc.gov/national center for health statistics**. Did Alzheimer's disease, heart disease, cancer, stoke, and COPD just go away? The news should show us Alzheimer's, diabetes, cardiovascular, COPD, and HIV/AIDS statistics if they were so concerned about our well-being. Things just are not adding up for me.

In 2019, ten million estimated tuberculosis cases were reported. Twelve percent (12%) or 1.2 million people died of tuberculosis **(ibid, WHO/tuberculosis/key facts)**. Why was there no urgency in that matter?

Why were we not we told to wear a mask back then? Nowadays, it is painfully evident that most people lack the ability to think for themselves. I am sure *COVID-19* was here several months before the WHO declared it as a global health emergency. Something just does not feel right. If *COVID-19* were as bad as they make it out to be the POTUS would have declared Martial Law. The National Guard would have been sent out. A State of Emergency would have been declared with mandatory quarantine and at the very least an international curfew.

Why is the system telling us the only way to get through *COVID-19* is by pushing the vaccine down everyone's throat? There are many herbs and herbal remedies that boost immunity. Ashwagandha decreases stress in the body and can adapt based on the specific needs of the body.

God created all kinds of herbs like Reishi, Rhodiola-rosea, Schisandra, Holy Basil, and Eleuthero to equip our immunity. In Daniel 1:3-15, Daniel and his three friends went on a plant based diet. In only ten days their health improved.

"...And at the end of ten days their countenances appeared fairer and fatter in flesh than all the children which did eat the portion of the king's meat."
– Daniel 1:3-15

When God created Adam and Eve, they were herbivores. God knew that mankind would eventually acquire the taste for animal flesh. After the flood of Noah God allowed mankind to devour animal flesh, but that was not his original design.

"And God said, behold, I have given you every herb bearing seed, which is upon the face of all the earth, and every tree, in the which is the fruit of a tree yielding seed; to you it shall be for meat."- Genesis 1:29

Animals get their protein from plants and many humans get their protein by eating animals. Humans who eat meat are consuming by-product protein from a secondary source. God intended our main source of protein come from vegetables, seeds, nuts, grains, fruits and plants. These are higher in protein than some meats. Our bodies need the purest form of protein for bio-availability.

I am not saying drop all your meat sources like that big juicy steak or hamburger. I just want you to understand you can become more healthy by putting more plant based foods in your diet. We all will die one day, but at least we can be healthy doing it. Aside from genetics we can avoid many diseases by keeping our bodies healthy.

God has given us an incredible defensive system within the body to heal. Foods are for healing and nourishing the body. Food is your medicine. The body needs help from you to feed it the right medicine. Are you taking the right medicine? You will know when you wake up every morning and look in the mirror. Numbers and mirrors do not lie.

In our age of decadence the White Horseman of the Apocalypse have convinced many to give their body what it wants, instead of what it needs. When you change your way of thinking it will change your way of eating, and then you will see the results. Eat foods that reduce inflammation. Inflammation is the precursor to many of the health issues we later encounter in life. You can have fast food, chicken, burgers, or pork. There is nothing wrong with eating candy or junk food. You can have these, but eat in moderation. If we consume excessive amounts of anything it can harm us. Consuming more than 2,000 mg of vitamin C daily may cause diarrhea.

Consuming excessive amounts of iron will lead to iron toxicity. Consuming anything in excessive amounts can be very bad for you regardless of what it may be.

"...there will be pestilences" – Saint Matthew 24:7

Since March 11, 2020 several variants of *COVID-19* have been discovered. Suffice it to say; fake news and propaganda is telling us in order to stop the spread of these variants at least 70% percent of earth's population must be vaccinated. For some not getting vaccinated is a religious issue. For others it may be a power, propaganda, and patents issue. Getting vaccinated is not a religious belief for me. It is a trust issue among other things. I need to be assured the vaccine is 100% percent effective with no side effects. I believe in immune therapies for those that need or want it.

COVID-19 variants require two shots plus a booster shot. The booster shot may become the normal every year. I do not want my immune system to become dependent on a yearly booster shot. This is why I chose not to be vaccinated. There are some that say everyone should get vaccinated. Even if you get vaccinated, you can still contract a *COVID-19* variant, and or die from it. The *COVID-19* vaccinations are for those with weak and compromised immune systems. These shots are good because they help create *COVID-19* antibodies on the front end. For an unvaccinated person with average to strong immunity, their immune system will create *COVID-19* antibodies on the back-end. If you are vaccinated and you contract a *COVID-19* variant, you become a carrier. If you are not vaccinated and you contract a *COVID-19* variant, you become a carrier. What is the difference? Someone is not telling these people the whole story. Because of media propaganda, constant change in herd immunity information, and misinformation, I believe it is more about patents and power, than your health. That is just my opinion.

I am already immune to the *COVID-19* virus, yet I am being punished for not getting vaccinated. I cannot go on a cruise vacation or travel outside of the United States. Is that fair? If or when push comes to shove and the government requires mandatory vaccinations (which I highly doubt), Christians must obey the law even if they disagree. However, if it is a strong religious personal conviction not to get vaccinated, stand up for your constitutional rights!

"Let every soul be subject unto the higher powers: for there is no power but of God: the powers that be are ordained of God. Whosoever therefore resisteth the power, resisteth the ordinance of God: and they that resist shall receive to themselves damnation." – Romans 13:1-2

The only exception to ignore these scriptures is when the government's cause is against God's word.

For example, if the government sanctioned murder, as a Christian would you murder? If the government sanctioned rape, as a Christian would you rape? If the government sanctioned theft, as a Christian would you steal? When you cannot buy or sell unless you are wearing a mask, or travel outside of your country unless you have the 'shot', you must realize we are moving towards a one-world-government. Today it is the 'shot'. Thirty-five years from now it will be the '**The Mark of the Beast**'. I believe *COVID-19* preparedness is another rung in the ladder of global control over the masses, but the *COVID-19* shot is not the Mark of the Beast. To get vaccinated is not a sin. As Christians we are God's children and his protection is upon us; but again, to each his own.

"Behold, I give unto you power to tread on serpents and scorpions, and over all the power of the enemy: and nothing shall by any means hurt you." – Saint Luke 10:19

Whether this virus was unleashed deliberately or by accident, the variants are out there. We are all connected. What affects one affects all. The sooner we get a handle on this epidemic the sooner we can get back to normal life. Even though I have immunity to *COVID-19*, if the government signed mandatory vaccinations into law, I will get vaccinated. Though I would be going against my deeply held belief in natural remedies and cures, this situation may become problematic in the very near future. My faith is in God, and I am under his protection (Romans 8:28).

"For God hath not given us the spirit of fear; but of power, and of love, and of a sound mind." – I Timothy 1:7

I do not know if some of these viruses are man-made or if it is just the systemic evolution of viruses. Between the bacteria, viruses, and evils we encounter during our lifetime, we are born into a virtual death trap from the day we are born into this fallen world. The wool is pulled over your eyes. All are born hood-winked by the god of this world. People invest in this world as if they are going to live forever. I do not know why people put so much stock in this world. The only thing you will carry with you into the next world is how much you love God or how less you love God. The only way of escape is to trust in the one True God (YAH), through his only begotten son; Jesus.

What good is it to invest in something that is not going to last? What good would it be to gain the whole world, but lose your soul? God has a better place and a better plan for your life. Jesus offers you an abundant life beyond this world. God wants to exchange your tired virus infected body and your measly eighty years with an immortal body and eternal life. What a deal!

I wrote this chapter because I want you to step outside of your box to see the big picture. Since the **1960's** we have changed our views on moral absolutes, freed ourselves from our moral responsibility to God, and have gone off to serve other gods. Today all acts of sexual promiscuity are shown on the big screen and television as though it is the norm. There is fake news, political agendas, global propaganda and thousands of false prophets manipulating the masses with their false doctrine – **(White Horse)**. God is angry with the (3rd) and 4th generation.

"Thou shalt not bow down thyself unto them, nor serve them; for I, the Lord thy God am a jealous God, visiting the iniquity of the fathers upon the children unto the third and fourth generation of them that hate me." – Deuteronomy 5:9

Since the **1970's** thousands of prisons have been built to enslave the innocent, further tearing away at the fabric of the family. To add insult to injury, legalized abortion, and Divorce and Family Court has caused psychological and generational traumas. The generations are growing up angrier and angrier. The way we treat our neighbor has changed. We now live in a generation where there is no love lost. Because conflict lives within the heart of man, this leads to all types of wars up to world wars. Today we live in a world of global unrest – **(Red Horse)**.

In the **1970's** we came off the gold standard, thus aggravating the value of our currency. It is not just the United States. All the countries of the world are no longer on a gold standard and are recklessly printing money. There is already economic instability in 3rd World countries – **(Black Horse)**.

In the **1960's** farms began to disappear. Corporations swooped in and took over the food industry. "Only 10 companies control almost every large food and beverage brand in the world." – **ibid, businessinsider.com/these 10 companies control everything you buy** – In the **1970's** GMOs came into play. The ways our foods are processed are different than the **1960's**. The fruits, vegetables, and grains are being sprayed with suspect chemicals that **may** have carcinogens. Our meats are pumped full of steroids, fillers, and suspect chemicals that are hard to identify. Today most of our diets are processed, microwaved, and fast foods.

In **1960** 13.3% of adults in the United States were categorized as obese when compared to BMI. Currently, 70% of adults in the United States fall into the category of being obese and overweight when compared to BMI. That would be an increase of 526%. In **1960** 0.91% of Americans had diabetes. Currently, 10.00% of Americans have diabetes. That is an increase of 1,099%. Since the **1960's**, heart disease, obesity, cancer, diabetes, and high blood pressure have risen significantly. What is the correlating factor? Could one of the factors causing chronic diseases be the foods we are consuming?

From **1978-1989**, kidney disease (ESRD) increased in males from 27,732 to 88,941 and females from 21,734 to 74,076. In a little over a decade those numbers increased 320% in males; 340% in females. − **ibid, ncbi.nlm.nih.gov/table 4-6**

Since then, a myriad of prescription drugs began rolling onto the market. Look at all the prescription drugs adults and even some children are taking just to stay alive. It is unprecedented. In the **1970's** drugs started flowing into our country like water. Look at all the drugs epidemics we had since then; the cocaine epidemic, the crack epidemic; the smack epidemic, and the opioid epidemic. People hooked on drugs walk around like the living dead because that is what drugs do. Back in the **1960's** there was no such thing as the suicide prevention hotline or drug addiction intervention − **(Pale Horse).**

Why am I telling you all this? So you may understand all these changes started in the **1960's**, **1970's** and **1980's**. The seeds of the Four Horsemen were planted about three generations ago. This highly orchestrated agenda by the dark forces of this world has been disrupting our family values, health equity, basic human needs, and the way we perceive. This paradigm shift by the devil and his generals have taken root into our thinking in slow increments over the past sixty years, converging slowly over time hoping we would not notice the changes. The writing is on the wall. How can you not notice? Their plans are to inflict so many traumas on the human race; mankind will ultimately look to any messiah regardless of whether this person is a saint or a devil.

- In the last sixty years thousands of cults and false teachers have come out of the wood-work. Satan has infiltrated many Churches with his false teachers who claim Jesus sent them. Mass manipulation and global propaganda run our lives with impunity. All these things are happening today (White Horseman).

- All around the world there is murder, today. People are losing their lives to suicide, drug use, and gun violence. The devil knows if he can destroy the family structure it will create a dysfunctional anarchic society (Red Horseman).

- All around the world some are experiencing starvation and hunger, today (Black Horseman).

- All around the world there are pestilences like mudslides, droughts, wildfires, hurricanes, tornadoes, volcanic eruptions, tsunamis, earthquakes and pandemics today (Pale Horseman).

All Four Horsemen are working tirelessly around the clock to ultimately achieve the devil's desired effect on humanity. The first Four Seals are clustered and sequentially connected; you cannot have one without the other. This means all Four Seals (Four Horsemen) will be occurring around the same time.

125

What makes these last days different is the severity and frequency of these occurrences. To better understand, we must view the Four Horsemen as personifications and metaphoric expressions. It is not only who they are, but what they represent. The White Horseman metaphor is **Delusion,** because the world has rejected Christ due to the 'Falling Away' and their disrespect for God.

"And for this cause God shall send them strong delusion, that they should believe a lie: that they all might be damned who believed not the truth, but had pleasure in unrighteousness." – 2 Thessalonians 2:11-12

The Red Horseman metaphor is **Contention,** because the love of many will wax cold. This will lead to all types of wars.

"And ye shall hear of wars and rumors of wars: see that ye be not troubled: for all these things must come to pass, but the end is not yet. For nation shall rise against nation, and kingdom against kingdom:" – Saint Matthew 24:6-7

- Drama wars – War on martyred Christians, World Wars
- Domestic wars – War on drugs – Cyber wars – Bullying
- Skirmishes – Covert wars – War on crime – Hate and Race wars
- War on terror – Legal wars – Political and Cold wars – Civil wars

"And because iniquity shall abound, the love of many shall wax cold." – Saint Matthew 24:12

The Black Horseman metaphor is **Famine.** We are going to have another Great Depression. Only this time it will be on a global scale. The Pale Horseman metaphor is **Death** by **pestilence,** murder, suicide, and such things. The Pale Horseman needs no introduction. Just look at how dependent our society is on pharmaceutical drugs. We have street drugs like meth, cocaine, and all the others that kill millions every year. When you compare the first four seals to **Saint Matthew 24:5-7**, these match up with one another perfectly.

WHITE HORSE	RED HORSE	BLACK HORSE	PALE HORSE
○	○	○	○
St. Matthew 24:5-6	St. Matthew 24:6-7	St. Matthew 24:7	St. Matthew 24:7
○	○	○	○
Take heed that no man deceive you.	Ye shall hear of wars and rumors of wars	There shall be Famines	And Pestilences
GLOBAL DECEPTION	**GLOBAL CONTENTION**	**GLOBAL FAMINE**	**GLOBAL PESTILENCE**

The principalities, powers, rulers of the darkness of this world, and the spiritual wickedness in high places will use the Four Horsemen like knights on a chess board. They will bring havoc and distress to the entire world. When it seems all hope is lost, Antichrist will swoop in like a messiah and save the world. The **Dark Forces** of this world will create the problem and then send their false messiah to fix the problem. These beings are very cunning and absolutely brilliant!

With every passing year, would you say things seem to be getting worse, not better? If you compare the state of our society between **1960** and **2020**, we have taken a 180° turn for the worst. Brothers and sisters, the **First Four Seals** have already been opened! The **First Four Seals** are not future prophecy; they are **now** prophecy. The Four Horsemen Seals was an agenda initiated about sixty years ago to usher in global chaos, which will eventually destabilize global democracies'. Global anarchy will become the norm.

Once this is achieved, the governments of the world will come to understand that in order for this planet and its people to survive, they must all ban together as one. Hermeneutically, the beginning of the end began in the year 1948 with the rebirth of the Israeli nation. Even if everyone woke up tomorrow and realized the Luciferian Agenda has been set into motion, it cannot be stopped.

The next event on the prophetic timeline **is not** the Millennial Reign of Jesus Christ. The next event on the prophetic timeline **is not** the wrath of God. The next event on the prophetic timeline **is not** the Rapture. The next event on the prophetic timeline **is not** the Great Tribulation. The next event on the prophetic timeline is the collapse of the global economy; which will initiate the beginning of sorrows. The collapse of the global economic system will amplify deception, contention, pestilence, and death, claiming the lives of two billion people.

These will be trying times for the sick, elderly, and those that depend on pharmaceutical drugs and medical equipment to survive. Hospitals will not be accessible to many of these people. People that cannot get access to life sustaining prescription medications and medical equipment will begin to die off by the thousands. Many thousands will kill and murder to survive. Many hundreds of thousands will die of starvation. Others will lose all hope and a wave of mass suicide will occur. By the time the nations of the world come together and pull themselves up by the bootstraps, the global death toll will be ¼ or 25% percent.

Two billion people dead is quite a large number. Two billion is 999,999,999 million + 1, multiplied by two. Give or take ten million, which is more than the entire populations of the United States, Russia, Indonesia, Brazil, Turkey, Japan, Pakistan, Philippines, Mexico, Egypt, Germany, Congo D.R., United Kingdom and Iran. One out of every four persons will perish.

Four Horsemen of the Apocalypse

1st Prince	Apateon	Deception
2nd Prince	Polemos	Contention
3rd Prince	Aplistia	Greed
4th Prince	Thanos	Death
And Hell	Followed	Hades

"...and power was given unto them over the fourth part of the earth, to kill with sword, and with hunger, and with death, and with the beasts of the earth." – Revelation 6:8

The converging of the first Four Seals will mark the beginning of sorrows. Many lukewarm Christians will mistake the beginning of sorrows for the great tribulation period and will mistake Antichrist as Jesus' second coming in the flesh. When the full force of the Four Horsemen of the Apocalypse converges, society as we know it will come to a crashing end. The beginning of sorrows will force global solidarity among all nations.

"And the Lord said, Behold – the people are one." – Genesis 11:6

Links in the Prophetic Chain

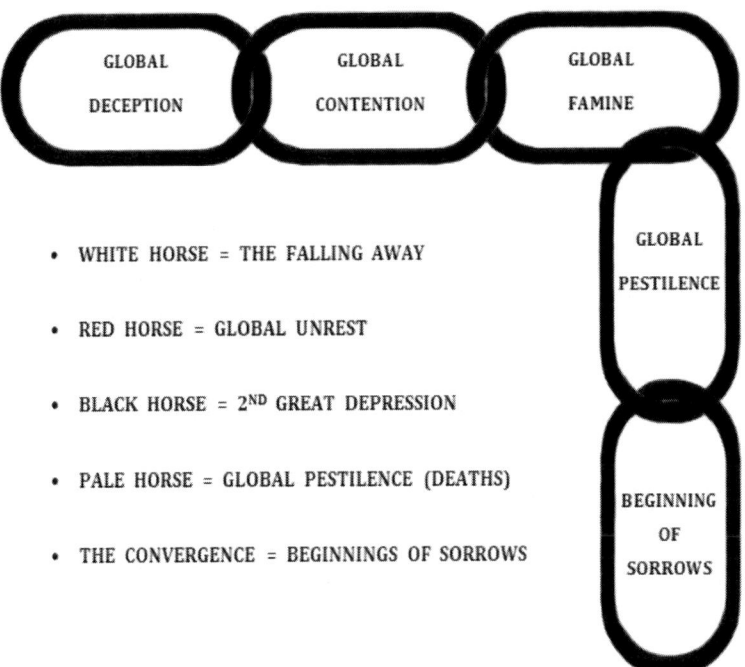

- WHITE HORSE = THE FALLING AWAY

- RED HORSE = GLOBAL UNREST

- BLACK HORSE = 2ND GREAT DEPRESSION

- PALE HORSE = GLOBAL PESTILENCE (DEATHS)

- THE CONVERGENCE = BEGINNINGS OF SORROWS

"All these are the beginning of sorrows." – Saint Matthew 24:8

Chapter Six
The New World Order

<u>The Mystery of Iniquity</u>

A mystery is a secret. Iniquity is wickedness or evil. The Mystery of Iniquity is the devil's master plan to deceive us into willingly surrendering our souls over to him, by gaining total control over the hearts and minds of men.

"And God said, Let us make man in our image, after our likeness: and let them have dominion over the fish of the sea, and over the foul of the air, and over the cattle, and over all the earth, and over every creeping thing that creepeth upon the earth." – Genesis 1:26

When God created Adam and Eve symbolically speaking, the Garden of Eden was their throne and earth was their dominion. Before their fall from grace, God instructed Adam and Eve to be fruitful and multiply (procreate), take dominion and cover the earth. Lucifer came onto the scene and made a deal with a snake in order to tempt Eve, and we know the rest of the story. Because Adam and Eve forfeited their eternal status, our direct contact with the Most High God was cut off.

Not only did Lucifer gain dominion over mankind, but the power of death and hell was put within his grasp. God restricted Lucifer's power by making a promise that he would one day make a way for our sins to be cleansed. Since mankind could no longer speak with God directly, God had to come down out of heaven to dwell with us through the Ark of the Covenant, teaching the Israelites his statues and commandments. When the Israelites sinned, God punished them because of their continuous need to commit spiritual fornication and worshiping other gods, but God always had men and women with a special connection with him. God used these individuals down through the ages to keep his truth secure. This is how the Holy Scriptures (Bible) came into existence.

"Knowing this first, that no prophecy of the scripture is of any private interpretation. For the prophecy came not in old time by the will of man: but holy men of God spake as they were moved by the Holy Ghost." –
2 Peter 1:20-21

Back in the Old Testament a servant of the Lord named Daniel prayed for answers concerning his people. An angel was dispatched from the Third heaven. Upon his arrival to earth the angel was met by demonic opposition in the exosphere. For twenty-one days the angel fought and eventually was assisted by Michael a chief angel (Daniel 10:12-13).

Daniel had a special connection with God to receive wisdom and understanding via angels, but Lucifer would always be there to dispatch one of his lieutenants to stop or delay God's truth. 2,000 years ago Jesus Christ came and delivered mankind through his shed blood, death, and resurrection. Through Christ's mediation, we now have direct access back to the throne of God. We now have God living on the inside of us through the Holy Spirit of promise.

Even though Lucifer lost the war and his spiritual hold over mankind, the game must play itself out. Initially, Lucifer directed all his forces to totally eradicate the first century Christians, but the Gospel of Jesus Christ began spreading as Christians scattered into different parts of the world. Even though some first century Christians were martyred, the Christian movement known as 'The Way' grew exponentially.

Lucifer's direct attack against the Word of Truth was a monumental failure, so he devised an elaborate scheme. If he could not beat the Word of Truth, he would corrupt the Word of Truth. Just a little lie here, a little lie there, a little twisting of God's word here and there, is the seed Lucifer needed to corrupt the Word of Truth down through the ages. Take the pagan gods of old and rebrand them with Christian labels. Lucifer's new mantra was infiltration instead of eradication. This plan was hatched over two thousand years ago. Jesus did not create denominations, we did. Jesus did not create cults, we did. Jesus did not create church cliques, we did. This is the first part of the devil's secret plan known as the Mystery of Iniquity.

"For the mystery of iniquity doth already work: only he who now letteth will let, until he be taken out of the way. And then shall that Wicked be revealed, whom the Lord shall consume with the spirit of his mouth, and shall destroy with the brightness of his coming:" – 2 Thessalonians 2:7-8

I am not a conspiracy theorist, but what I am going to say will seem a little weird. Somewhere on this planet is a clandestine organization of political, economic, scientific, and military operations systematically bent on the subterfuge of mankind. I refer to this unnamed organization as the Organism. In the last sixty years or so the Organism has revved up its' attack on humanity.

- 1960s – Popularization of television

- 1970s – Political agendas and movements were set into motion

- 1980s – Music started to take on a different tone

- 1990s – Computer systems and game systems became popularized

- 2000s – Google and Facebook was born

- Today there is A.I., quantum computing and cybernetics systems

Does it seem strange in about 7,000 years mankind has been on earth; suddenly there is an explosion of technology? What we could not accomplish in 6,940 years, we accomplished in only 60 years? That does not sound right to me. Technology just did not fall out of the sky: or did it? Hmm?

Deception on a Global Scale

"For many shall come in my name, saying I am Christ; and shall deceive many." – Saint Matthew 24:5

The seed of deception was planted centuries ago and has infiltrated every aspect of religion. The devil's master plan has already taken root in all aspects of human thinking, reasoning, and apostate teachings. We can clearly see this in the Book Revelation Chapters 2 and 3. The most popular televangelists today represent themselves as the go-between for Christ and there are many deceivers in the pulpits. Some of these men and women are being paid off and used as the devil's pawns to confuse us more and more. The devil understands the psychology of a human to yield oneself to an authority figure or father figure. People obey their pastor because God speaks through this man or woman. My question is, *"Which god?"*

The First Seal Judgment is step#1 in the Luciferian agenda. Little by little the forces of darkness will lull humanity into spiritual sleep slowly moving us away from the Word of Truth. Haven't you seen a deviation from Christ as the head of the Church to the pastor as the head of the Church? Haven't you seen a deviation from Christ as the head of the Church to the elders as the head of the Church? In these last days, many false teachers of God's word will arise, and many will be deceived. These prophetic warnings are happening today.

All the reality television shows, sitcoms, music, and entertainment we have and enjoy are skillfully used against us to occupy us away from the truth of the gospel and their hidden agenda. If you have noticed, most of our pleasures appeal to our emotions, not our logic. As long as our minds are tuned into these pleasures, we are happy, but deep down inside some are dysfunctional and empty.

The Second Seal Judgment is step#2 in the Luciferian agenda. Lucifer's plan is to cause us to fight among ourselves. He wants it to be a global occurrence right down to disharmony within the family structure or what is left of it. As you can see with every Seal broken things seems to get worse and worse.

The Third Seal Judgment is step#3 in the Luciferian agenda. As we speak, we are enjoying the pleasures of life and all the comforts technology provides. We do not have to grow our own food, milk our own cows, or skin our own chickens.

Corporations provide us with everything we need, like a parent to her children. Well, my friend, that is not going to last. Once we are lulled into a passive state, the devil will hit us so hard with pain, sorrow, and suffering, we will not know what to do. A global famine is headed our way to which the world has never seen, courtesy of the powers of darkness. We have become so dependent on the system to take care of our every need we will not know what to do or how to survive when the Second Great Depression hits us. We will be like little lost sheep. Society is like the fatted calf waiting to be slaughtered.

The Fourth Seal Judgment is step#4 in the Luciferian agenda. For this plan to work the population must be decreased by about twenty-five percent. There are about eight billion people worldwide. As it stands now, that is just too many people to control. For the second half of this plan to work effectively there must be global tragedy. The world will be brought to its' knees by chaos, mayhem, death, destruction, and madness. The devil will just sit back and watch the Four Horsemen of the Apocalypse have their way. Through natural disasters, mass suicide, murders, killings, diseases, famines, wars, and such-like, over two billion people will lose their lives.

By this time, the world will be crying out for a savior. When it seems like all hope is lost and the precipice of human annihilation seems sure, Lucifer will capitalize on the world's emptiness and introduce Antichrist to the world. The entire world will be brought together through global tragedy. Antichrist will make his appearance between the 4th and 5th Seal. He will not come with fangs and horns on his head. He will come in peace with a halo on his head.

Antichrist only asks one small thing; that you become a part of the system. To do that, you must be branded with his mark of technology. Antichrist and his Mark will be welcomed with arms wide open. All humanity whose names are not written in the Book of Life will happily sell their souls to the devil. It is a brilliant well thought out plan; create the problem and come onto the scene to fix the problem. Antichrist will deliver all that he promises for a little while and bring the world back from the brink of destruction. Antichrist will be the 'John Connor' of the New World Order.

Only he who now letteth will let – II Thessalonians 2:7

For now, Jesus is restraining Antichrist from moving into a power position. In our rebellion, sin, and hardness of heart, the world has mocked the Son of the Most High God who gives us salvation freely. Mankind's incessant need to follow his own heart leaves Jesus no choice but to step aside out of respect for mankind's wishes. Jesus said, *"He that is unjust, let him be unjust still. He that is filthy, let him be filthy still. He that is righteous, let him be righteous still. He that is holy, let him be holy still." – Revelation 22:11*

In layman's terms, God gives people over to the consequences of their actions, because there is no repentance. Jesus will allow the wicked heart of mankind to have their false doctrines, false messiahs, and false teachers. Jesus will allow the 'Mystery of Iniquity' to deceive the hearts and minds of men, because men love evil. We see this time and again with the Israeli Nation when God let their enemies take them away into captivity because of their sins.

Until he be taken out of the way – II Thessalonians 2:7

The **Holy Ghost** cannot be taken out of the way. **Jesus** cannot be taken out of the way. **God the Father** cannot be taken out of the way. All members of the Godhead are Omnipresent. **"He"**; refers to Antichrist. When Antichrist is assassinated, **he** will be taken out of the way.

And then shall that Wicked be revealed – II Thessalonians 2:8

Antichrist will not plunge mankind into World War III, but on the contrary, he will avert World War III with the peace armistice. Revelation 6:1-8, reveals the devil's entire plan in the first Four Seals. After the Four Horsemen of the Apocalypse prepare the way for Antichrist's rise to power, he will be assassinated. When Antichrist resurrects from the dead, the Beast (that **Wicked**) will show his true colors during the second half of the global peace armistice; which is when the Abomination and Great Tribulation will begin.

It is plain as day if you understand what you are reading. Revelation is the prophetic map of end-time events. What good is having a map if you do not know how to read it? Since this false pretribulation teaching has been drilled into our skulls, we downplay the Four Horsemen of the Apocalypse and confuse the White Horseman with Antichrist. If you have studied ancient war tactics you will understand the king always rides in a chariot, and the horses are before the chariot. The Four Horsemen of the Apocalypse comes before Antichrist, not after. Before Antichrist can even show his face the Four Horsemen must prepare the way with war, famine, pestilence, and death. Antichrist will not bring the chaos. The chaos (Convergence) will already be here.

Whom the Lord shall consume with the spirit of his mouth, and shall destroy with the brightness of his coming – II Thessalonians 2:8

Antichrist will wage two wars. The first war will be against the Christians and Jews (Daniel 7:25 and Revelation 13:7). The second war will be at the Battle of Armageddon (Revelation 16:16), but he will be defeated upon Jesus' return to earth (Revelation 19:20).

New World Order

"After this I saw in the night visions, and behold a fourth beast, dreadful and terrible, and strong exceedingly; and it had great iron teeth: it devoured and broke in pieces, and stamped the residue with the feet of it: and it was diverse from all the beasts that were before it; and it had ten horns. I considered the horns, and, behold, there came up among them another little horn..." – Daniel 7:7-8

Beasts are one-world governments. The fourth beast was the Roman Empire. The ten horns are symbolic of the New World Order. The little horn is symbolic of Antichrist. As you can see from scripture Antichrist came up within the New World Order **(There came up among them another little horn)**. Daniel 7:7-8 tells us Antichrist will be a little horn (powerful leader) that will rise within the New World Order political system. Antichrist **will not set up a one world government**, nor ignite the world against God. The New World Order is already here and the world is already against God. It is global solidarity that will make the New World Order official.

When Antichrist comes along to offer the world their best life now, they will be like putty in his hand. Antichrist will put food in the bellies of the hungry, eliminate crime, introduce new cures for diseases, and restore the economy, so if it were possible that even the very Elect of God would be fooled. Sadly, Christians that do not know what is in the Bible will be fooled by the False Prophet, false prophets, false teachers, and Antichrist with their signs and lying wonders.

Until this day comes the Jews will still be waiting on their Deliverer clothed with a purple robe and fine jewels. The Muslims will still be waiting on their Imam-Mahdi. Christians will still be waiting for the Rapture, Buddhists for their Maitreya, Arabs for their Al-Masih, Hindus for Vishnu, and the Roman Catholics will still be praying to Mother Mary.

The foundation of the New World Order was established more than sixty years ago. The many things that have occurred behind closed doors since then to push the New World Order into fruition would shock you. Unofficially the New World Order is already here, and it is here to stay. The invisible 'Powers That Be' have been planning this for quite some time. Just look on the back of your one-dollar bill. To the left under the all-seeing eye of technology you have **'Novus Ordo Seclorum'** or **New World Order**. To the right you have above the eagle **'E. Pluribus Unum'** or **'Out of many comes one'**. When the many become one, God will once again confound their language; only this time, it will be in his wrath and sore displeasure.

135

Lucifer knows Jesus is coming back soon to vanquish him and the powers of darkness, set up his thousand-year reign on earth, and restore the House of Jacob. The devil's ultimate goal is to drag as many people to the Lake of Fire with him as he possibly can before Jesus returns, because he knows he only has a short time to work his magic on humanity. This is the purpose for which the Mystery of Iniquity was devised.

We trivialize and marginalize the power of the Four Horsemen, but we must realize they will play a significant role in destabilizing the old-world order. The sorrows of the 'Convergence' will touch every man, woman, and child regardless of sex or age, free or bond, or economic social class, except for the rich. After the 4th Seal is opened, but before the 5th Seal is opened, Novus Ordo Seclorum will rise from the ashes of the old-world order. In a frenzy all the world leaders for the first time in history will come together to solve the global crisis. In the game of chess, one must first strategically position their pieces then go in to squash their opponent. Lucifer's Four Horsemen of the Apocalypse are the knights on Lucifer's chess board.

- 1st Seal = White Horse – Global Deception = The Conditioning (Global Propaganda)

- 2nd Seal = Red Horse – Global Contention = International, National, Civil, Domestic

- 3rd Seal = Black Horse – Global Depression = Stock Market Crash (2nd Great Depression)

- 4th Seal = Pale Horse – Global Pestilences = Man-made Diseases and Natural Disasters (Death on a mass scale)

The United Nations was formed in 1945 in response to World War II. The two bombs dropped on Hiroshima and Nagasaki Japan, the bombing of Pearl Harbor, and many other atrocities took the lives of over 85 million people. The idea was if all the countries can work as one, the wars, famines, crimes of humanity, and things that bring down world peace could be abolished. The solution was to institute a global republic of nations. Under the charter of the United Nations the world will be averted from destruction.

In the New World Order cultural influences and forms of political structures will not change. There will still be Prime Ministers, Presidents, Supreme Leaders, General Secretaries, Kings and Queens, but the United Nations will be the top authority that will create new laws, rules, and a global constitution that will become policy for the world.

As of 2014 the United Nations has adopted (Sustainable Developments Goals) or SDGs. So far, no one has been aggressively able to carry out the SDGs. The SDGs is the 2030 Agenda for Sustainable Development. - **ibid, transforming our world: The 2030 Agenda for Sustainable Development**

The problem is no one person knows how to implement them all, given our current global disunity. The world must first see how it is in dire straits. There are global border issues, global domestic wars, myriad of famines and pestilences around the world, Third World countries economics are failing, and hate relations run rampant globally. In my opinion reaching the SDGs 2030 goal is wishful thinking. However, when Antichrist makes his appearance he will fulfill the United Nations SDGs. For the record I want to say the United Nations is not an evil organization bent on world domination. The nations of the world are not doing it to hatch some clandestine plan. The clandestine plan lies in the lap of the Evil One. The nations of the world will band together out of necessity. The United Nations and the New World Order is one link in the prophetic chain. The United Nations Security Council Mandates are:

- "To maintain international peace and security"

- "To develop friendly relations among nations"

- "To cooperate in solving international problems and promoting respect for human rights"

- "And to be a center for harmonizing the actions of nations" **ibid, www.un.org/mandate**

The United Nations will implement a system of global surveillance to understand precisely what is happening all around the world. Artificial intelligence will have the ability through its quantum analytics to survey and formulate algorithms to solve the global crisis. Artificial intelligence will not be the demise of mankind, but rather the savior of mankind. As I speak, Artificial intelligence is processing vast amounts of data to offer viable sustainable solutions for tomorrow. Artificial intelligence will take away some jobs, but it will also make things better.

During the early 20th century farmers needed to physically measure their land to grow crops and human labor to harvest and transport those crops. With technology and automation, farming has greatly diminished over the past fifty years. Technology has produced weed resistant seeds and the hardware is specifically tailored to plant and harvest the crops in a fraction of the time. During the early 20th century factory jobs were in abundance until most of these jobs moved overseas.

Like the farming industry, factory jobs have become automated as well. In the early 20th Century, an assembly line of humans would assemble the product. Today machines do the assembling.

The Tesla Company already has the technology for autonomous vehicles. Truck drivers, delivery drivers, public transportation drivers, and taxi drivers may have to find a new line of work in the next twenty years. Autonomous vehicles do not need rest, take breaks, and GPS sensor technology attentiveness is 24/7. Car manufacturers will soon be equipping their vehicles with driverless technology. Just tell the vehicle where you want to go, and it will drive you there.

Fifty percent of cashiers have already been replaced with self-checkout scanners. Technology of the future will link a person's bank account with instant purchasing. A consumer will be able to walk into a store or supermarket, take an item(s) and just walk out. No worries as their money will be debited from their account. When scanner technology is fully deployed the job of cashier will disappear. No more obnoxious customer service situations and no wait times. Just walk in, grab what you want, and walk out.

The main challenge in the New World Order will center on the stabilization of the economy. With the rise of technology, it is estimated the workforce will be greatly reduced by Artificial intelligence, A.I. drives down costs and increases productivity. Most unskilled jobs like a fast-food worker, security guard, bartender, and such will probably be replaced by Artificial intelligence in the next twenty years. Growing automation of technologies will create lower wages and more unemployment. The SGDs will have to find a way to level the playing field. This sustainable goal of the New World Order is to:

- "Achieve higher levels of economic productivity via diversification, technological upgrading and innovation, including through a focus on high-value added and labor-intensive sectors." ibid, 8.2

- "Promote development - oriented policies that support productive activities, decent job creation, entrepreneurship, creativity and innovation, and encourage the formalization and growth of micro-, small- and medium-sized enterprises, including through access to financial services." ibid, 8.3

- "Achieve full and productive employment and decent work for all women and men, including for young people and persons with disabilities, and equal pay for work of equal value." ibid, 8.5

- "Substantially reduce the proportion of youth not in employment, education or training." ibid, 8.6

- "Take immediate and effective measures to eradicate forced labor, end modern slavery and human trafficking and secure the prohibition and elimination of the worst forms of child labor, including recruitment and use of child soldiers, and end child labor in all its forms." ibid, 8.7

- "Protect labor rights and promote safe and secure working environments for all workers, including migrant workers, in particular women migrants, and those in precarious employment." ibid, 8.8

- "Devise and implement policies to promote sustainable tourism that creates jobs and promotes local culture and products." ibid, 8.9

- "Strengthen the capacity of domestic financial institutions to encourage and expand access to banking, insurance and financial services for all." ibid, 8.10

- "Increase Aid for Trade support for developing countries, in particular least developed countries, including through the Enhanced Integrated Framework for Trade-Related Technical Assistance to Least Developed Countries." ibid, 8.10a

- "Develop and operationalize a global strategy for youth employment." ibid, 8.10b

The New World Order will have to implement policies to make the job market fair and equitable. One way would be to take those doing unskilled labor and placing them in other tasks Artificial Intelligence cannot do. I do not see that happening, but what I do see is mankind and Artificial Intelligence working side by side to bring Third World countries up to fair living standards. The end goal of the New World Order will be to bring all Third World countries up to equal footing economically, socially, and technologically. Infrastructures like roads, tunnels, cell towers, sewage irrigation, bridges, clean water, transportation, and such are vital to raise equitable standard of living. Building up under-developed countries will add positive value to the GDP (Gross Domestic Product), and it will be a great way to balance the overall economic pie.

Since the United States is an already developed country, employment in Third World countries will be in abundance. With humans and Artificial Intelligence working together, infrastructures in developing countries will be built much faster. This sustainable goal of the New World Order is to:

- "Develop quality, reliable, sustainable and resilient infrastructure, including regional and trans-border infrastructure, to support economic development and human well-being, with a focus on affordable and equitable access for all." ibid, 9.1

- "Promote inclusive and sustainable industrialization and, by 2030, significantly raise industry's share of employment and gross domestic product, in line with national circumstances, and double its share in least developed countries." ibid, 9.2

- "Increase the access of small-scale industrial and other enterprises, in particular in developing countries, to financial services, including affordable credit, and their integration into value chains and markets." ibid, 9.3

- "Upgrade infrastructure and retrofit industries to make them sustainable, with increased resource-use efficiency and greater adoption of clean and environmentally sound technologies and industrial processes, with all countries taking action in accordance with their respective capabilities." ibid, 9.4

- "Enhance scientific research, upgrade the technological capabilities of industrial sectors in all countries, in particular developing countries, by encouraging innovation and substantially increasing the number of research and development workers per 1 million people and public and private research and development spending." ibid, 9.5

The most vulnerable underdeveloped landlocked countries or regions like small islands will be targeted first. To bring the New World Order into prosperity for all, its' policies must be fair, universal, and inclusive to all. Disadvantaged and marginalized populations must be treated fair, open, honest, and equal. To reduce inequalities the goal of the New World Order will be to:

- "Progressively achieve and sustain income growth of the bottom 40% of the population at a rate higher than the national average." ibid, 10.1

- "Empower and promote the social, economic and political inclusion of all, irrespective of age, sex, disability, race, ethnicity, origin, religion or economic or other status." ibid, 10.2

- "Ensure equal opportunity and reduce inequalities of outcome, including by eliminating discriminatory laws, policies and practices and promoting appropriate legislation, policies and action in this regard." ibid, 10.3

- "Adopt policies, especially fiscal, wage and social protection policies, and progressively achieve greater equality." ibid, 10.4

- "Improve the regulation and monitoring of global financial markets and institutions and strengthen the implementation of such regulations." ibid, 10.5

- "Ensure enhanced representation and voice for developing countries in decision-making in global international economic and financial institutions in order to deliver more effective, credible, accountable and legitimate institutions." ibid, 10.6

- "Facilitate orderly, safe, regular and responsible migration and mobility of people, including through the implementation of planned and well-managed migration policies." ibid, 10.7

Another strategy that should be put in place to bolster, sustain, and stabilize the economy is an idea known as UBI or Universal Basic Income. UBI is a monthly stipend from the government that covers a person's basic living needs. The money is tax free with no strings attached. In addition, a person would also be able to work without being penalized. No matter the social or economic class, everyone would receive this stipend, unless they decide to opt out.

Under Pennsylvania's current MBI or Minimum Basic Income guidelines a single person can receive six types of government assistance if he or she makes less than $904 a month. When employment is obtained even at minimum wage ($7.25hr × 40hrs = $290 minus taxes = $203 week = $10,556 Year), this would put a single person at risk for losing all their benefits. So, I ask you, *"Where is the incentive to work?"*

UBI is not a cure all solution, but rather an incentive to empower those who want to live a better lifestyle. People want to work if given fair wages. Why go out and find a job working 60 hours a week, not being able to make ends-meet? You would do better on Public Assistance and have a side gig working under the table. MBI penalize people for wanting a better life, chastises you for wanting to make ends meet, creates negative reinforcement, and creates an environment of feeling trapped with no way out.

The impoverished, assisted poor, working poor and lower middle class seemed stuck in a system that keeps them psychologically, emotionally, and mentally trapped in a spider's web. The government has lost touch with reality and does not understand what it is all about. For the working poor and those living in poverty it is all about survival. It is frustrating not being able to pay your bills on time or not being able to buy healthier foods for you and your family. At no time in my fifty years on this planet have I ever heard a person say they like being poor. UBI would break this vicious cycle of oppression by allowing people to be proactive knowing they will not be penalized for wanting a better life.

Acquiring employment along with receiving a UBI stipend would make a person's financial circumstances better. More money opens more opportunities to make ones' lifestyle better, especially if the money is not taxed. This will empower people to do more like spend more time with the kids, open an online business, look for a better job, or go to school. Just imagine how UBI would be a major stress reliever on many low-income households. I often hear people say, *"If only I had an extra $500 or $800 a month."* In my opinion, UBI will not eliminate the poor, but it will bring up their quality of living which would be a vast improvement over our current MBI system.

Proponents against UBI advocate that a UBI stipend would make many lazy and ruin the economy. Apparently, these individuals are not looking at the current economic situation. A UBI system will create confidence in the governments of the world; add positive reinforcement, and positive psychological dependence on the system. UBI would not only be a financial incentive, but an emotional and psychological incentive as well. Of course if UBI is implemented the stipend should come with the agreed upon narrative the person must be employed nine months out of every year.

Money cannot buy you happiness, but it can make your life happier. The happier you are the better you feel. The better you feel the more confidence you have in the government. When people feel the government is looking out for their best interest it creates dependence and security. This is the same tactic Franklin Delano Roosevelt employed and it brought America out of the Great Depression. When I receive my income tax check every year my confidence in the government reaches an all-time high. Economic sustainability is psychological not monetary. The government has not figured this out yet, but Antichrist will.

By implementing social protection systems, providing fair affordable equal access to economic resources and basic services like healthcare, food, shelter, and sanitation. This sustainable goal of the New World Order is to:

- "End hunger and ensure access by all people, in particular the poor and people in vulnerable situations, including infants, to safe, nutritious and sufficient food all year round." ibid, 2.1

- "End all forms of malnutrition, including achieving, by 2025, the internationally agreed targets on stunting and wasting in children less than 5 years of age, and address the nutritional needs of adolescent girls, pregnant and lactating women and older persons." ibid, 2.2

- "Double the agricultural productivity and incomes of small-scale food producers, in particular women, indigenous peoples, family farmers, pastoralists and fishers, including through secure and equal access to land, other productive resources and inputs, knowledge, financial services, markets and opportunities for value addition and non-farm employment." ibid, 2.3

- "Ensure sustainable food production systems and implement resilient agricultural practices that increase productivity and production, that help maintain ecosystems, that strengthen capacity for adaptation to climate change, extreme weather, drought, flooding and other disasters and that progressively improve land and soil quality." ibid, 2.4

- "Maintain the genetic diversity of seeds, cultivated plants and farmed and domesticated animals and their related wild species, including through soundly managed and diversified seed and plant banks at the national, regional and international levels, and promote access to and fair and equitable sharing of benefits arising from the utilization of genetic resources and associated traditional knowledge, as internationally agreed." ibid, 2.5

In some Third World countries poverty is so extreme. To have basic needs met would be a luxury. Eating and having clean drinking water is a day-to-day struggle. In Third World countries about eighty percent of people live on less than ten dollars a day. Thirteen out of every hundred people in America are living an inferior quality of life. This means hand to mouth existence, and utter destitution. Food insecurity, lack of shelter, water, and clothing should not be a way of life for about 43 million people living in America. – **ibid, https://global issues.org**

Artificial intelligence will examine the Old World Order's past failures and will create a series of 'One Solution for All' algorithms for the redistribution of global wealth.

This will eliminate much red tape, bureaucracy, and wasteful spending. Discrimination against the lower middle class, poor, and impoverished will be a thing of the past. The new economic system will be fair, open, honest, and transparent. Instituting this economic system will not be geared toward the political elite. Its' sole purpose is to make the global system fair.

One of the many algorithms Artificial intelligence will write will correct the imbalance in food produce. The U.S.D.A. pays farmers not to produce goods to control food prices while millions of Americans go to bed hungry. Why not give away the surplus to those in need? All the food Americans throw away every day, and all the families that go to bed hungry will become a thing of the past. Science will play a significant role in the foods of the future. Most of the beef, chicken and pork that we love to consume will be one hundred percent plant based. These plant-based meats will be less taxing on the environment (greenhouse gases).

In our consumer driven society people buy too much, eat too much, and waste too much. Foods of the future will be produced cheaper and will be healthier. These foods will have more protein and fiber necessary for a healthy body. Plant-based foods are becoming more and more popular these days as scientists move closer to make plant-based foods taste like real meats. People want to eat healthier because they want to feel healthier. I moved to plant-based foods for this reason. Eventually, innovation will make plant-based foods taste just as good as real meats by improving texture, taste, and smell.

As more and more farmers are fading out of existence, part of our agricultural produce will be grown by future farms inside vertical urban high rises. Fruits, vegetables, and grains will be grown through aeroponics and lamps that produce photosynthesis. This ingenuity will save space, increase yields, productivity, and create a sustainable food supply. The best part about future foods is they will be one hundred percent organic.

When you shop at the supermarket you will find that foods will be tailored to your physiology. Through some type of smart watch device worn on your wrist, an onscreen display at the supermarket will give you all relevant information about products. Information such as: Distributor, weigh, health benefits, cost, recipes, vitamin and mineral facts, how and when it was grown, and which vertical farm produced the item. These onscreen displays will even tell you if you are allergic to certain types of foods based on your physiology. You simply bag your groceries and walk out the door as there will be no cashiers. Scanners in the supermarket will know exactly who you are and what you purchased. The funds will come directly out of your bank account. In a cashless society this will eliminate most shoplifting, theft, and robberies.

The New World Order will ensure good health, well-being, and life expectancy. The aim of the World Health Organization is to eradicate a wide range of diseases, communicable or otherwise. Funding will be provided for scientific research studies in nanotech biology. Artificial Intelligence has already mapped the human genome. Through quantum analytics of medical data, Artificial Intelligence will assimilate all medical information in the world that has ever existed. Heart rate, body mass index, blood pressure, and even your daily activities will be analyzed to ensure a healthy and wholesome lifestyle. This sustainable goal of the New World Order is to:

- "Reduce the global maternal mortality ratio to less than 70 per 100,000 live births." ibid, 3.1

- "End preventable deaths of newborns and children under 5 years of age, with all countries aiming to reduce neonatal mortality to at least as low as 12 per 1,000 live births and under-5 mortality to at least as low as 25 per 1,000 live births." ibid, 3.2

- "End the epidemics of AIDS, tuberculosis, malaria and neglected tropical diseases and combat hepatitis, water-borne diseases and other communicable diseases." ibid, 3.3

- "Reduce by one third premature mortality from non-communicable diseases through prevention and treatment and promote mental health and well-being." ibid, 3.4

- "Strengthen the prevention and treatment of substance abuse, including narcotic drug abuse and harmful use of alcohol." ibid, 3.5

- "Halve the number of global deaths and injuries from road traffic accidents." ibid, 3.6

- "Ensure universal access to sexual and reproductive health-care services, including for family planning, information and education, and the integration of reproductive health into national strategies and programs." ibid, 3.7

- "Achieve universal health coverage, including financial risk protection, access to quality essential health-care services and access to safe, effective, quality and affordable essential medicines and vaccines for all." ibid, 3.8

- Substantially reduce the number of deaths and illnesses from hazardous chemicals in air, water and soil pollution and contamination." ibid, 3.9

All medical and biological data will be connected to the Cloud and interpreted through digital monitoring in real time. Artificial Intelligence will be able to detect any abnormalities in a person's health. If or when something negative occurs, your smart devices will be alerted in real-time. In the future your smart glasses, scale, comb, Fitbit, hair brush, toothbrush, or contacts will send the data directly to A.I. systems. In turn, you will be alerted of your current health status. Every single item in the world will have connectivity to Artificial Intelligence via ioT (internet of things). Everything from family history, chronic diseases, surgeries, ailments, and such will be scrutinized. Artificial Intelligence will discover new cures for many of our current diseases that hold our lives hostage today. Preventing diseases before they occur will be the first goal.

The second goal will be curing diseases. In the technological utopia of the New World Order, science will have the ability to look inside of your body on a sub-atomic level. These technological advancements will be able to repair your DNA. Just imagine having your failing heart restored to youthfulness or being cured of cancer in one day. Medicine will be technologically advanced to detect any abnormalities in the human body to prevent disease, cure disease, and will provide personalized treatment to avert any side effects. Medical care will not be general, but targeted and uniquely based on the individual.

Antibiotic resistance will become a unique problem in the near future unless nanotech steps in and develops a super antibiotic. Super antibiotics drugs would only target the bad bacteria and highly reduce the chances of antibiotic resistance. As we speak scientists and researchers are working to create super drugs.

Regenerative medicine will be able to regenerate organs and cells that have been damaged. Do you need a new leg, hand, or arm? No problem. These limbs can be created in a lab and will fit your body perfectly. Need a new heart or kidney? No problem. You will not have to worry about organ rejection or blood types because the organ will be tuned to your physiology. Future regenerative medicine will be able is to create and or replace any part of the human body that has been injured: organs, tissue, an ear, a nose, eyes, cartilage, liver, kidneys, heart, skin, etc.

3D imaging will allow doctors and surgeons to see far more detail in a person's body, invisible to the naked eye. Minute tumors, veins, arteries, nerves, blood flow, and even cells can be seen in real-time through 3D imaging technology. No more long waits or exams for results.

Your health will be monitored in real-time via Healthcare Management Intelligence Systems (HMIS), which will instantly forecast the prognosis and offer an accurate diagnosis. From a single drop of blood, the doctor will detect potential diseases like cancer, diabetes, viruses, cardiovascular disease, HIV, influenza, and such diseases within seconds. Just imagine detecting diseases in their infancy and instantly receiving a diagnosis. Detecting a problem before it becomes chronic will save the lives of millions. Diseases will become a thing of the past. As Artificial Intelligence continues to learn more about the human genome, science will predict potential diseases and life expectancy in newborns. The end result of mapping the human genome will be to create a one-pill solution to cure all diseases. Nano-tech will play an important role in the medicine of the future.

Having a good standard of living and health is a great thing, but it means nothing if earth's inhabitants continually contaminate the atmosphere with Greenhouse gases. Clean types of energy must be found to create an atmosphere of mental and emotional well-being. A great deal of our energy consumption is fossil fuels. In about thirty years or so our energy consumption will double.

Since the technological revolution began in the early 20th century, factories, power plants and automobiles have bombarded Earth's atmosphere with greenhouse gases like nitrous oxide, carbon dioxide, and methane. These byproducts from oil, coal, gas, and such reduce oxygen levels and warm our atmosphere. Industries cannot keep taxing the environment. We need new and innovative ways to heal the planet. Earth always finds a way to heal itself, but it needs time to rest.

At the North and South poles, advocates of global warming say the ice is beginning to melt, increasing sea levels. Advocates of global warming push the carbon dioxide threat, but nitrous oxide is the real culprit of global warming because it does not dissipate in our atmosphere. Scientists are looking into the idea of fusion power that can duplicate the processes of the sun by smashing two or more atomic nuclei to produce energy. When the sun converts the protons of hydrogen into helium the result is a mass output of energy. If scientist can duplicate the processes of the sun, we would have an infinite source of clean energy.

The first Tokamak fusion test reactor was built in 1980. Presently, thirty-five nations are working together to build the largest Tokamak fusion reactor in the world. Unlike a nuclear reactor which produces radioactive waste, a Tokamak reactor produces little to no waste, because its' energy is created by a magnetic field. It would be the perfect power source with no greenhouse gases, no atomic waste, and no worries about reactor meltdown.

147

Another source and one that is becoming very popular is solar energy. Special panels capture free energy from the sun and convert it into useable energy. A 3'×5' (feet) solar panel produces 250 watts of power per hour. Using 8 hours of sunlight per day, a basic solar panel produces 2,000 watts per hour (2 kilowatts). Realistically the average American home uses about 33.75 kilowatts per day. In total the kilowatt usage per year would be 12,327 kilowatts to satisfy the average appliance household. To solar power your home you would need 255 square feet and 17 solar panels. Solar panels only capture about 20% of the sun's energy. That will soon change with up-and-coming pioneering inventor and architect Andre Broessel. He is one of the co-founders of a company called Rawlemon.

Rawlemon created a multi-junction solar optical panel that concentrates the power of the sun to increase yield up to four times greater than a solar panel. – **bid, https://rawlemon.com.** This multi-junction cell is an optical solar panel that produces the same energy output, whose technology is about ten times smaller as a regular solar panel. You would need 17 solar panels and the square footage would be significantly smaller. One panel would be 3½" × 6" (inches) instead of 3'×5' (feet). To solar power the average home with Rawlemon technology you would need 25-30 square feet instead of 255 square feet. Rawlemon claims their multi-junction cell technology can even absorb the sun's energy on a cloudy day. Very soon car manufacturers will be equipping their products with solar technology.

Another form of clean and sustainable energy making its' way onto the scene is technology called Ocean Thermal Energy Conversion. Earth is covered by almost seventy-five percent water. If someone found a way to convert water into energy, we would have a plentiful supply of energy as well.

Duke Hartman is an employee of Makai Ocean Engineering. This company has found a way to harness heat from ocean water, to create electrical energy. Makai's apparatus current test trials using only sunlight and sea water has produced 100,000 up to 5,000,000 watts of power. This is just a small-scale model. When OTEC is globally deployed, it too may be one of many solutions for sustainable clean energy. This sustainable goal of the New World Order is to:

- "Ensure universal access to affordable, reliable and modern energy services." ibid, 7.1

- "Increase substantially the share of renewable energy in the global energy mix." ibid, 7.2

- "Double the global rate of improvement in energy efficiency." ibid, 7.3

- "Enhance international cooperation to facilitate access to clean energy research and technology, including renewable energy, energy efficiency and advanced and cleaner fossil-fuel technology, and promote investment in energy infrastructure and clean energy technology." ibid, 7.3a

- "Expand infrastructure and upgrade technology for supplying modern and sustainable energy services for all in developing countries, in particular least developed countries, Small Island developing States, and land-locked developing countries, in accordance with their respective programs of support." ibid, 7.3b

In the near future urban planning, parks and recreation, transportation services, and housing institutions will collaborate to design better cities. Today's cities are too big and congested. The trick will be to balance the traffic of the population, so people will not be stepping on each other's toes. The less crowded you feel the better you feel. Future cities will be designed differently to reduce the levels of stress by promoting a sense of well-being. Elements like:

- Walk-able access to parks or jobs
- Around the clock garbage and trash removal services
- Better subway and transport systems
- More recreational programs for young teenagers
- UBI for persons interested in starting a home-base business
- Even ideas to incorporate hydroponics inside city buildings

This sustainable goal of the New World Order is to:

- "Ensure access for all to adequate, safe and affordable housing and basic services and upgrade slums." ibid, 11.1

- "Provide access to safe, affordable, accessible and sustainable transport systems for all, improving road safety, notably by expanding public transport, with special attention to the needs of those in vulnerable situations, women, and children, persons with disabilities and older persons." ibid, 11.2

- "Enhance inclusive and sustainable urbanization and capacity for participatory, integrated and sustainable human settlement planning and management in all countries." ibid, 11.3

- "Strengthen efforts to protect and safeguard the world's cultural and natural heritage." ibid, 11.4

- "Significantly reduce the number of deaths and the number of people affected and substantially decrease the direct economic losses relative to global gross domestic product caused by disasters, including water-related disasters, with a focus on protecting the poor and people in vulnerable situations." ibid, 11.5

- "Reduce the adverse per capita environmental impact of cities, including by paying special attention to air quality and municipal and other waste management." ibid, 11.6

- "Provide universal access to safe, inclusive and accessible, green and public spaces, in particular for women and children, older persons & persons with disabilities." ibid, 11.7

To remedy overcrowding and to house the populations of the future, cities in the New World Order will be vertical communal high rises with flexible reinforced materials capable of withstanding earthquakes on the Richter scale of 7.0-7.9. The Richter scale measures the power of earthquakes by logarithmic. A low scale number will produce less damage. The higher the number, the more damage the earthquake will produce. As each number on the Richter scale goes up, the magnitude increases. With high magnitude earthquakes in mind, the cities of now and the future are being designed with dampers and shock absorbers to control seismic sway.

These enable high rise buildings to withstand wind gusts of up to 145 mph and resist massive seismic quakes. Some vertical cities will be so massive they will be considered a city within a city. Adopted with cruise ship ideology in mind, a mega-city will have swimming pools, shopping centers, restaurants, stores, malls, parks, entertainment venues and recreational activities. Thirty years from now our cities will be technological marvels.

As work will be plentiful on a global scale these infrastructure projects will be aimed at the poorest countries. The ghettos of Haiti, Ethiopia, Mozambique, Uganda, Kyrgyzstan, Uzbekistan, and such will be at the top of the list. The rich class, medium class, and poor class will still exist, but the guidelines for the cost of living will be more than adequate for Third World countries and all poverty will be all but eliminated. By this time the word 'Poor' will be relative.

The greatest achievement for the New World Order will be to establish a peaceful, prosperous and a sustainable world for all. The New World Order will be a place of clean energy, electric and hybrid self-driving cars, and an abundant food supply. Plenty employment will be available, and a monthly stipend will help with expenses without a person having to worry about how they are going to pay their bills.

Smart IQ technology will make everyone lives better. There will be convenient shopping, direct and instant access to information and technology. Crime will be all but eliminated through the all-seeing eye of technology. Once all technologies are integrated, economic and gender equality, sustainable cities, environmentally friendly materials, and technological singularity will make the New World Order a technological utopia. With these great new infrastructures in place everybody will profit. In the New World Order everybody will be a winner!

I disagree with the devil on everything, but a One World Government makes a lot of sense. And yes, I know the one thing you cannot do is sleep on the devil. Now, do not kill the messenger because Lucifer is a brilliant creature, and you must give credit where credit is due. The New World Order will offer all that it promises, except for a couple major details. You will have to give up your privacy and soul for the greater good. The devil will offer the world its best life now if it means taking as many to the Lake of Fire as possible.

There are other sustainable goals: Education, protecting wildlife and marine life, and forming long lasting global partnerships. If you would like to research all seventeen sustainable goals go on the United Nations website @ sustainable development.un.org.

The Coming World Dictator – Revelation 6:9-11

The plan has already been set in motion. It is not a question of if it is going to happen, but when. Sometime during this new period of global restoration, a new leader will come onto the scene. The Bible calls this man the Antichrist. The New World Order is Lucifer's MAD (Mutually Assured Destruction) strategy.

Antichrist will be a strategic genius with exceptional intellectual abilities. He will bring original ideas and advancements to the world. The world governments will be screaming out for a messiah to usher in total peace and prosperity. Through deceit and political maneuvering, Antichrist will move into a position of total power. When Antichrist moves into absolute power, he will set into motion a series of events that will cause the world to worship him as God, devastate Christians, Jews, and profane the Jewish temple. The Bible calls this event the Abomination of Desolation or the Great tribulation.

Links in the Prophetic Chain

THE CONVERGENCE

RISE OF THE NEW WORLD ORDER

RISE OF ANTICHRIST

GLOBAL PEACE ARMISTICE

RISE OF THE BEAST

- FOUR HORSEMEN = OLD WORLD ORDER ENDS

- GLOBAL SOLIDARITY

- THINGS START TO GET BETTER

- PEACE AND SAFETY FOR ALL

- JACOB'S TROUBLE OR ABOMINATION OF DESOLATION OR THE GREAT TRIBULATION PERIOD

Revelation 6:8	The Old World Order Ends	4th SEAL
○	The New World Order Begins	○
Revelation 6:9	Abomination of Great Tribulation	5th SEAL

Chapter Seven
The Two Witnesses

"One witness shall not rise up against a man for any iniquity, or for any sin, in any sin that he sinneth: at the mouth of two witnesses, or at the mouth of three witnesses, shall the matter be established." – Deuteronomy 19:15

"And when he had opened the fifth seal, I saw under the altar the souls of them that were slain for the word of God, and for the testimony which they held: And they cried with a loud voice, saying, how long, O Lord, holy and true, dost thou not judge and avenge our blood on them that dwell on the earth? And white robes were given unto every one of them; and it was said unto them, that they should rest yet for a little season, until their fellow servants also and their brethren, that should be killed as they were should be fulfilled." – Revelation 6:9-11

Revelation 6:9-11 is when believers will be killed for the cause of Christ. This period is the Abomination of Desolation (Jacob's Trouble), when the Gentiles occupy Jerusalem and the Jewish temple. Revelation 11:1-3 tell us the two witnesses will rise when the Jewish temple is occupied by Antichrist. This occupation will last for 1,260 days. This is the first half of Daniel's Seventieth Week, which is the remaining 3½ years of Antichrist's covenant. It is during this time Christians will begin to experience great tribulation. Before God brings wrath upon the disobedient, he always gives a warning. God's wrath only comes after warnings of judgment. It is during this time two men will rise to oppose the Antichrist, False Prophet, and the New World Order. The Bible refers to these two men as two witnesses.

"And I will give power unto my two witnesses, and they shall prophesy a thousand two hundred and threescore (1,260) days, clothed in sackcloth." – Revelation 11:3

There is much speculation about these two individuals. The widely accepted belief is one of these individuals will be Moses. I have heard it said it will be Moses because he did not die. Moses did die; so, we can rule out Moses coming back.

"Moses the servant of the Lord died there in the land of Moab..." – Deuteronomy 34:5

I have heard it said it will be Elijah because he must come a second time to prepare the way for Christ. The Bible already told us Elijah's second coming was fulfilled through the ministry of John the Baptist. The Bible does not speak of Elijah coming back a third time. So, we can rule out Elijah coming back.

"And his disciples asked him, saying, why then say the scribes that Elijah must first come? And Jesus answered and said unto them, Elijah truly shall first come, and restore all things. But I say unto you, that Elijah is come already, and they knew him not, but have done unto him whatsoever they listed. Likewise shall also the Son of man suffer of them. Then the disciples understood that he spake unto them of John the Baptist." – Saint Matthew 17:10-13.

The least popular view is these two individuals are just two random guys that come in the power of Elijah and the power of Moses. Lastly, others believe it will be Enoch and Elijah because they were translated.

"So God created man in his own image, in the image of God created he him; male and female created he them. And God blessed them, and God said unto them, be fruitful, and multiply, and replenish the earth, and subdue it..." – Genesis 1:27 & 28

Replenish (Maw-Lay: Hebrew) means to procreate. It is sexual intercourse. Yes, God created sex. Hypothetically speaking, if Adam and Eve had not fallen eventually the entire world would become full of immortal beings. The question is, *"Since there would be no death, how would attrition of population control take place?"* In our sinful world attrition is through death, but in a world without sin attrition would have been through translation. Most leave this world by death, but a few down through the centuries have left by translation. For all living when Jesus comes in the clouds, the Raptured is a type of translation.

"And all the days of Enoch were 365 years: And Enoch walked with God: and he was not; for God took him." – Genesis 5:23 & 24

"By faith Enoch was translated that he should not see death; and was not found, because God had translated him: for before his translation he had this testimony, that he pleased God." – Hebrews 11:5

"And after six days Jesus taketh Peter, James, and John his brother, and bringeth them up into a high mountain apart, and was transfigured before them: and his face did shine as the sun, and his raiment was white as the light." – Saint Matthew 17:1 & 2

The Moses and Elijah theology is based on the Mount of Transfiguration event. Translation and transfiguration are not the same. People confuse these two processes. Enoch and Elijah were translated; Jesus was transfigured. Jesus transfigured his physical body to a higher form. This process is called transmutation. Jesus controlled his transmutation ability by stepping up to his higher form and stepping down to his physical form, because he is God. Transmutation ability was under Jesus' complete control because he was not born in sin nor shaped in iniquity. We do not possess this ability because our bodies are sinful.

154

Unlike transfiguration, translation is transferal from a physical body to a spiritual body, in which the individual skips over the process of death. Translation is to transition from the physical to the spiritual. One may assume translation equals a physical body. It does not. All saints past, present, and up to the Rapture, will receive a new body at the Rapture. Anyone translated does not yet have a physical body. From the beginning of Adam until now, no one has a new physical body yet, except Jesus. That is why Jesus is the first born from the dead (Colossians1:18).

"For as in Adam all die, even so in Christ shall all be made alive; but every man in his own order: Christ the first-fruits; afterwards, they that are Christ's at his coming." – I Corinthians 15:22

- Resurrection of Jesus Christ (#1)
- Resurrection / Rapture (#2)

Romans 8:30 explains the progression of Jesus Christ's plan for all his saints.

"Moreover, whom he did predestinate, them he also called: and whom he called, them he also justified: and whom he justified, them he also glorified." – Romans 8:30

The last stage is a glorified body. Those who died or were translated, presently rest in Paradise, awaiting the First Resurrection. This includes Moses and Elijah. In the Rapture the dead will resurrect first, and if you are alive your body will automatically be changed into a physical glorified body (I Thessalonians 4:16-17). Up to the point of the Rapture, translation does not negate the three physical laws of sin and death.

"...absent from the body, present with the Lord." – II Corinthians 5:8

"...for dust thou art, and unto dust thou shalt return." – Genesis 3:19

"...flesh and blood cannot inherit the kingdom of God." – I Corinthians 15:50

The sinful body cannot enter heaven, because God cannot and will not allow sin in his presence. The sinful body must return to the dust of the Earth. Enoch, Elijah, or anyone that was translated did not take their physical body into heaven. It does not matter if a person died in the Old or New Testament, or if a person was translated in the Old or New Testament; the sinful body must remain here. Whoever was translated, Genesis 3:19 kicked in, and in the twinkling of an eye, their physical body returned to the dust of the ground. If the physical body can be changed in the twinkling of an eye at the Rapture, it can also return to the dust of the earth in the twinkling of an eye if God commands.

A body absorbed into earth will eventually become part of the food chain. At the Rapture, God is not going to track down every molecule and piece you back together. God will just form a new glorified body for you out of the dust of the earth or wherever He is going to get the material. Now you do not have to figure out how God is going to resurrect that guy that was eaten by a shark two hundred years ago, or those ashes spread into the ocean for fish food after being cremated.

Because we are born in sin and shaped in iniquity, death is a one-way ticket; translation is a one-way ticket; and the Rapture is a one-way ticket. Once we leave earth through any process, God will purpose us with a glorified body at the First Resurrection (I Corinthians 15:51-55). Even people that were born and did not sin are also subject to the three physical laws of sin and death.

"Nevertheless death reigned from Adam to Moses, even over them that had not sinned after the similitude of Adam's transgression..." Romans 5:14

First Corinthians 15:51, states that we shall all be changed. Changed or Allasso in Greek means to do away with the former, but also means to exchange with the newer. We misunderstand the resurrection and rapture process. Just as God will destroy the old earth and create a new one, he will destroy the old body and create a new body. The DNA of this planet and your body carries the stench of sin. Compared to the glorified body, your physical body is a pile of manure. Your identity is not in your old body, it is in your soul. The resurrection is not a resurrection of the old body, but your soul resurrecting into a new body. When Jesus raises us from the dead it is not the old body he will raise, but rather raising the spiritual body into a new glorified physical body.

Food For Thought

"And I will give power unto my two witnesses, and they shall prophesy a thousand two hundred and threescore (1,260) days, clothed in sackcloth." – Revelation 11:3

'I will give' is future tense. It has not happened yet, but will happen in the future. Why would God give Moses and Elijah power they already have? So, does God take back his power from Moses and Elijah only to give that power back to them? Is God an Indian giver? If you read the above scripture a million times, it does not state once these two witnesses are Moses or Elijah. If these two men are Old Testament prophets, the scripture would read like this.

"And I will give power unto my two prophets, and they shall prophesy a thousand two hundred and threescore days, clothed in sackcloth."

OR

"And I will give my power back to Moses and Elijah, for they are my prophets. They shall come back to life after 3,000 years and they shall prophesy a thousand two hundred and threescore days, clothed in sackcloth."

OR

"I have already given power unto my two witnesses, and they shall prophesy a thousand two hundred and threescore days, clothed in sackcloth."

For the record I just want to say neither I nor God is trying to confuse you. If it is going to be Moses, Elijah, Enoch, a cat, dog or a stone, God would have said it. This philosophy is reading into something that is not there. Just because Moses and Elijah appeared to Jesus on the Mount of Transfiguration someone created a the-ology around it. When I explain this to people they still hold on to the theory of Moses and Elijah being the two witnesses because it is so widely accepted. They always come up with the same answer: God can do anything. That is not true. God can do everything, but God cannot do anything. God cannot violate his Word or sin. Some believe widely accepted theology is true even though it is nowhere in the Bible. If it is not specific or hermeneutically consistent in the Bible, it is false doctrine. For some reason, out of all the unscriptural doctrines I have heard, the Moses and Elijah theology irritates me the most! It is just **bad theology**.

"And Elijah took his mantle, and wrapped it together, and smote the waters, and they were divided hither and thither, so that they two went over on dry ground." – 2 Kings 2:8

Elijah had a student by the name of Elisha. Elijah's time was coming to be taken up into heaven by God. Elijah took his mantle and hit the waters of the Jordan River and the waters parted so they both walked across on dry land.

"And it came to pass, when they were gone over, that Elijah said unto Elisha, ask what I shall do for thee, before I be taken away from thee. And Elisha said, I pray thee, let a double portion of thy spirit be upon me. And Elijah said, thou hast asked a hard thing: nevertheless, if thou see me when I am taken from thee, it shall be so unto thee; but if not, it shall not be so." – 2 Kings 2:9-10

"And it came to pass, as they still went on, and talked, that, behold, there appeared a chariot of fire, and horses of fire, and parted them both asunder; and Elijah went up by a whirlwind into heaven. And Elisha saw it, and he cried, my father, my father, the chariot of Israel..." – 2 Kings 2:11-12

157

"He (Elisha) took up also the mantle of Elijah that fell from him, and went back, and stood by the bank of the Jordan River." – 2 Kings 2:13

"And he took the mantle of Elijah that fell from him, and smote the waters, and said, where is the Lord God of Elijah? And when he also had smitten the waters, they parted hither and thither: and Elisha went over." – 2 Kings 2:14

Elisha took Elijah's mantle, hit the waters of the Jordan River, and crossed back over on dry land. Elisha did the same miracle Elijah did. God anointed Elisha with the same power as Elijah. What comes up in my mind is, if God anointed Elisha, why not anoint the two future witnesses? Why an elaborate scheme of reaching into the past to resurrect Moses and Elijah? First, God would be violating his three physical laws of sin and death. Second, Elijah would have to come back to die a physical death, and Moses would have to come back to die a physical death twice. That is a lot of work.

"And the Lord said unto Joshua, this day will I begin to magnify thee in the sight of all Israel, that they may know that, as I was with Moses, so I will be with thee." – Joshua 3:7

"And as they that bare the ark were come unto Jordan, and the feet of the priests that bare the ark were dipped in the brim of the water... that the waters which came down from above stood and rose up upon an heap very far from the city, and the priests that bare the ark of the covenant of the Lord stood firm on dry ground in the midst of Jordan, and all the Israelites passed over on dry ground until all the people were passed clean over Jordan." – Joshua 3:15-17

When Moses died the mantle of leadership passed to Joshua. The priests lifted the Ark of the Covenant of God. When they walked into the Jordan River the waters split apart. This was essentially the same miracle Moses did when he parted the Red Sea. As you can clearly see God did not resurrect Moses to part the Jordan River. God anointed Joshua with the same power.

"Then spake Joshua to the Lord in the day when the Lord delivered up the Amorites before the children of Israel, and he said in the sight of Israel, Sun, stand thou still upon Gibeon; and thou, Moon, in the valley of Ajalon. And the sun stood still, and the moon stayed, until the people had avenged themselves upon their enemies. Is not this written in the book of Jasher? So the sun stood still in the midst of heaven, and hasted not go down about a whole day." – Joshua 10:12-13

Joshua parted the Jordan River. Not only that; Joshua delivered the Children of Israel into the Promise Land; Not only that; Joshua commanded the moon to stand still; and not only that; Joshua commanded the sun to stand still.

What comes up in my mind is, why bring back Moses 1.0 when God can bring back Joshua 2.0? Why bring back Elijah 1.0 when God can bring back Elisha 2.0? Elisha had a <u>double portion</u> of Elijah's spirit. I do not know who contrived this fairytale of Moses and Elijah being the two witnesses, but to teach, claim, or substantiate this theory without any credible scriptures is unbiblical. Why would God bring back anyone from the past when he can clearly anoint any two people to carrying out his work?

"And when they (two witnesses) shall have finished their testimony, the beast that ascendeth out of the bottomless pit shall make war against them, and shall overcome them, and kill them." – Revelation 11:7

Now, look at the flip side from a common sense perspective. If God gave Enoch a new body and Elijah a new body when they were translated it must be a glorified body. If Enoch and Elijah will be the two witnesses how will the Beast kill them in Revelation 11:7? A glorified body is impervious to death. Can you see where I am going with all this?

For Moses to be killed he would have to come back in a regular human body through childbirth. God could do this without contradicting His Word, but that would be reincarnation! These controversial points I am making should provoke you to study more. We need to stop listening to all this nonsense. When you add common sense, does this nonsensical theology make any sense? Because theories such as these sound spectacular, are full of awe and grandiose, we just outright abandon the truth. Parroting anecdotal theology has become the normal amongst many Christians. It is blind faith. Contrary to popular belief, faith is not blinding following a person and believing everything they say. Humans being are fallible.

Let me tell you the problem with blind faith. A woman is disgusted in her marriage and wants to get rid of her husband. She goes to a close male friend and says her husband abuses her emotionally, mentally, physically, and psychologically. Her male friend wants to protect the woman and eventually winds up killing the husband. This male believed her because it sounded so convincing without one single shred of proof to back up her claims. Many Christians fall into the same trap. Hearsay sounds so convincing until you ask questions and apply common sense. If this guy had asked the right questions and checked out the facts for himself, the husband would still be alive. One of the many reasons Christians get caught up with misinformation is they do not sift through the doctrine to confirm if it is true or not. These people reason, if it is coming from someone with high biblical authority, then it must be correct. Usually a theory built on one scripture, or no scripture(s) is 99 times out of 100 not backed up by the scriptures. We must do away with rumor, assumption, fabled doctrine, and fairytales.

159

"...Thou shalt be a good minister of Jesus Christ, nourished up in the words of faith and of good doctrine, whereunto thou hast attained. But refuse profane and old wives' fables, and exercise thyself rather unto godliness." – I Timothy 4:6-7

Because it sounds goods, feels convenient, and everyone is accepting it, we once again jump on the bandwagon. Who is making all this stuff up? These anecdotal teachings are not biblical. Moses is not coming back! Elijah is not coming back! Enoch is not coming back! They did their time. For heaven's sake let them rest! All through the Old and New Testament God raised and anointed men with power to carry out his will. What, did God run out of power? God can give you this same power by simply breathing on you.

"And when he had said this, he breathed on them, and saith unto them, receive ye the Holy Ghost..." – Saint John 20:22

Do you think Moses, Elijah or Joshua did those miracles? The Holy Spirit did those miracles. The Holy Spirit is the Power of God. God does not have to invent some elaborate scheme. What is easier: breathing on someone or getting a pick-and-shovel to excavate a 3,000-year-old corpse? God can anoint whomever he pleases. The same way he has always done it in the past.

"For I am the Lord, I change not..." – Malachi 3:6

For many years I would not study the Book of Revelation because I wanted to unlearn what I heard through the years by pastors and teachers. I wanted to study the Book of Revelation with a clean slate unhindered by any previous bias. This is what I discovered.

- Preterism – False
- Seven-year tribulation – False
- Pre-tribulation Rapture – False
- Mid-tribulation Rapture – False
- Post-tribulation Rapture – False
- The 7 Churches are 7 Church Eras – False
- The Rapture can happen at any time – False
- The 2 witnesses are Moses and Elijah – False
- The gospel will be preached by the 144,000 – False
- The 7-year peace armistice is the last 7 years of Daniel – False
- The White Horseman of the Apocalypse is the Antichrist – False

Find one scripture in the Bible from Genesis to Revelation where it states the White Horseman is Antichrist the man; Moses and Elijah are the two witnesses; the Rapture can occur at any moment; the 144,000 will preach the gospel during the <u>seven-year tribulation</u> period? My apologies, I meant the 1,260 days of great tribulation. As a matter of fact, the 144,000 will not be sealed until after the Great Tribulation, but right before God's wrath. So how can the 144,000 preach during the Great Tribulation if they are not sealed until after the Great Tribulation? Is any of this making sense to you? Stop believing in all these myths, fairytales, and biblical fables. Understanding, Knowledge, and Faith, are not blind. To determine who the two witnesses are we must simply use the process of elimination.

Who are the 2 Witnesses?

"And he gave some, apostles; and some, prophets; and some, evangelists; and some, pastors and teachers; for the perfecting of the saints, for the work of the ministry..." – Ephesians 4:11-12.

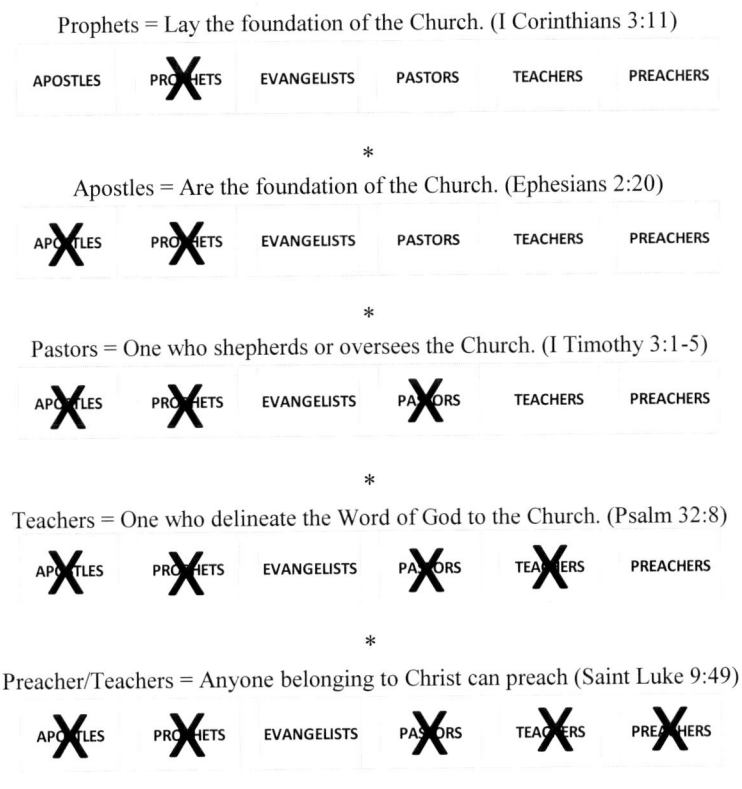

Prophets = Lay the foundation of the Church. (I Corinthians 3:11)

| APOSTLES | PROPHETS | EVANGELISTS | PASTORS | TEACHERS | PREACHERS |

*

Apostles = Are the foundation of the Church. (Ephesians 2:20)

| APOSTLES | PROPHETS | EVANGELISTS | PASTORS | TEACHERS | PREACHERS |

*

Pastors = One who shepherds or oversees the Church. (I Timothy 3:1-5)

| APOSTLES | PROPHETS | EVANGELISTS | PASTORS | TEACHERS | PREACHERS |

*

Teachers = One who delineate the Word of God to the Church. (Psalm 32:8)

| APOSTLES | PROPHETS | EVANGELISTS | PASTORS | TEACHERS | PREACHERS |

*

Preacher/Teachers = Anyone belonging to Christ can preach (Saint Luke 9:49)

| APOSTLES | PROPHETS | EVANGELISTS | PASTORS | TEACHERS | PREACHERS |

"And I will give **power** unto my two **witnesses**..." – Revelation 11:3

*"But ye shall receive **power**, after the Holy Ghost is come upon you: and ye shall be **witnesses** unto me both in Jerusalem, and in all Judea, and in Samaria, and unto the uttermost part of the earth." – Acts 1:8*

"Go ye therefore, and teach all nations, baptizing them in the name of the Father, and of the Son, and of the Holy Ghost: teaching them to observe all things whatsoever I have commanded you..." – Saint Matthew 28:19-20

The job of an evangelist is to **witness** to an unbelieving world. Before God brings His wrath, He will send two witnesses to testify the Truth of Jesus Christ to an unbelieving world? This is exactly what the two witnesses will be doing. A witness is an evangelist. Now that we know these two men are operating in the office of evangelism, why do teachers call them prophets? Because the Moses and Elijah theology have been pounded into our heads and shoved down our throats repeatedly. Due to this widely accepted belief many accept this theology as fact. Theology is theoretical. It only becomes concrete with proper exegesis and hermeneutics.

Elijah called fire down from heaven and parted the Jordan River. Moses called down hail-fire and parted the Red Sea. If Moses or Elijah wanted it to rain cats, dogs, and hamburgers, they could have done that too. I always hear preachers say the power of Elijah or the power of Moses. It took power to bring the universe into existence. Where were Moses and Elijah when God laid the foundations of the Earth? Where were Moses and Elijah when God divided the waters from the waters? Where were Moses and Elijah when God set the sun, moon and stars in their places?

It is an offense to the Most High God to even suggest such ludicrous that it is Moses' or Elijah's power. To even speak this nonsense just 'Ruins the ride'. *The Power of Elijah - The Power of Moses*; give me a break! The power is God's before, now, and will continue to be God's. God can give you, Elijah, Moses, Joshua, a donkey, a flea or a stone that same power. The power of God is the power of God. Please stop limiting the power of God.

The White Horseman is so good at distorting the truth of God's word even impressionable Christians prefer to believe science fiction over sound doctrine. If you believe God must reach into the past to resurrect two long dead prophets (something the Bible never implies nor teaches) to violate his Holy Word, '**The Illusion**' already has you. Many Christians get stuck in a loop because of nonsensical theology. Most Christian comments I get on YouTube are negative. These people want Revelation to be masked in mystique, because they are not looking for the truth.

162

They hold on to the seven year tribulation and Pre-Tribulation Rapture theology even though these teachings are clearly not in the Bible. Anecdotal end time teachings are one of the White Horseman's greatest techniques against Christians. Your mind is like a computer. A computer can be programmed. The White Horseman has mastered the art of human psychology, and his power is quite amazing. Just like the world, Christians with deeply engrained preconceived notions cannot think past their programming. Bias dictation is not objective truth. Objective truth is truth, whether you believe it or not.

<u>Power of the two witnesses</u>

- Endued with power for only 42 months **(Revelation 11:3)**

- Preach repentance **(Revelation 11:3)**

- Preach salvation **(Revelation 11:3)**

- Preach the wrath of God **(Revelation 11:3)**

- 2 Olive Trees = 2 Anointed Ones **(Revelation 11:4)**

- 2 Candlesticks = 2 Lights of Evangelism **(Revelation 11:4)** 2 Spirits of God = Spirit of Power. Spirit of Might

- Verbally speak spontaneous combustion **(Revelation 11:5)**

- Power to stop the rain **(Revelation 11:6)**

- Power to turn water into blood **(Revelation 11:6)**

- Power to smite the earth with plagues **(Revelation 11:6)**

The Jewish candlestick called the Menorah holds seven candlesticks. The seven candlesticks represent the seven Spirits of God. Saint Mark 8:24 symbolized men as trees walking. We get olive oil from an olive tree. The oil represents the anointing. The two witnesses will be anointed with the Spirit of Power and the Spirit of Might to carry out this specific ministry. As you can see, God created this temporal office for this time, place, and location. Think of the two witnesses on special assignment from God.

God can achieve this without contradicting his word. In Ephesians 4:11-12, it says he gave some evangelists, not all evangelists. Occasionally, desperate times call for desperate measures. In the Greek language there may be more than one meaning for a word. Angel, for example is a messenger of God, but it can also refer to an angelic being. Love has several meanings in Greek also. The two Greek words for prophet are Präfət or evangelist: One who proclaims the words of the Lord openly before the world or Profitis or Seer: One who prophesies future events. These two witnesses are Präfəts. We must not confuse the two.

163

"Now the acts of David the king, first and last, behold, they are written in the book of Samuel the seer, and in the book Nathan the prophet, and in the book of Gad the seer." – I Chronicles 29:29

These two witnesses will be two men anointed by God with supernatural abilities to be his last and final light to the world before God brings global wrath and vengeance. As these two men are witnessing to a godless world under the rule of the Antichrist, these two evangelists will need supernatural power to contend with the Antichrist and False Prophet. The two witnesses will preach both sides of the gospel of life in Christ and death and hell. They will preach the wrath to follow if the world does not repent, and the second coming of Jesus. Through their ministry many eyes will be opened, and hundreds of millions will reject the Beast and his lies.

"Who opposeth and exalteth himself above all that is called God, or that is worshiped; so that he as God sitteth in the temple of God, showing himself that he is God." – II Thessalonians 2:4

The Abomination of Desolation occurs when the Fifth Seal is opened. It is at this time all Christians will have to make a choice to go with the program (New World Order) or be killed for their faith. This period will be the inquisition of those who reject the New World Order. It is during this time the line will be drawn in the sand. It is during this period Christians, Jews, or infidels will be killed on mass.

"And when he had opened the fifth seal, I saw under the altar the souls of them that were slain for the word of God, and for the testimony which they held. And they cried with a loud voice, saying, how long, O Lord, holy and true, dost thou not judge and avenge our blood on them that dwell on the earth?" – Revelation 6:9-10

(1) ABOMINATION	ST. LUKE 21:20	5th SEAL	3 ½
The 2 WITNESSES	REVELATION 6:9-11	REVELATION 11:1-13	Years
1st Half	**of Daniel's**	**Seventhieth (70th)**	**Week**

The Abomination of Desolation is antecedent to God's wrath. The Wrath of God has not occurred yet, but will occur at the opening of the Seventh Seal; which contains the seven plagues of God's wrath (Revelation 15:1). The martyred saints are asking God to avenge their deaths by his wrath. But before God's wrath can fall more saints will be martyred. God will not allow Antichrist to murder all Christians. The remaining Christians will be raptured at the opening of the Sixth Seal in Revelation 6:12-13.

"And shall not God avenge his own elect, which cry day and night unto him, though he bear long with them? I tell you that he will avenge them speedily..." – Saint Luke 18:7-8

"And white robes were given unto every one of them; and it was said unto them, that they should rest yet for a little season, until their fellow serv-ants also and their brethren, that should be killed as they were, should be fulfilled." – Revelation 6:11

During this time Antichrist will change the laws, oppress the Christians, and double-cross the Israeli nation by going on a murderous rampage, and set up his idols in the temple of God. Revelation 11:4-13 tells us what the two witnesses will be doing during Antichrist's occupation in Jerusalem. Daniel 11:31-45 dual parallel speaks of Antichrist's rebellion against the Most High God.

Daniel 11:31

"And arms shall stand on his part, and they shall pollute the sanctuary of strength, and shall take away the daily sacrifice, and they shall place the abomination that maketh desolate."

| ↑ | COMPARE | ↓ |

Revelation 11:2 & 3

"But the court which is without the temple leave out, and measure it not; for it is given unto the Gentiles: and the holy city shall they tread under foot 42 months. And I will give power unto my two witnesses, and they shall prophesy 1,260 days (42 months)..."

(Given unto the Gentiles = Occupied by the Gentiles)

(1) ABOMINATION	ST. LUKE 21:20	5th SEAL	3 ½
The 2 WITNESSES	REVELATION 6:9	REVELATION 11:1-13	
1st Half of Daniel			Years

The False Prophet will lead many astray with his miracles. God will send the two witnesses to challenge the False Prophet. The two witnesses will make the False Prophet and all other false prophets look weak. People will hate these two men and come against them. Earth's inhabitants will come to realize the two witnesses have the power to only speak the word "FIRE", and a person will spontaneously burst into flames. These two men will also have the ability to invoke drought, turn water into blood, and to smite the earth with many plagues.

165

"And if any man will hurt them, fire proceedeth out of their mouth, and devoureth their enemies: and if any man will hurt them, he must in this manner be killed. These have the power to shut heaven that it rain not in the days of their prophecy: and have power over waters to turn them to blood, and to smite the earth with all plagues, as often as they will." – Revelation 11:5-6

By this time in the future Third World countries telecommunications infrastructure will be established via the instant global communications network. Through social media, world news and satellite technologies, the preaching of the two witnesses will go to the ends of the earth. Through the miracle of technology their message will easily be translated into all languages. The two witnesses will become known as the infamous two.

*"And this **gospel** of the kingdom **shall be preached** in all the world for a **witness** unto all nations; and then shall the end come." – Saint Matthew 24:14*

- Then shall the end come = Then shall God's wrath come.

The two witnesses will draw media attention not only for their evangelism; but mainly for their supernatural abilities. The two witnesses will work the miracles of God for 1,260 days. The two witnesses do not mete out God's wrath when they smite the Earth. Their plagues will be a precursor of what will soon come on all the Earth. God's wrath cannot begin until the two witnesses finish their ministry.

"And when they shall have finished their testimony, the beast that ascendeth out of the bottomless pit shall make war against them, and shall overcome them, and kill them." – Revelation 11:7

Around midnight on the 1,260[th] day, the blood moon will appear directly over the Middle East. The ground will quake, and hundreds of shooting stars and several thousand particles of space debris will light up the Middle Eastern sky like a Christmas tree. Jesus told us in Saint Matthew Chapter 24 verses 29-31, immediately after the 1,260 days of great tribulation the Rapture will take place. Later that very same day, Antichrist will kill the two witnesses.

"Immediately after the tribulation of those days shall the sun be darkened, and the moon shall not give her light, and the stars shall fall from heaven, and the powers of the heavens shall be shaken:" – Saint Matthew 24:29

(2) RAPTURE   ST. MATTHEW 24:29-31   REVELATION 6:12   6th SEAL

"And then shall appear the sign of the Son of man in heaven: and then shall all the tribes of the earth mourn, and they shall see the Son of man coming in the clouds of heaven with power and great glory. And he shall send his angels with a great sound of a trumpet, and they shall gather together his elect from the four winds, from one end of heaven to the other."
– Saint Matthew 24:30-31

The bodies of these two individuals will lie in the streets of the Holy City for another three and a half days because people will be scared to touch their dead bodies. God allows this as a testimony to the world to what would soon follow upon the resurrection of his two witnesses. God does not want to send his wrath, but like the days of Noah mankind has corrupted himself. What more can God do. After sending his judges, teachers, prophets, mighty warriors, Jesus, apostles, pastors, evangelists, Christians, and the two witnesses, God will still give the world fifteen additional days to repent before the day of his awful wrath. Mankind has left God no Choice but to destroy it. It is during this fifteen day grace period God will seal the 144,000.

(1) ABOMINATION 1st Half of Daniel	REVELATION 6:9	5th SEAL	3 ½ Years
(2) RAPTURE	REVELATION 6:12-14	6th SEAL	○
(3) 144,000	REVELATION 7:1-8	SEALED	○
(4) WRATH of GOD 2nd Half of Daniel	REVELATION 8:6-13 REVELATION 9:1-21 REVELATION 11:15,19	7th SEAL	3 ½ Years

The focus of the two witnesses is to preach the gospel of God's love and forgiveness, but also to warn against God's wrath that would come if the world rejected the gospel of truth. For the next three days the people of earth will celebrate, give one another gifts, and worship their false messiah's victory until…

"And after three days and a half the Spirit of life from God entered into them, and they stood upon their feet; and great fear fell upon them which saw them…and the same hour was there a great earthquake, and the tenth part of the city fell, and in the earthquake were slain of men seven thousand: and the remnant were affrighted, and gave glory to the God of heaven." – Revelation 11:11-13

Revelation Chapter Six ends after opening the Sixth Seal. The Sixth Seal is the Rapture.

Revelation Chapter Seven seals the 144,000 and shows us a great multitude in heaven. This great multitude is the raptured and great tribulation saints.

Revelation Chapters Eight and Nine reveal the Seventh Sealed Judgment, containing the first Six Trumpets of God's wrath.

When we get to **Revelation Chapter Ten**, there is a break in the continuity of the story. Chapter 10 gives us a narrative of an angel giving John a little book to eat.

Revelation 11:1-13, comes into play as parenthetical verses which occur during the **Fifth Seal** (The two witnesses during the Abomination of Desolation).

An example of parenthetical would be like watching a movie where it starts off by showing you the ending first, then proceeds to show you the rest of the movie leading up to the ending. You can also think of parenthetical as prequel or a before-thought that is inserted as an afterthought. It does seem as if Revelation Chapter 11:1-13 is occurring during God's wrath, but it is not. We know this because Revelation 16:18 & 21, and Revelation 11:19 tells us God's wrath ends with a global earthquake and hailstorm. When the two witnesses are murdered on the 1,260th day, there is no global earthquake or hailstorm. On the contrary, when the two witnesses are killed, the world will celebrate for three and one-half days.

"And they that dwell upon the earth shall rejoice over them, and make merry, and shall send gifts one to another; because these <u>two prophets</u> tormented them that dwelt on the earth." – Revelation 11:10

Another fact the two witnesses' ministry cannot be occurring during God's wrath is Revelation 9:1-4 introduces the 5th Judgment of super locust. Everyone on earth will be tormented by these super locusts except them that bare the seal of God in their foreheads. Only the 144,000 of all the tribes of Israel will bare this mark. The two witnesses will not have the *Seal of God* in their forehead. Thus, the locust will attack and torment them. That would not make any sense because God's children are not targeted for wrath.

"And he opened the bottomless pit; and there arose a smoke out of the pit, as the smoke of a great furnace; and the sun and the air were darkened by reason of the smoke of the pit. And there came out of the smoke locusts upon the earth: and unto them was given power, as the scorpions of the earth have power. And it was commanded them that they should not hurt the grass of the earth, neither any green thing, neither any tree; but only those men which have not the seal of God in their foreheads." – Revelation 9:1-4

"For God hath not appointed us to wrath, but to obtain salvation by our Lord Jesus Christ." – I Thessalonians 5:9.

Revelation Chapter 11:14-19, jumps forward, which culminates in the finality of God's wrath with the Seventh Trumpet.

I do not know why the Bible was written in this manner. If you are not careful this writing style may confuse you. As I stated before the King James 1611 was not a smooth translation. Even words in italics are not from original Hebrew and Greek, but were added for your reading pleasure.

When Jesus comes to rapture his sheep, it will be a rapture of the righteous. The only two groups left behind will be the 144,000 and reprobate unbelievers. The only exception will be unsaved people that reject the Mark of Beast but, came to repentance after they missed the Rapture. These will still be eligible for salvation. These will be few, far and in between though. After the Rapture and sealing the 144,000, God's wrath will fall.

God will create hellish conditions on earth to punish the wicked. I have heard some say the Seven Trumpet Judgments of God's wrath is to get people of earth to repent. His wrath is not intended to bring sinners to repentance, but to show the unrepentant sinner he is God. God will do to that last future generation what he did to Pharaoh; harden their hearts. God will unleash seven plagues of wrath on mankind, and mankind still will not repent. On the contrary, they will curse and blaspheme God. As a matter of fact, mankind will be so twisted the armies of the earth will assemble at the Battle of Armageddon to fight God!

"And men were scorched with great heat, and blasphemed the name of God, which hath power over these plagues: and they repented not to give him glory." – Revelation 16:9

In Genesis 6:5-13, God's wrath fell in Noah's day because the world waxed thoroughly corrupt. Corruption is to be continually evil, and is associated with a reprobate state of mind. Jesus explained when God's wrath would fall in the last days people would be just as wicked as the people in Noah's day; corrupt and reprobate. In these 'Last Days' every imagination and heart of mankind will be evil continually. Today –

- People Are Deceived - 2 Timothy 3:13
- People Are Boastful and Proud, etc. - 2 Timothy 3:1-5
- People Live Their Lives Apart from God - Saint Matthew 24:37-38

The Christians are gone, the two witnesses are gone, and the Jews were scattered several years earlier.

169

The 144,000 are hidden away under the protection of Michael the Arch Angel and his angels. I have heard some theologians preach the 144,000 will evangelize the world after the Christians are raptured. This means the 144,000 will be preaching the gospel during the Wrath of God. These theologians say the 144,000 are the only believers left, so they must preach the gospel. It sounds good on paper, but it is not biblical. It was God who sent unbelievers the spirit of strong delusion so they should believe Antichrist and the False Prophet to accept the Mark, so they might all be damned.

"And for this cause God shall send them strong delusion, that they should believe a lie: That they all might be damned who believe not the truth, but had pleasure in unrighteousness." – 2 Thessalonians 2:11-12

Why would God turn right back around and send anybody to preach the gospel to a world full of reprobates that cannot repent nor receive the gospel even if they wanted to. The people of Antichrist's kingdom are indwelled with the spirit of Delusion. They are perdition. After seven horrible plagues the people in Antichrist's kingdom do not repent. So, the question is, *"Preach the gospel to whom?"*

"...Nevertheless when the Son of man cometh, shall he find faith on the earth?" – Saint Luke 18:8

During God's wrath there will be no more preaching, no more teaching, no more reasoning with the world. The opportunity for grace is over. God is not going to keep talking. Everyone has their limit, even God. There will be only wrath after the two witnesses are gone.

"And I will dash them one against another, even the fathers and the sons together, saith the Lord: I will not pity, nor spare, nor have mercy, but destroy them." – Jeremiah 13:14

Did preaching continue when God closed the door on Noah's Ark? Did preaching continue after the angels dragged Lot out of Sodom? Did preaching continue when the angel of death visited the first born of Egypt? Did preaching continue when Korah and those that rebelled with him were swallowed up by the Earth? Did Peter preach to Ananias and Sapphira after their greed was uncovered? If that is the case God should let everyone out of Hell right now. The time to repent is now, not after! This is your window of opportunity. Once your window of opportunity closes, that is it!

The second half of Daniel's Seventieth Week will initiate with God's wrath. When the Antichrist kills the two witnesses, he will proclaim peace and safety for millennia.

As the world celebrates in jubilation, suddenly destruction will come on them. God is not one to be trifled with. Love God with all your heart, mind, soul, and strength. Kiss the Son lest he be angry and serve only him. The world's inhabitants will not sorely be afraid of the two witnesses coming back to life, nor the earthquake, but rather the wrath to come. Cabinet members, presidents, joint chiefs, dictators, soldiers, famous people, the incarcerated, and such will retreat to their places of refuge and say to themselves, *"The words of the two witnesses have come true. Hide us from the face of the Lord, for the apocalypse of God's wrath will soon be upon us."*

"And the kings of the earth, and the great men, and the rich men, and the chief captains, and the mighty men, and every bondman, and every free man, hid themselves in the dens and in the rocks of the mountains; and said to the mountains and rocks, Fall on us, and hide us from the face of him that sitteth on the throne, and from the wrath of the Lamb: For the great day of his wrath is come; and who shall be able to stand." – Revelation 6:15-17

Links in the Prophetic Chain

RAPTURE OF THE CHURCH

THE TWO WITNESSES ARE MURDERED

THE TWO WITNESSES ARE RESURRECTED

SEALING OF THE 144,000

THE WRATH OF GOD BEGINS

- EPISUNAGOGE (RAPTURE) = 6TH SEAL

- THE 2 WITNESSES ARE KILLED

- THE 2 WITNESSES ARE RESURRECTED

- 144,000 SEALED = BETWEEN 6TH AND 7TH SEAL

- SEVEN ANGELS BEGIN TO SOUND = 7TH SEAL

171

Chapter Eight
The Rapture Equation

$$R = \frac{r\,\text{Sun}\ \text{-}r\,\text{Earth}}{d\,\text{Sun}\ \text{-}d\,\text{Earth}\ \text{-}d\,\text{Moon, when FOTL} = P} \quad \text{Simplified}$$

Personally, I feel that we only have about sixty years left. Looking at society today, how much time would you say we have left before the world comes to an end? I asked several of my friends and family members, giving them multiple-choice of 20, 40, or 60 years when they think Jesus may return for his Church. Like a broken record, I get the same verse pushed in my ear time and again. *"But of that day and hour knoweth no man, no, not the angels which are in heaven, neither the Son, but the Father only." - Saint Mark 13:32.* No one knows that day or hour is preached from the pulpit as though it is set in stone. But believe me, it is not.

Harold Camping was an American Christian radio broadcaster and evangelist that prophesied Jesus would come to rapture the Church and that God's wrath would fall on humanity on May 21, 2011, at 6 pm. When nothing happened Harold Camping explained Jesus did come and the Rapture did occur, but it was a spiritual coming not a physical coming. One of Harold Camping's followers did not understand why he was not raptured. After all, Harold Camping speaks for God. Harold Camping then went back to revise his prophecy to October 2011, which also came and went.

"When a prophet speaketh in the name of the Lord, if the thing follow not, nor come to pass, that is the thing which the Lord hath not spoken, but the prophet hath spoken it presumptuously..." – Deuteronomy 18:22

There are many YouTube videos expressing the Rapture view. These teachers spend about an hour trying to explain when the Rapture will occur. It should not be what I, you, or they believe; it is what the Bible teaches. Most teachings in the churches today are very emotional and based in personal bias. You hear things like:

- "I believe what this is saying is…"

- "This is the only reasonable explanation because…"

- "Many teachers believe as I do."

- "It must happen this way because…"

- "That's just symbolic!"

- "So, because it's this, then it must be that."

172

I have heard it said the Rapture can happen at any time; it can happen tomorrow or next week or next year. In an earlier chapter I explained how teachers try to make the Bible fit their theology, and they themselves are not even sure of what they are saying themselves (I Timothy 1:7). When people do predict when Jesus is coming in the Rapture these predictions fall flat. These predictions fall flat for three reasons.

#1– The wrong variables are being used. These teachers misinterpret scriptures by parroting, on purpose, or simply by ignorance. They do this to make their teaching on the Rapture fit their theology.

#2–Teachers will often quote First Corinthians 15:51-52 or First Thessalonians 4:15-17. These scriptures tell us what is happening at the time of the Rapture, but do not give us the when. Teachers will throw **their 'when'** theology in there for a sweet convenient sermon to tickle the ears of their congregation, but ignore other scriptures that give us the 'when' of the Rapture. First Thessalonians 4:15-17 and First Corinthians 15:51-52, tell us what happens at the Rapture. Second Thessalonians Chapter 2 verses 1-4 give us the timing of the Rapture.

*"Let no man deceive you by any means: For **that day** (Rapture) shall not come, except there come a falling away first, and that man of sin be revealed, the son of perdition; who opposeth and exalteth himself above all that is called God, or that is worshiped; so that he as God sitteth in the temple of God, showing himself that he is God." – 2 Thessalonians 2:3-4*

Paul makes it clear, **that day** (Rapture), will not happen until the falling away happens first and Antichrist (Beast) of the New World Order comes into power over the entire world. Paul clearly stated the rapture of the Church will occur after Antichrist rises to power, not before. Up to this point, before Antichrist comes into power the Rapture **CANNOT HAPPEN AT ANY TIME!** Added to the fact, in order for Antichrist to sit in the Jewish temple and proclaim himself as God, there must be a Jewish temple. As of the year 2021, to my knowledge, the third temple in Jerusalem has not been built yet. There has to be a Jewish temple for Antichrist to sit in. So I reiterate, "How is the Rapture imminent?" "How can the Rapture happen at any time?" "How can the Rapture happen tomorrow?" #It Can't! Read the Bible and stop believing every wind of doctrine.

Even before the saints are raptured, the New World Order and Antichrist will be here. In the New World Order Antichrist will already have a position in politics, but will eventually rise into a position of supreme political power. Antichrist will come second with his deceptive global peace armistice. By this point in time the Elect of God will know who he is. Eventually Antichrist will usher in the Abomination of Desolation (or the great tribulation period). When the Beast is revealed in Second 2 Thessalonians 2:3-4, the Great Tribulation will begin.

This is when the Beast will make war with the Jews and Christians. Up to this point in time the Rapture has not occurred. Jesus tells us the Rapture will occur after the great tribulation period.

*"**Immediately after the tribulation of those days** shall the sun be darkened, and the moon shall not give her light, and the stars shall fall from heaven, and the powers of the heavens shall be shaken... And he shall send his angels with a great sound of a trumpet, and they shall gather together his elect from the four winds, from one end of heaven to the other." – Saint Matthew 24:29-31*

Yes, brothers and sisters, we will go through the great tribulation period of 1,260 days. Please, do not kill the messenger. For some I know it is a hard pill to swallow after everything you have been taught, but it is what it is.

#3–*"No man knows that day or hour."* is cryptic. For many years, *"No man knows that day or hour."* has mistakenly been taught wrong. *"No man knows that day or hour."* is a Hebrew idiom. *"No man knows that day or hour."* is a riddle.

When I first read the phrase, *"No man knows that day or hour, but the Father only."* there was always a little splinter in my mind. I have heard it said only God the Father knows when Jesus is coming back to rapture the Church. That did not make much sense to me, because Jesus knows everything. Jesus is the Word of God born into humanity. Think about what I just said and throw your common sense into it. 95% percent of the time Jesus always taught in parables, idioms, and cryptic language.

"In the beginning was the Word, and the Word was with God, and the Word was God." – Saint John 1:1

*"But God hath revealed them unto us by his Spirit: for the Spirit searcheth all things, yea, the **deep things of God**. For what man knoweth the things of a man, save the spirit of man which is in him? Even so the things of God knoweth no man, but the Spirit of God." – I Corinthians 2:10-11*

God knows everything. As God, Jesus does not know the day of the Rapture? The Holy Ghost is the Spirit of God. As God, the Holy Ghost does not know the day of the Rapture? Hmm? To imply Jesus does not know all things strips him of his Deity. To imply the Holy Ghost does not know all things strips him of his Omniscience. Scripture must support other scriptures or balance other scriptures. How can Jesus know all things, but not know the day of the Rapture? Obviously, this phrase meant something else. Listen to what the disciples told Jesus.

174

*"His disciples said unto him, lo, now speakest thou plainly, and speakest no proverb. Now are we sure that thou **knowest all things**, and needest not that any man should ask thee: by this we believe that thou camest forth from God." – Saint John 16:29-30*

'Camest forth from God' or Emmanuel means God with us or God in human form. Notice Jesus did not say, *"You are right with one exception. I don't know when I'm coming back to rapture the Church."* Jesus never disputed that statement in verses 29 and 30. On the contrary, Jesus is telling us when he is coming back by his response in Saint Mark 13:32 and Saint Matthew 24:36. Through the years the phrase *'**No man knows that day or hour**'* has been misinterpreted from a Gentile perspective.

Rosh Hashanah starts the Jewish month known as Tishrei, which is the Jewish New Year. Our New Year starts on the first of January every year, but Tishrei begins sometime around the fall season. Unlike our Gregorian calendar which is based on solar years the Jewish calendar is based on lunar years. Rosh Hashanah is also known as the Festival of Trumpets which is the sounding of the shofar (blowing of the rams' horn), and is also known as Yom Teruah, or the day of the blast. In Jewish tradition the shofar is a call to battle, to crown a king, to alert the people of danger, or to gather in a special place. One Christian Jew referred to the shofar as a wake up from sleep and slumber. The blowing of the shofar has three main types of blasts: Tekiah, Shevarim, and Teruah.

"For the Lord himself shall descend from heaven with a shout, with the voice of the archangel, and with the trump of God…" – I Thessalonians 4:16

"Behold, I show you a mystery; we shall not all sleep, but we shall all be changed, in a moment, in the twinkling of an eye, at the last trump: for the trumpet shall sound, and the dead shall be raised incorruptible, and we shall be changed." – I Corinthians 15:51-52

This trumpet blast is not the trumpet blast spoken of in Revelation, but rather the blast of the shofar. The last trumpet is not referring to the last trumpet in Revelation 11:15, but is the last Tekiah-Gedolah blast of the ram's horn which is the longest blast. The trump or shofar always occurs on the Jewish New Year, but we never know what day the Jewish New Year will fall on based on our Gregorian calendar. If we do not know the **day,** then we will not know the **hour.** Today's preaching is predicated on this misassumption. Based on our Gregorian calendar, Independence Day, Veterans Day, Christmas, and New Year's Day all fall on the same calendar date each year.

175

We celebrate George Washington's birthday on the third Monday in February; Memorial Day on the last Monday in May; Labor Day on the first Monday in September; and Columbus Day on the second Monday in October. We always know what days our holidays will fall on, but Jewish holidays are not on the same dates as our Gregorian calendar. On our Gregorian calendar Rosh Hashanah will always fall on different dates every year. On September 29, 2019, Rosh Hashanah was on Sunday.

- (Rosh Hashanah) Saturday - September 19, 2020
- (Rosh Hashanah) Tuesday - September 07, 2021
- (Rosh Hashanah) Monday - September 26, 2022
- (Rosh Hashanah) Saturday - September 16, 2023
- (Rosh Hashanah) Thursday - October 03, 2024
- (Rosh Hashanah) Tuesday - September 23, 2025

"...If therefore thou shalt not watch, I will come on thee as a thief, and thou shalt not know what hour I will come upon thee." – Revelation 3:3

Revelation means to reveal. Why Jesus would give us the book of revealing, but not reveal the date of the Rapture or his second coming? That is not logical to me. Just because everyone is teaching and believes no one knows the date of the Rapture, it does not make it true. Jesus gives us a warning in Revelation 3:3. If you are not watching for the Rapture, you will not know when Jesus is coming back. Inference implies that if you are watching for the Rapture, you will know when Jesus is coming back. In order for us to watch, we must know what date to watch for.

As children my brothers, sisters and I knew what time my parents would come home from work. Just before my parents would arrive home, we would make sure we did every last chore. The home would become spotless and undisturbed just before they walked in the door. We knew when they would arrive because we were watching. In my studies I found there were only three things Jesus did not reveal. If you find more, please let me know.

- Date of the 2nd Great Depression
- Identity of the 24 Elders
- What the 7 Thunders uttered in Revelation 10:4

*"But of the **times and the seasons**, brethren, ye have no need that I write unto you. For yourselves know perfectly that the day of the Lord so cometh as a thief in the night." – I Thessalonians 5:1-2*

"A thief in the night." is also taken out of context. Many think it to mean Jesus will come back at a time we do not know when. *"A thief in the night."* is a metaphor. Paul is telling us the Rapture will occur at night-time. The thief comes in the wee hours of the morning before daylight. Paul also alludes and confirms Jesus' idiom by telling us not to be ignorant of the timing of the Rapture; which will occur during the times and seasons. The question is, *"What are the times and the seasons?"* – The times and seasons are referring to the Feasts Days of the Lord. Let me put this Hebrew idiom into the proper context for you.

- **The Disciples:** Jesus, when will the Rapture occur?

- **Jesus:** No angel in heaven or man on earth knows. I know, the Holy Ghost knows, and the Father knows. Here is a riddle. If you can figure it out, then you will know too. I will come back to rapture my sheep on the day of one of our festival traditions that we celebrate every year known as *"No Man Knows That Day or Hour."*

"No man knows that day or hour." is a Hebrew idiom for seven sacred Jewish Holy Days called Divine Appointments. There are three in the **fall season** and four in the **spring season**. Jews celebrate Shavuot fifteen days from Passover. Christians celebrate Pentecost seven weeks after Easter. Jesus will rapture the Church on one of these Holy Days. This is the first part of the Rapture Equation.

Fall Festivals

- Rosh Hashanah – Feast of Trumpets

- Yom Kippur – Day of Atonement

- Sukkoth – Feast of Tabernacles

Spring Festivals

- Passover – Day of Unleavened Bread

- Chag Hamatzot – Feast of Unleavened Bread

- Chag Shavuot – Feast of Weeks

- Pentecost – First-Fruits

Many last day prophecies are being linked or combined together when they should be separated. Jesus said end-time events would occur in stages. For example, people confuse the second coming of Jesus with the Rapture. The Rapture is not Christ's second coming. The Rapture is the Rapture, and the second coming is the second coming. People also confuse the 'sign of thy coming' with the end of the age. The three phrases below are synonymous. They all mean the same thing, but have nothing to do with Christ's Second Coming.

177

- Sign of thy coming is the Rapture

- The Day of the Lord is the Rapture

- Sign of the Son of Man is the Rapture

The end of the age is the end of our era. The end of our era ends with the beginning the 7th Trumpet Blast in Revelation 11:15, when the kingdoms of this world become the kingdoms of our Lord. The second coming of Jesus Christ is the precursor to the Millennial. Presently there are end time signs to let us know Jesus is coming back soon, but the major **sign** of Jesus' Second Coming is the Rapture. Jesus' Second Coming is when he comes back to earth <u>on a white horse</u> with all his saints to set up his millennial kingdom.

"Jesus, when he had cried again with a loud voice, yielded up the ghost. And, behold, the veil of the temple was rent in twain from the top to the bottom; and the earth did quake, and the rocks rent; and the graves were opened; and many bodies of the saints which slept arose, and came out of the graves after his resurrection, and went into the holy city, and appeared unto many." – Saint Matthew 27:50-53

I have heard it said these are the Old Testament Saints coming back with Jesus at the Rapture. This is not the case. God allowed this miracle to show the unbelieving Jews and the Romans that Jesus was who he said he was; the Son of God. For now, the Old and New Testament Saints do not have glorified bodies yet. When Jesus rewards us with new bodies it will be at the Rapture. First Thessalonians 4:16-17 tell us there will be a resurrection immediately before the Rapture. Together with the past saints and those raptured, it will be billions, not just **Many Bodies.**

The Rapture will occur first when all past saints are resurrected and the Elect of God which are still alive will be caught up into the **clouds** to meet up with Jesus, and taken into heaven. Jesus does not come back to earth to punish or to rule at that time, only to retrieve his faithful followers. From that point on we will be with Jesus forever. Wherever Jesus is, that is where we will be. We will be with Jesus after we are raptured, and we will be with Jesus when he returns at his second coming.

So, there is a difference between the Rapture, Second Coming, and the end of our era. In Saint Matthew 24:3, Jesus' disciples specifically asked him what **the sign of his second coming** would be, **not his second coming**. The events of the Rapture, Second Coming, and the end of our era were the three questions Jesus clarified for his disciples. If you are confused, do not be. I will break everything down in my sequel book titled, *"Revelation – God's Wrath Cometh"*.

There are some teachers that combine the Rapture in Saint Matthew 24:29-31 and the Second Coming in Revelation 19:11-14 together. I have heard others teachers say those coming back with Jesus are angelic armies dressed in fine linen, white and clean? These are not angels; these are the saints of God.

*"And the armies which were in heaven followed him upon white horses, **clothed in fine linen, white and clean**." – Revelation 19:14*

*"Let us be glad and rejoice, and give honor to him: for the marriage of the Lamb is come, and his wife hath made herself ready. And to her was granted that she should be **arrayed in fine linen, clean and white**: for **the fine linen is the righteousness of saints**." – Revelation 19:7-8*

For us to come back with Jesus, we have to be with Jesus, which means he has to rapture us first. We cannot be waiting on earth for the Rapture and be coming back with Jesus at the same time. Inference implies the second coming of Jesus Christ and the Rapture are different events.

*"To the end he may establish your hearts unblameable, in holiness before God, even our Father, **at the coming of our Lord Jesus Christ** <u>with all his saints</u>." – I Thessalonians 3:13*

<u>Rapture vs Second Coming</u>

*"But I would not have you to be ignorant, brethren, concerning them which are asleep, that ye sorrow not, even as others which have no hope. For if we believe that Jesus died and rose again, even so them also which sleeps in Jesus will God bring with him. For this we say unto you by the word of the Lord, that we which are alive and remain **unto the coming of the Lord** shall not prevent them which are asleep...*

For the Lord himself shall descend from heaven with a shout, with the voice of the archangel, and with the trump of God: and the dead in Christ shall rise first: Then we which are alive and remain shall be caught up to-gether with them in the clouds to meet the Lord in the air: and so shall we ever be with the Lord. Wherefore comfort one another with these words." – I Thessalonians 4:13-18

In this particular portion of scripture teachers are lumping 1st Thessalonians 4:15 **(Unto the coming of the Lord)** with 1st Thessalonians 3:13 **(At the com-ing of our Lord)** as the same event. Because the 'Coming of the Lord' is am-biguous in this particular portion of scripture we must understand the mood in which it is being relayed. 'At' means the action is happening at that moment. 'Unto' means the action has not occurred yet, but will occur in the future. This means **'at'** and **'unto'** are two different events. The Greek uses three forms for the 'Coming of the Lord' in verse 15.

The first is the Aorist Subjunctive Active, which is an undefined action. In other words it can refer to the Rapture or the Second Coming of Jesus Christ. The second form is the Subjunctive Mood, which adds uncertainty to the 'Coming of the Lord', because the action has not occurred yet. The third form is the Active Voice, which distinguishes the subject matter.

The aorist subjunctive active is undefined and the subjective mood is uncertain. To determine what Paul is conveying we must move to the 'Active Voice' that distinguishes the subject matter. How do we distinguish the subject matter? We read the scripture to determine the subject matter. In 1st Thessalonians 4:13-18 the subject matter is Christ returning for all his believers; which is the Rapture. The 'Coming of the Lord' in this particular passage is referring to the Rapture, but the 'Coming of the Lord' in 1st Thessalonians 3:13 refer to his Second Coming with all his Saints. It is just a simple matter of reading the text.

*"Now we beseech you, brethren, by the **coming of our Lord Jesus Christ**, and by **our gathering** together unto him." – II Thessalonians 2:1*

*"That ye be not soon shaken in mind, or be troubled, neither by spirit, nor by word, nor by letter as from us, as that <u>the **day of Christ**</u> is at hand." – II Thessalonians 2:2*

*"Let no man deceive you by any means: For **that day** shall not come, except there come a falling away first, and that man of sin be revealed, the son of perdition." – II Thessalonians 2:3*

*Verse 1 – "Now we beseech you, brethren, by the **coming of our Lord Jesus Christ**, and by **our gathering together unto him**."*

The first thing Paul differentiates is: 'Coming of our Lord Jesus Christ' – The Greek interprets this phrase as Parousia or Jesus Christ's Second Coming.

*** From ***

'Our gathering together unto him' – The Greek interprets this phrase as The Gathering or Episunagoge (Rapture).

*Verse 2 – "That ye be not soon shaken in mind, or be troubled, neither by spirit, nor by word, nor by letter as from us, as that the **day of Christ** is at hand."*

In verse two, Paul refers to the Rapture as the **'Day of Christ'**, or **'That Day'** in verse three. Parousia in Greek is connected to Christ's second coming, and unveils his glorious power to the entire world. Apokalupsis in Greek is connected to Christ's second coming, but pertains to his judgment.

Paul said, *"Coming of our Lord Jesus Christ, **and** our gathering together unto him"* If you have an apple **and** a banana you are speaking of two different things.

Paul clearly makes the distinction between **'Parousia – Second Coming' and 'Episunagoge – Rapture'.** The coming of our Lord Jesus Christ and our gathering together unto him are two different events, but as I just mentioned, these two events are being confused and lumped together by many teachers.

The Day of the Lord

As I stated earlier, the Day of the Lord is the Rapture. However, the Day of the Lord has a dual component. The first component is the Rapture. The second component is the Wrath of God. The Day of the Lord is when God judges the wicked, but preserves the righteous. When you go back into biblical history with Noah, Lot, and the firstborn of Egypt, you will see and understand that immediately before judgment fell there was a type of (rapture) or saving of those that believed; but also a day of punishment for those that did not believe. This day will preserve the righteous from wrath while judging the wicked. Christians will experience tribulation, but not God's wrath.

"The Lord knoweth how to deliver the godly out of temptations, and to preserve the unjust unto the Day of Judgment to be punished." –
2 Peter 2:9

Component #1 – God saved Noah +7 (Genesis Chapters 7 and 8)
Component #2 – God destroyed every living creature on dry land (wrath)
Component #1 – God saved Lot +2 (Genesis Chapter 19)
Component #2 – God destroyed Sodom and Gomorrah (wrath)
Component #1 – God spared the first-born of Israel (Exodus Chapter 12)
Component #2 – God killed the first-born of Egypt (wrath)
Component #1 – Rapture – I Thessalonians 5:2
Component #2 – Wrath of God – Isaiah 13:6-9

The sign of the Son of Man is the first component of the Day of the Lord. The Wrath of God is the second component of the Day of the Lord. The Bible teaches the Rapture will come like a thief in the night, but also teaches the Day of the Lord will also come with wrath. The Day of the Lord is twofold.

(Rapture) = *For yourselves know perfectly that <u>the day of the Lord</u> so cometh as a thief in the night. – I Thessalonians 5:2*

(Wrath) = *"Howl, ye; for <u>the day of the Lord</u> is at hand; it shall come as a destruction from the Almighty... Behold, the day of the Lord cometh, cruel both with wrath and fierce anger, to lay the land desolate: and he shall destroy the sinners thereof out of it." – Isaiah 13:6-9*

Rapture Date Revealed?

"And I beheld when he had opened the sixth seal, and lo, there was a great earthquake; and the sun became black as sackcloth of hair, and the moon became as blood; and the stars of heaven fell unto the earth, even as a fig tree casteth her untimely figs, when she is shaken of a mighty wind." – Revelation 6:12-13

COMPARE SAINT MATTHEW 24:29 WITH REVELATION 6:12-13

"Immediately after the tribulation of those days, shall the sun be darkened, and the moon shall not give her light, and the stars shall fall from heaven, and the powers of the heavens shall be shaken." – Saint Matthew 24:29.

In Revelation 6:12-13, we see something happen to the sun, moon and stars. In Saint Matthew 24:29, we see something happen to the sun, moon and stars. These two scriptures are describing the same astronomical event. This event is the Rapture. We know it is the Rapture because Saint Matthew elaborates with verses 30 and 31 as our gathering together unto him.

*"...And then shall appear the sign of the Son of man in heaven...and they shall see the Son of Man coming in the clouds of heaven with power and great glory. And he shall send his angels with a great sound of a trumpet, and they shall **gather together his elect** from the four winds, from one end of heaven to the other." – Saint Matthew 24:30-31*

I did not have to play a guessing game with date setting or predictions for the Rapture. I did not get the Rapture Equation by going into a deep trance or meet Jesus on a mountain. The angel Gabriel did not come to my house to tell me. And I did not receive the Rapture Equation in a dream. In Revelation 6:12, Jesus told us the exact year, month, day, hour, and minute of the Rapture. Many people read right over verse 12 without giving it a second thought because it is cryptic. Revelation 6:12 is the second part of the Rapture Equation. I will explain what it means.

The black sun is a total solar eclipse, and the blood moon is a total lunar eclipse. A total solar eclipse occurs when the moon is aligned with the sun casting its' shadow on earth (when the moon is between the sun and earth). A total lunar eclipse occurs when earth is aligned with the sun casting its' shadow on the moon (when the earth is between the sun and moon). You cannot have a total solar eclipse and a total lunar eclipse at the same time. Inference implies these are different events. The Blood Moon initiates the Rapture and the Black Sun initiates God's wrath. All the scriptures below are the second component of the Day of the Lord, and are associated with God's wrath. Down through history and even today total solar eclipses have been viewed as omens.

Amos 5:18 (Choshekh)	Dark obscurity, dusk, or darkness
Joel 3:15 (Qadar)	Dark colored, made black, to darken sun or stars
Isaiah 13:10 (Chashakh)	To grow dark, be obscured, made dark or darken
Zephaniah 1:15 (Choshekn)	A day of darkness. It's figurative meaning is Judgment

"The sun shall be turned into darkness **(Wrath of God)***, and the moon into blood* **(Rapture)***, before that great and notable day of the Lord come." – Acts 2:20*

Because of these scriptures we now know the total solar eclipse (component #2) represents the wrath of God. Inference applies the total lunar eclipse (component #1) represents the Rapture. The total lunar eclipse will occur at the opening of the **6th Seal (Blood Moon)**. – *"And the moon became as blood."*

Just to reiterate, two events are happening on the Day of the Lord: The Rapture and the Wrath of God. The Wrath of God occurs immediately after the total solar eclipse (black sun) and the Rapture will occur at the total lunar eclipse (blood moon). As you can see the day of the Lord is an event that will occur about two weeks apart, spanning fifteen days. **That day** (Rapture) will commence with a great earthquake, shooting stars, and a total lunar eclipse. The stars falling to earth are shooting stars. The Day of the Lord is an idiom; it is not just one day.

Syzygy, in Greek means yoked together. Eclipses occur in a pair. Eclipses generally occur four times a year, but can occur up to seven times a year. There are seven types of eclipses: Annular, Lunar, Partial, Penumbral, Solar, Total, and Transits. A Syzygy eclipse is a full total solar and full total lunar eclipse pair. This means syzygy eclipses are very rare.

183

What calculates days, nights, years, celestial signs, and seasons? Answer: Math. The Earth's 24 hour 365.25-day revolution around the sun is math. The moon's 27-day synchronous rotation around planet earth is math. Solar and lunar eclipses are math. What measures days, nights, signs, and seasons? Answer: Math. The rotation of satellites, stars, constellations, galaxies, and planets is known as the astronomical star chart. The star chart is God's universal time clock. Like everything else, biblical prophecy works on God's universal time clock. The universe is one perfect mathematical equation. Biblical prophecy and math are related. The two are mutually inclusive. I hope you are excited because I intend to show you what I discovered. But before I go on, I need you to do one thing for me: **ABANDON ALL YOUR PRECEIVED NOTIONS!!!**

"Thus saith the Lord, which giveth the sun for a light by day, and the ordinances of the moon and of the stars for a light by night..." – Jeremiah 31:35

*"And God said, let there be lights in the firmament of the heaven to divide the day from the night; and let them be for **signs**, and for **seasons**, and for **days**, and **years**." – Genesis 1:14*

*"Now when Jesus was born in Bethlehem of Judea in the days of Herod the king, behold, there came wise men from the east to Jerusalem, saying, where is he that is born King of the Jews? For we have seen his **star** in the east, and are come to worship him." – Saint Matthew 2:1-2*

In Saint Matthew 2:1-2, how did the Magi know the exact year, month and day Jesus would be born? They knew because they understood biblical prophecy and mathematics are related. They calculated where and when the star would appear, and journeyed from the East. Jesus told us the Rapture will occur at a syzygy eclipse. To calculate the date of the Rapture, all we need to do is check the eclipse data. Timeanddate.com created an algorithm calculating eclipses up to the year 2199. We are only concerned with the dates that reflect a full total solar and a full total lunar eclipse pair. From Y2K up to the year 2199, there will be 954 eclipses. Out of these 954 eclipses, there will be 250 total/partial solar and total/partial lunar eclipses. Out of 250 total/partial solar and total/partial lunar eclipses, only 12 will be a Syzygy. The years are: 2033, 2043, 2044, 2050, 2061, 2072, 2073, 2090, 2091, 2167, 2167, 2185, and 2195.

Believers will not experience God's wrath (black sun). This means the total lunar eclipse must occur first. When I first studied the eclipse chart, I believed that a solar eclipse always occurs first, and then a lunar eclipse always follows. On further study I learned that lunar eclipses can and do occur first followed by a solar eclipse. The dates below are when the Blood Moon occurs first.

BLOOD MOON - RAPTURE	BLACK SUN - WRATH
March 25th, 2043	April 9th, 2043
May 6th, 2050	May 20th, 2050
April 5th, 2061	April 20th, 2061
August 29th, 2072	September 12th, 2072
September 8th, 2090	September 23rd, 2090
July 22nd, 2195	August 5th, 2195

Between you and me, I do not think the world is going to make it into the 22nd century. If the rapture of the Church occurs in the year 2090, at most we only have about seventy years left. To find out the year, month, day, hour, and minute of the Rapture, all we need to do is use the process of elimination. Out of these six occurrences only three will appear directly over the Middle East.

(Rapture of the Church)   (Wrath of God)

BLOOD MOON - RAPTURE	BLACK SUN - WRATH
o	o
May 6th, 2050	May 20th, 2050
o	o
April 5th, 2061	April 20th, 2061
o	o
September 8th, 2090	September 23rd, 2090

The total solar eclipse (black sun) will follow fifteen days later on May 20, 2050, April 20, 2061, and September 23, 2090. During this fifteen-day grace period God will stop the prophetic time clock to seal the 144,000 and to welcome all the Saints into heaven.

"...And lo a great multitude, which no man could number, of all nations, and kindreds, and people, and tongues, stood before the throne, and before the Lamb, clothed with white robes, and palms in their hands...And he said unto me, these are they which came out of great tribulation..." – *Revelation 7:9,13-14*

"And after these things I saw four angels standing on the four corners of the earth, holding the four winds of the earth, that the wind should not blow on the earth, nor on the sea, nor on any tree.

185

*And I saw another angel ascending from the east, having the seal of the living God: and he cried with a loud voice to the four angels, to whom it was given **to hurt the earth and the sea**, Saying, **hurt not the earth, neither the sea, nor the trees,** till we have sealed the servants of our God in their foreheads." – Revelation 7:1-3*

"And I heard the number of them which were sealed: and there were sealed a hundred and forty and four thousand of all the tribes of the children of Israel." – Revelation 7:4

The Day of the Lord will come like a thief in the night, literally. On this particular night, the earth will shake. Jesus will come in the sky; break through the atmosphere bringing down hundreds of our man-made satellites along with several thousand particles of space debris culminating in the greatest fireworks show ever experienced by man. Billions of Saints in their new glorified body will turn night into daylight. And every eye will see Jesus in the clouds. Hopefully, you are not seeing the fireworks show from the ground. If you are, then you have already missed being raptured, because the Rapture will occur in a millisecond.

Seven years prior to the Rapture Antichrist will ratify a global peace armistice on behalf of the nation of Israel. Three and one-half years later Jerusalem will be besieged, and its temple desecrated by the Antichrist. During these three and one-half years of great tribulation the goal of Antichrist will be to wipe out the Jews along with anyone professing to know Jesus Christ.

*"When ye therefore shall see the abomination of desolation, spoken of by Daniel the prophet, stand in the holy place, **(whoso readeth, let him understand)**...For then shall be great tribulation, such as was not since the beginning of the world to this time, no, nor ever shall be." – Saint Matthew 24:15 & 21*

"And he shall confirm the <u>covenant</u> with many for <u>one week</u>: and <u>in the midst</u> of the week he shall cause the <u>sacrifice and the oblation to cease,</u> and for the over spreading of abominations..." – Daniel 9:27

- Covenant = Antichrist will ratify a global peace Armistice
- One Prophetic Week = 84 months or 7 years
- In the midst of the week = 42 months later or 3½ years later
- Sacrifice and the oblation to cease = Desecration of the Jewish Temple

The countdown to the Rapture will be seven years from the time the global peace armistice is ratified. If the peace armistice is ratified in the year:

186

- 2043, we know the Rapture will occur on May 6, 2050
- 2054, we know the Rapture will occur on April 5, 2061
- 2083, we know the Rapture will occur on September 8, 2090

The Bible gives us four clues for the timing and the day of the Rapture:

- After Antichrist sits in the Jewish Temple
- Immediately after the great tribulation period
- On one of the Seven Annual Sacred Feasts
- On the day of a total lunar eclipse

The Bible states everything must be done in decency and in order. Jesus also knows the day of the Rapture, but the Father will give him the go-ahead. Jesus told us the Rapture will occur on the day of a total lunar eclipse. Paul told us the Rapture will occur on one of the sacred Holy Days of the Lord. This is how we determine the day of the Rapture. In other words the Rapture (Blood Moon) and a Holy sacred day will share the same year, month, and day. In the next 180 years only three dates are available.

May 6, 2050 and September 8, 2090 do not fall on any Divine Appointment. April 5, 2061 is the only date that remains. In the year 2061 on a Tuesday April 5th, the Holy Jewish Holiday will be **Passover**. Jesus died on Passover, and he will rapture his true believers on Passover. The date on the Jewish calendar will be Nisan 15, 5821. Some believe no man knows that day or hour is the Feast Day Rosh Hashanah because it is the next Feast Day to be fulfilled on the prophetic calendar. This makes sense, but Paul said **times** and **seasons** (plural); referring to all seven sacred Holy Days. As you can see in the year 2090, Rosh Hashanah and the Syzygy eclipse do not fall on the same date or day.

May 06, 2050 – Friday	Lag Baomer, May 9th, 2050
April 05, 2061 – Tuesday	**Passover, April 5th, 2061 - Tuesday**
September 08, 2090 – Friday	Rosh Hashanah, September 25th, 2090

On the East Coast it will be April 4, 2061, 5:56 p.m. On April 5, 2061, @12:56 a.m., it will be Israeli Daylight Time. This is when the Rapture will take place. Israeli Daylight Time is seven hours ahead of Eastern Time. The total solar eclipse will follow fifteen days later on Wednesday April 20, 2061, @5:55 am, Israeli Daylight Time.

187

The Rapture will come like a <u>thief in the night</u>, but we also know the Day of the Lord will also come like a <u>thief in the night</u>. It is ironic Jesus would choose the Blood Moon as a reminder to Earth's inhabitants of his shed blood for their sins.

Unlike other predictions, April 5, 2061, **is not prediction** or date setting. These calculations are based on the biblical text of Saint Matthew 24:36, the cryptic idiom given by Jesus in Revelation 6:12, the times and seasons of the Divine Appointments given by Paul in 1st Thessalonians 5:1-2, and the eclipse data. Now you know when the Rapture will occur. Now you know when the resurrection of those who sleep in Christ will take place: If you are watching.

I was skeptical about telling anyone about April 5, 2061, until I came across a documentary titled *"The Coming Convergence"*, by Ingenuity Films. One of the producers by the name of Brent Miller Sr. has a YouTube channel titled, *"Brent Miller Sr.: The Coming Convergence, Part 2"*. In this eschatological documentary several top theologians discussed end-time events. This documentary is the **best** I have ever come across, and the glue I needed to piece together the chronology of end-time events. *"The Coming Convergence"* helped me exegesis the Book of Revelation and fill in missing clues I needed to solve the Rapture Equation.

In this documentary several theologians quoted, *"No man knows that day or hour."* They went on to explain this Jewish saying is a Hebrew idiom that has been grossly taken out of context, and is being taught by many end-time teachers as literal. They further stated *"No man knows that day or hour."* is referring to the Feasts of the Lord found in Leviticus Chapter 23.

I began studying the Feasts of the Lord. I crossed referenced April 5, 2061, with all the feast dates in 2061. I discovered on April 5th, 2061, the Passover Feast is the exact same day as the total lunar eclipse described by Jesus in Revelation 6:12 and Saint Matthew 24:29. At this juncture I still felt apprehensive about revealing April 5, 2061, as the day of the Rapture. Trust and believe I do not want God to brand me as a false prophet. However, confirmations from the theologians are there, the Passover 2061 Divine Appointment is there, the eclipse data is there, and the math is there. Even still, I was not quite convinced.

As I was about 85% percent convinced of all the information, I decided to do one more thing. I asked Google – *"Is no man knows that day or hour a Hebrew idiom?"* This is the response I received – *"No man knows that day or hour is a Hebrew idiom."* WOW! That is when I knew my Rapture Equation was correct! 'R' represents Rapture. The top half of my equation is the Blood Moon. The bottom half of my equation is the Feast Day (Passover). As you can see for yourself the Rapture Equation has absolutely nothing to do with predictions or date setting, and everything to do with mathematics.

It took me about six months of studying the eclipse data and cross referencing other information to figure out the Rapture Equation. Like so many others that came before me, I do not want you to think I pulled this date out of thin air. This is why I showed you the math. Believe me, I thought long and hard about this matter. To confirm what I am saying, just check it out for yourself. Ask Google these four questions:

- "Eclipse 2061?"
- "Passover 2061?"
- "Feasts of the Lord 2061?" – Sanctus.org
- "Is no man knows that day or hour a Hebrew idiom?"

Better yet, go to www.timeanddate.com and check for a syzygy eclipse to appear directly over Jerusalem. You will discover there will be only three within the next 180 years. One syzygy eclipse is 14½ days. One syzygy eclipse is 15½ days. The syzygy eclipse on April 5, 2061, has exactly fifteen days and it will be on the sacred Jewish holiday of Passover.

When I revealed the date of the Rapture to my Aunt, she thought I was non compos mentis. I am sure back in the first Era of humanity they thought Noah was looney tunes for building an ark when it never rained before. I am sure they thought Isaiah was crazy when he stripped and walked around naked for three years (Isaiah 20:2-3). I am sure they thought John the Baptist was eccentric for living in the wilderness feasting on wild honey and locust. I am not sure why God gave me the ability and understanding to figure out the date of the Rapture, but I am glad he did. When I gave a few of my Christian friends the date of the Rapture they looked at me like I was crazy. But when I explained to them how I arrived at this date the wheels in their head start turning. They never looked at the Rapture from a different perspective.

The Mathematics of Revelation

There is another way to understand biblical prophecy. I see the Bible, life, and situations through logic, common sense, and reasoning. Everything I say in this book is backed by scripture and confirmed by mathematical deduction. Remember that math problem in junior high school; when Billy had to travel by train 300 miles from Texas to California? If the train is traveling 100 miles per hour, how long would it take Billy to get to California? We can apply this same rule to the Book of Revelation.

The Book of Revelation is mathematical, and the variables are embedded within its' text. If you can locate the correct variables (scriptures) and understand how to do the math, you will be able to understand the Book of Revelation. I had to unlearn what had been taught about Revelation, and start from scratch.

I had to forget what I thought I knew and learn all over again. I learned that understanding the math of the Book of Revelation is the key. When I understood this simple basic rule and did the math, all other prophetic dates and numbers fell in line. For example, if I have one cupcake and I eat half the cupcake, how much cupcake do I have left? The answer is one-half of a cupcake. If I have seven years, and three and one-half years are peaceful, how many years are not peaceful? The answer is three and one-half years of unrest. If I have a 7 year covenant and the first 3½ years are peaceful, how many years left is great tribulation? Answer: 3½ years. Do not just buy what they are selling; apply your common sense and study. For example; 3+3=6. The solution will always be 6. Do not believe everything you hear. Do the math.

The pre-tribulation seven year lie is telling people if they ate half of one cupcake, they would still have one whole cupcake left. What they are saying is one-half of seven years is literally seven years. #Huh? It is not rocket science. It is basic math. Do you see my point? Get off the theological bandwagon, do the math and think for yourself. It is a serious matter when Christians are so easily fooled by false doctrine. If the theology does not fit, you must omit. Understand that I did not apply hermeneutics to the seven year tribulation theology. I applied basic math. Not only does basic math totally dismantle the false teaching of a seven year tribulation, but it also dismantles the Pre, Mid, and Post tribulation theory as well. Because this seven year lie is confusing so many Christians we must oust the Pre, Mid, and Post tribulation theory altogether.

I break down scripture for what it is. I do not run with the crowd. I think for myself. I just do not believe because it is a fad, accepted view, or because it makes me feel good. If the majority believes in something that is unknown, does it means it cannot be known? Study to show yourself approved means to analyze, not believe what you hear, what everyone thinks, and run with it. I jumped off the theological anecdotal bandwagon a long time ago. When you study the Bible from a logical, common sense, and mathematical perspective it will allow you to think outside the box. When studying God's word always ask yourself these seven questions: Who? What? Why? Where? When? Which? How?

Paul referred to the Feast Days. Logic dictated I should study the Feasts Days of the Lord. Jesus spoke of the total lunar/total solar eclipse pair in Revelation 6:12. Joel spoke of the total lunar/total solar eclipse pair in the Book of Joel Chapter 2:31. Peter spoke of the total lunar/total solar eclipse pair in Acts 2:20. Logic dictated I check the eclipse chart. Father God, Jesus, and the Holy Spirit know all things. Logic dictated *"No man knows that day or hour, but my Father only."* is not a colloquial phrase. When I realized the Book of Revelation is mathematical, solving the Rapture Equation became fairly easy.

190

In my future sequel book titled, *"Revelation: God's Wrath Cometh"*, I solve for the Mark of the Beast (666) in Revelation 13:18, and the City of Mystery Babylon in Revelation 17:18. As I solve for the seven mountains on which the woman sits in Revelation 17:9, you will realize the seven mountains have absolutely nothing to do with the Seven Hills of Rome. Not only do I reveal just how gigantic the new earth will be, but I also reveal the year, month, and day of Jesus Christ's Second Coming. When I counted all the days leading up to Christ's Second Coming, I have to tell you Jesus has a sense of humor. You will be surprised what day it is.

All these answers are embedded as mathematical equations in scripture. The Book of Revelation is not as complicated as you think. It is filled with so many embedded equations; Jesus is practically giving us all the answers. It is like an open-book test. You just need to look in the right place, find the right variables, and do the math. It is not a hard puzzle to solve. Daniel 9:27 is just one example.

"And he shall confirm the <u>covenant</u> with many for <u>one week</u>: and <u>in the midst</u> of the week he shall cause the <u>sacrifice and the oblation to cease,</u> and for the over spreading of abominations..." – Daniel 9:27

Variable #1	∘	PEACE ARMISTICE	*equals*	7 YEARS
Variable #2	2ND HALF	ABOMINATION	*equals*	3½ YEARS
Remainder	SOLVE FOR	X, OR REMAINING	?	3½ YEARS

The first variable is 7 years. The second variable is the great tribulation period which is 3½ years and it occurs in the middle. Therefore, we do not include the first 3½ year period of peace as part of Daniel's last pr ophetic week. 'X' means there is an additional 3½ year period unaccounted for that completes the Seventieth Week of Daniel. 'X' = God's Wrath. Here is another misinterpreted scripture.

"Then shall two be in the field; the one shall be taken, and the other left. Two women shall be grinding at the mill; the one shall be taken, and the other left." – Saint Matthew 24:40-41

The first variable is *"2"* or 100% percent. The second variable is *"1"* or 50% percent. 100% percent minus – 50% percent = 50%. 50% is ½ of something. If you apply the 'Matthew 2441 Equation' to the Rapture, it means half of the people on earth will go up in the Rapture. That is about four billion people. We know that will not be the case. This theological reasoning may stem from the ten virgins in Saint Matthew 25:1-13. Half were wise and half were foolish. About two billion people claim Christianity in some form or fashion.

191

Even then we know a greater percentage of that two billion will not make it into heaven based on what Jesus said in Saint Matthew 7:21-23.

Variable #1	2	100%	8 BILLION _ PEOPLE	
Variable #2	1	50%	4 BILLION _ RAPTURED	ONE TAKEN
Remainder	1	50%	4 BILLION _ NOT RAPTURED	THE OTHER LEFT

Saint Matthew 24:1-44 is in chronological order. The Rapture occurred in verses 29-31, and referenced in verse 36. In verse 37 Jesus said, "But as the days of Noah were, so shall also the **coming of the Son of man** be." The Greek for Coming (Parousia) speaks of his second coming to set up his millennial reign. Verses 40 and 41 occur around the time of Jesus' Second Coming, which is nearly four years (1,335 days) after the Rapture. Verses 29-31 and verses 40-41 are often combined, just as the coming of our Lord and are gathering together unto him are often combined. All four of these events are separate. Verses 40 and 41 are **not referring the Rapture.** It is referring to something else. I did solve this equation, but I reveal it in my next book which will be released at a future date.

The Rapture Equation is a bit more complex, but it works on the same principle. If you look at the 'what' only or the 'how' only, you will never be able to solve for the 'when'. Including both 'what' and 'how' will lead you to solve for the 'when'. Because some are not following this formula, they create their own variables. All the variables in the Bible are set in stone and they cannot be substituted to fit one's own personal theology. The Bible gives us 'X' or 'When' of the Rapture by the scriptures below. The When:

- Acts 2:20 – Dark sun; Blood moon

- Joel 3:15 – Sun and moon darkened

- II Thessalonians 2:3 – After Antichrist comes to power

- Revelation 6:12 – Sun black as sackcloth; Moon as blood

- Saint Mark 13:24 – Sun darkened; Moon will not give her light

- I Thessalonians 5:1-2 – Times and Seasons (Divine Appointments)

- Saint Matthew 24:29 - Sun darkened; Moon will not give her light

192

X	(+)	7	(=)	12
WHEN		WHAT		HOW
Solve for X		Variable #1	(=)	Variable #2
(When) The Rapture	(+)	(What) The Rapture	(=)	(How) The Rapture
Acts 2:20		I Corinthians 15:51-53		I Thessalonians 4:13-18
Joel 3:15				
Revelation 6:12				
Saint Mark 13:24				
I Thessalonians 5:1-2				
II Thessalonians 2:3				
Saint Matthew 24:29-31				
X = 5	(+)	7	(=)	12

There are many types of equations in the Book of Revelation. Some equations are addition and subtraction, and some division and multiplication. There are algebraic equations, worded equations, cryptic equations, common sense equations, deduction equations, fragmented equations, fragmented parenthetical equations, and antecedent equations. An antecedent equation gives you the 'what', 'when', and 'how', but not the 'whom'. Here is an example of an antecedent equation.

"And now ye know what with-holdeth that he might be revealed in his time." – 2 Thessalonians 2:6

"For the mystery of iniquity doth already work: only **he** *who now letteth will let, until he be taken out of the way." - 2 Thessalonians 2:7*

I am not going to call any names, but I have heard it said 'he' is the Holy Ghost. The problem I have with some theology is only part of the scripture is being read. You must read all of the scripture which pertains to the subject matter.

"And then shall that Wicked be revealed, whom the Lord shall consume with the spirit of his mouth, and shall destroy with the brightness of his coming:" – 2 Thessalonians 2:8

"Even him, whose coming is after the working of Satan with all power and signs and lying wonders..." – 2 Thessalonians 2:9

"And with all deceivableness of unrighteousness in them that perish; because they received not the love of the truth, that they might be saved." – 2 Thessalonians 2:10

Most people study the Bible from the front end. I study scripture from the back-end first. The front-end may only contain one layer. Reading this portion of scripture from the back-end will give us a clearer understanding of this entire text and who 'he' is.

2nd Thessalonians 2:10 – With all deceivableness of unrighteousness... - "If it were possible, they shall deceive the very elect." – Saint Matthew 24:24
Who shall try to deceive the very elect? – Many antichrists.

2nd Thessalonians 2:10 – In them that perish, because they rejected the truth. – "For the wrath of God is revealed from heaven against all ungodliness of men, who hold the truth in unrighteousness." – Romans 1:18
Who will reject truth to accept the Mark of the Beast? – The ungodly.

2nd Thessalonians 2:9 – Even him whose coming is after the working of Satan... - "And the dragon gave him his power..." – Revelation 13:2
To whom did Satan give power? – Antichrist (Beast).

2nd Thessalonians 2:8 – Whom the Lord shall consume with the spirit of his mouth, and shall destroy with the brightness of his coming. - "And the beast was taken, and with him the false prophet...These both were cast alive into a lake of fire burning with brimstone." – Revelation 19:20
Who is going to be cast into the Lake of Fire? – Antichrist & False Prophet.

2nd Thessalonians 2:8 – Then shall that wicked be revealed. – "Let no man deceive you by any means: for that day shall not come, except there come a falling away first, and that man of sin be revealed, the son of perdition." – 2 Thessalonians 2:3
Who is the Man of Sin? Who is the Son of Perdition? – Antichrist.

2nd Thessalonians 2:7 – Until he be taken out of the way. – "And causeth the earth and them which dwell therein to worship the first beast, whose deadly wound was healed." – Revelation 13:12 - What is a deadly wound? – Assassination. The Beast cannot come forth until Antichrist is murdered (taken out of the way). The Antichrist will confirm the covenant. The Beast will break the covenant.

2nd Thessalonians 2:7-10 gives us many antichrists; Mark of the Beast, Antichrist, Antichrist, Antichrist (Beast), and Antichrist. In these four verses **'he'** or the antecedent is Antichrist (Beast).

Now let us continue to solve the antecedent in verses six and seven.
2nd Thessalonians 2:6 & 7 – Only he who now letteth will let. And now ye know what with-holdeth that he might be revealed in his time.

Now letteth or with-holdeth means to restrain. We know no one on earth is powerful enough to restrain Antichrist from moving into a position of power, because Antichrist is given power over all kindreds, nations, and tongues. Therefore we must conclude the one restraining the Beast of Revelation 13:1-2 is not of this world. In verses six and seven **'he'** or the antecedent is Jesus.

"And Jesus came and spake unto them saying, all power is given unto me in heaven and earth." – Saint Matthew 28:18

I call this technique re-engineering scripture. The formula I use is algebraic. Because the back-end may contain other layers, you cannot study the Bible from one dimension. You must study the Bible from all sides and angles. As you study the Book of Revelation you will begin to realize there are layers within layers. In some cases the Book of Revelation is straight forward, but in most cases it is not. The hardest equations I solved were Revelation 13:18 and Revelation 17:11. The easiest was how long the Great Tribulation would last. And of course the most involved and thought provoking was the Rapture Equation. The math is basic until you get into the meat and potatoes from Revelation Chapters 8-22. Far too many assumptions have been made over the years concerning the Book of Revelation. If the Bible does not specify you must not prophesy. The best thing about math is:

- It is not bias.
- Math does not speculate
- It is not prideful or arrogant
- Math never lies and cannot be deceived.
- Math is precise and always tells the truth.
- It does not choose sides or have preconceived notions.

Most of the YouTube comments I receive are full of accusation, confrontational, and rude. I expect this kind of behavior from the world, not Christians. Where is the love? It seems like I am reading these comments from a parrot. All these comments are exactly alike: seven years of tribulation and even Jesus does not know the day when he will Rapture the Church. It sounds like a broken record. Jesus said he has all power in heaven and earth:

Omniscience = All Knowing; Omni*Present = All Aware; Omnipotent = All Powerful.

Some Christians get a little scripture in them and they begin to boast. People that understand biblical theology know when they are right, but do not understand enough about biblical theology to know when they are wrong. We have all been there.

You read that scripture ninety-nine times, but the one hundredth time you see something you never saw previously. I thought I knew the ends and out breaking down the Word of God, but I really did not. When I realized this I realized I was an imbecile, because I was duped by parrot theology.

As I said before, I believe the best Bible you can ever have in your studies is the Hebrew-Greek Key Study Bible by AMG Publishers. Without it, this book would have never been written. You must let go of preconceived notions, because it will limit your ability to see what God needs you to see. As long as a person holds on to their deeply engrained preconceived notions they will never come to a full understanding of the Book of Revelation. Just let go and take a leap of faith. You will be fine.

Everyone told me it would be impossible to figure out the date of the Rapture, because no one knows that day or hour. #No pun intended. One man quoted it best: *"Once you eliminate the impossible, whatever remains, no matter how improbable, must be the truth." – Sir Arthur Conan Doyle*

Time Dilation

"Then I heard one saint speaking, and another saint said unto that certain saint which spake, how long shall be the vision concerning the daily sacrifice, and the transgression of desolation, to give both the sanctuary and the host to be trodden under foot? And he said unto me, unto two thousand and three hundred days; then shall the sanctuary be cleansed." – Daniel 8:13-14

One saint told the other saint that it would be 2,300 days until the sanctuary would be delivered out of the hands of the Antichrist. We already know these are not literal days, but prophetic days. One prophetic week equals seven years, this means that one prophetic day equals one year. The 2,300 days equals 2,300 years. The saint however did not give us a point of reference in time. So the question is, "2,300 years from what point in time?" Unfortunately, I cannot produce an equation because I do not have all the variables. You are on your own on this one. All hope is not lost though. In Daniel 9:25-27, the angel Gabriel explained God would be dealing with his people for 490 years. So, we do have something to go on.

I know 2,300 days being 2,300 years seem contradictory, but it is not. Scoffers and atheists believe the Bible to be full of errors and contradictions, but this is furthest from the truth. God's thoughts are not our thoughts and God's ways are not our ways. The biggest problem with human beings is we are taught at an early age to think one dimensionally. A perfect example is some people think heaven is some place Christians go after they die, and they are floating on a cloud with wings in a fairytale place called La-La land.

196

Jesus told us that in his Father's house there are many mansions, and he was going away to prepare a place for us and would come back for us. We need to stop thinking one-dimensionally and step up our game. The Father's house is the universe and mansions are planets. The spiritual world is not a cloud in La-La land and our loved ones that have passed on are not floating on a cloud. Heaven is the politically correct name for other worlds. Is there other life in the universe? Of course there is other life in the universe! There are more stars (sun) systems in the universe than there are grains of sand on earth.

Out there in the vast universe God created trillions times trillions of worlds suitable for all types of life whether physical or spiritual. Some angels are here on earth as ministering spirits, and other angels are on other worlds in the different sectors of the universe. Heaven is that which is above or beyond us. Heaven is a very big place. There are four tiers of heaven. The first three tiers were created. The fourth tier called Unapproachable Light is beyond space and time.

"The Lord is high above all nations, and his glory above the heavens." – (Psalm 113:4).

When Christians die their physical body remains here and their spiritual body goes to the other world Jesus affectionately called Paradise.

"And one of the malefactors which were hanged railed on him, saying, if thou be Christ, save thyself and us. But the other answering rebuked him, saying, Dost not thou fear God, seeing thou art in the same condemnation?" – Saint Luke 23:39-40

"And we indeed justly; for we receive the due reward of our deeds, but this man hath done nothing amiss. And he said unto Jesus, Lord, remember me when thou comest into thy kingdom. And Jesus said unto him, Verily I say unto thee, today shalt thou be with me in paradise." – Saint Luke 23:41-43

"I knew a man in Christ above fourteen years ago, (whether in the body, I cannot tell; or whether out of the body, I cannot tell: God knoweth; such an one was caught up to the third heaven…he was caught up into paradise and heard unspeakable words, which it is not lawful for a man to utter." – 2 Corinthians 12:2-4

- 1st Tier = Our atmosphere (The Sky)
- 2nd Tier = Our galaxy (Milky Way)
- 3rd Tier = Paradise (Beyond our galaxy)
- 4th Tier = Unapproachable Light (Origin of God)

197

In the year 1905, Albert Einstein introduced his theory of special relativity which included gravitational time dilation. What his theory purposed is that time is relative depending on your universal location. Just as earth has different time zones, the universe also has different time zones. All places in the universe are not running on the same clock and all-time in the universe do not tick at the same rate. Think of time as a river. All rivers do not flow at the same rate. Gravity affects the flow of time just as gravity affects the flow of a river. Think of it as different rivers of time located in different sectors of the universe.

Let us say for instance that angels lived on a planet named Flora. One minute on earth would be equivalent to one second on planet Flora. And one second on planet Flora would be equivalent to one minute on Earth. If I traveled to planet Flora, I would then be subjected to their universal time clock. It is similar to traveling overseas. Once I do I become subject to that time zone. For every hour on earth I would only age one minute on planet Flora. For every 60 hours on earth I would only age one hour on planet Flora. For every 150 days on earth I would only age 2½ days on planet Flora. You get the idea.

Scientists would lead you to believe they know everything about the universe, but they know little. They always use words like, such as, may have been, might be, could be, what if, possibly, etc. Skeptics, atheists, and the unbelieving accuse the Bible of being contradictory, but it is not. In all reality these people neither understand the knowledge, wisdom, or power of Almighty God, nor the nature of the universe.

The problem is not God or the Bible; the problem is us. Even if God explained it to you, you probably would not understand it anyway. God is not trying to confuse us. Einstein got it right. Heaven's time clock is not the same as Earth's. His theory is no longer a theory. Hard data has been collected from our GPS satellites (atomic clocks) rotating in orbit at 8,700 MPH, experience a faster time rate than the clocks on Earth. The further you move away from Earth's gravitational field; time moves at a different rate for you. Time dilation is not a dream of a mad scientist. Both 2,300 days and 2,300 years are correct depending on time dilation. Time dilation is real, and based on the scriptures I am going to prove it to you.

"And when he had opened the seventh seal, there was silence in heaven about the space of half an hour." – Revelation 8:1

When Jesus loosed the 7th Seal there was silence in heaven for about ½ an hour. During this ½ hour in heaven no one spoke a single word, for they all knew what was about to happen on planet earth would be cataclysmic. The ½ an hour of silence is use in the aorist form (past tense), which implies this ½ hour occurs between the 6th and 7th Seal.

198

We know the 6th Seal is the Rapture and the 7th Seal is the Wrath of God. On earth the Blood Moon is the Rapture, and the Black Sun is the Wrath of God. On earth fifteen days pass by between the syzygy total eclipse pair. During this space of time:

- Four angels on earth wait before they hurt the earth – Revelation 7:1-3
- God seals the 144,000 – Revelation 7:4-8
- The saints receive their white robes – Revelation 7:13-15
- The seven angels in heaven are given one trumpet each – Revelation 8:2
- The two witnesses are resurrected – Revelation 11:11

"And I saw another angel ascending from the east, having the seal of the living God: and he cried with a loud voice to the four angels, to whom it was given to hurt the earth and the sea. Saying, hurt not the earth, neither the sea, nor the trees, till we have sealed the servants of our God in their foreheads." – Revelation 7:2-3

By these scriptures we now know time is relative between Heaven and earth, because ½ hour passes by in heaven in relation to fifteen days on earth. The higher the heavenly tier, the more time dilation is skewed. ½ hour in the 3rd Tier of heaven is fifteen days on Earth. One hour in the 3rd Tier of heaven would be thirty days on Earth. I refer to this hour as a prophetic hour. For every day spent in the 3rd heavenly tier (Paradise), two years pass by on earth. Time moves faster on earth than in Heaven.

Third Heavenly Tier	Earth
½ Hour =	15 Days
1 Hour =	30 Days
12 Hours =	One year
24 Hours =	Two Years

My wife, my heart, my love whom God took home five years ago has literally been in heaven for only 2½ days. If God let me live out the rest of my days until I am seventy years old, it would be twenty five years since I last seen my wife. From her time perspective less than two weeks would have passed since she last saw me. In the 4th tier a 24 hour day is 1,000 years on earth (Psalm 90:4). There are even sectors in the universe called outer darkness where time does not exist.

"But, beloved, be not ignorant of this one thing, that one day is with the Lord as a thousand years, and a thousand years as one day." –2 Peter 3:8

Fourth Heavenly Tier	Earth
• ½ Hour =	About 20 Years
• 1 Hour =	About 40 Years
• 12 Hours =	500 Years
• 24 Hours =	1,000 Years

"...And he said unto me, unto two thousand and three hundred days; then shall the sanctuary be cleansed." – Daniel 8:13-14

Second Heavenly Tier	Earth
• ½ Hour =	7.5 Days
• 1 Hour =	15 Days
• 12 Hours =	6 Months
• 1 Day =	1 Year
• 2,300 Days =	2,300 Years

<u>The Great Multitude in Heaven</u>

"After this I beheld, and, lo, a great multitude, which no man could number, of all nations, and kindreds, and people, and tongues, stood before the throne, and before the Lamb, clothed with whites robes, and palms in their hands..."

"And cried with a loud voice, saying, Salvation to our God which sitteth upon the throne, and unto the Lamb. And all the angels stood round about the throne, and about the elders and the four beasts, and fell before the throne on their faces, and worshiped God, saying amen:"

"Blessing, and glory, and wisdom, and thanksgiving, and honor, and power, and might, be unto our God forever and ever. Amen" – Revelation 7:9-12

They wore white robes and had palms in their hands. They all cried aloud giving honor to Jesus and God for saving them. This great multitude stood before the throne of God. All around God's throne stood the angels, and upon His throne the Twenty-Four Elders and the Four Beasts. Every being around God's throne fell on their faces in worship.

After the Rapture, Revelation 7:9-17 shows a great multitude no man could tell just how many there are in one glance. This multitude of people is from all nations, languages, and cultures.

All believers will be raptured. Those individuals blessed enough to escape the clutches of the Antichrist are also included in this great multitude.

"There is neither Jew nor Greek, there is neither bond nor free, there is neither male nor female: for ye are all one in Christ Jesus." – Galatians 3:28

"And other sheep I have, which are not of this fold: them also I must bring, and they shall hear my voice; and there shall be one fold, and one shepherd." – Saint John 10:16

"Therefore are they before the throne of God, and serve him day and night in his temple: and he that sitteth on the throne shall dwell among them. They shall hunger no more, neither thirst anymore; neither shall the sun light on them, nor any heat. For the Lamb which is in the midst of the throne shall feed them, and shall lead them unto living fountains of waters: and God shall wipe away all tears from their eyes." – Revelation 7:15-17

These loved Jesus more than they loved themselves even to death. God has given them the right to become his sons and daughters and to serve in his temple always. Jesus will feed them, shine on them, and give them living water.

Unfortunately, not all Christians that say they are Christians will make it to heaven. Jesus said there are three different types of Christians (Saint Matthew 13:18-30). There are Christians with stony hearts. These get offended easily and when tribulation or persecution comes, they fold like a piece of paper. There are Christians with thorny hearts. These get caught up with the pleasures of this world and go after other gods thinking they can have their cake and eat it too. Then you have the true believers that receive the good and bad things, knowing God is fully in control. All three of these types of Christians are in the Church today. God will purge the Church by the fire (Great Tribulation) to see who belongs to him. Judgment will start at the house of God (I Peter 4:17). One-third of Christians will endure, and two-thirds will not.

"And it shall come to pass, that in all the land, saith the Lord, two parts therein shall be cut off and die; but the third shall be left therein. And I will bring the third part through the fire, and will refine them as silver is refined, and will try them as gold is tried: they shall call on my name, and I will hear them: I will say, it is my people: and they shall say, The Lord is my God." – Zechariah 13:8-9

Statistical data from the Pew Research Center shows Christianity at about 2.2 billion worldwide. The Roman Catholic Church retains about 1.3 billion, giving a total of 1.9 billion Christians.

If we base John's account of the multitude that came out of the Great Tribulation on this figure, and Zechariah 13:8-9, the multitude John saw was about 635,000,000 million believers that will come out of the Great Tribulation.

Not at any other time in human history have there been so many people going to heaven in a short span of time. In my eyes the Great Tribulation is also the Great Revival. People killed because they reject Antichrist, and his system will be counted among the martyred because they loved not their lives unto death. God will impute this act of martyrdom as righteousness.

If we do a calculation based on the figures above, we will get a rough estimate of how many people are going to heaven and how many people are going to hell. After the Four Horsemen ride he earth there will be about six billion people left. 635 million divide by 6 billion = about 10% percent. Out of every 100 people only about 10 will make it to heaven. Would you say 10 out of 100 is a few? God will wipe away all tears for those we knew and love that did not make it to heaven. God may have to wipe our memories of them as well. Please prepare yourself for the next fifty years. You have an important choice to make.

"Enter ye in at the strait gate: for wide is the gate, and broad is the way that leads to destruction, and many there be which go in there at: because strait is the gate, and narrow is the way, which leads unto life, and few there be that find it." – Saint Matthew 7:13-14

Reconciliation of Days – Jacob's Trouble (The Great Tribulation)

To calculate the date of the great tribulation period, all we need to do is count backwards 1,260 days. Let us do the math.

Ends * April 5th, 2061		Tuesday 15th of Nissan	
Jewish Month	**Year**	**Gregorian Month**	**Days**
Iyar – Nissan	2061	May – April	4
Nissan – Adar	2061	April – March	31
Adar I – Adar II	X	Jewish Leap Year	X
Adar – Shevat	2061	March – February	28
Shevat – Tevet	2061	February – January	31
Totals			**94 Days**

Jewish Month	Year	Gregorian Month	Days
Tevet – Kislev	2060	January – December	31
Kislev – Cheshvan	2060	December – November	30
Cheshvan – Tishrei	2060	November – October	31
Tishrei – Elul	2060	October – September	30
Elul – Av	2060	September – August	31
Av – Tammuz	2060	August – July	31
Tammuz – Sivan	2060	July – June	30
Sivan – Iyar	2060	June – May	31
Nissan	2060	April	30
Adar I – Adar II	2060	Jewish Leap Year	31
Adar – Shevat	2060	March – February	29
Shevat – Tevet	2060	February – January	31
Totals			366

Jewish Month	Year	Gregorian Month	Days
○	○	○	○
Tevet – Kislev	2059	January – December	31
Kislev – Cheshvan	2059	December – November	30
Cheshvan – Tishrei	2059	November – October	31
Tishrei – Elul	2059	October – September	30
Elul – Av	2059	September – August	31
Av – Tammuz	2059	August – July	31
Tammuz – Sivan	2059	July – June	30
Sivan – Iyar	2059	June – May	31
Iyar – Nissan	2059	May – April	30
Nissan – Adar	2059	April – March	31
Adar I – Adar II	2059	Jewish Leap Year	X
Adar – Shevat	2059	March – February	28
Shevat – Tevet	2059	February – January	31
○		○	○
Totals			365

Jewish Month	Year	Gregorian Month	Days
○	○	○	○
Tevet – Kislev	2058	January – December	31
Kislev – Cheshvan	2058	December – November	30
Cheshvan – Tishrei	2058	November – October	31
Tishrei – Elul	2058	October – September	30
Elul – Av	2058	September – August	31
Av – Tammuz	2058	August – July	31
Tammuz – Sivan	2058	July – June	30
Sivan – Iyar	2058	June – May	31
Iyar – Nissan	2058	May – April	30
Nissan – Adar	2058	April – March	31
Adar I – Adar II	2058	Jewish Leap Year	X
Adar – Shevat	2058	March – February	28
Shevat – Tevet	2058	February – January	31
○		○	○
Totals			365

Jewish Month	Year	Gregorian Month	Days	Sub Totals
○	○	○	○	○
Tevet – Kislev	2057	January – December	31	
Kislev – Cheshvan	2057	December – November	30	61 Days
Cheshvan – Tishrei	2057	November – October	9	(+9 Days)
		12/31/2057 - 10/23/2057	Total	70 Days
○		○	○	○
Year	2058	12/31/58 - 1/1/2058		365 Days
Year	2059	12/31/59 - 1/1/2059		365 Days
Year	2060	12/31/60 - 1/1/2060		366 Days
Year	2061	4/5/2061 - 1/1/2061		94 Days
○		○	○	○
			Totals	1,260 Days
The Great Tribulation Period		Abomination of Desolation		Ministry of the two Witnesses
Begins* Tishrei 25, 5818		October 23nd, 2057		Tuesday

Sometime in October 2057, the Time of Jacob's Trouble will be signed into Law.

The Book of Revelation tells us what happens before it happens. Imagine if you had a book from the future with all the winning lottery numbers? You would want that book. Biblical prophecy gives us time to prepare us for what is coming; not to frighten us. Better to be informed than uninformed. I already know that two-thirds of Christians who read this book will not be able to accept what I am saying, but one-third will. Whether the two-thirds want to hear it or not, biblical objective truth is truth. Jesus said it, so you better take heed.

Chapter Nine
Seventy Weeks of Daniel

<u>Time, Times, and Half a Time</u>

King Nebuchadnezzar had a dream that troubled him, so he gathered together all the magicians, astrologers, Chaldean scientists, and soothsayers. None of them knew what he dreamt, nor could explain his dream. King Nebuchadnezzar knew that Daniel was a prophet that received visions and dreams from God, so he summoned Daniel. Daniel knew exactly what the dream was and what it meant.

"...behold a tree in the midst of the earth, and the height thereof was great. The tree grew, and was strong, and the height thereof reached unto heaven, and the sight thereof to the end of all the earth. The leaves thereof were fair and the fruit thereof much, and in it was meat for all: the beasts of the field had shadow under it, and the fowls of the heaven dwelt in the boughs thereof, and all flesh was fed of it." – Daniel 4:10-12

"I saw in the visions of my head upon my bed, and behold, a watcher and a holy one came down from heaven; He cried aloud, and said thus, Hew down the tree, and cut off his branches, shake off his leaves, and scatter his fruit: let the beasts get away from under it, and the fowls from his branches:" – Daniel 4:13-14

"Nevertheless leave the stump of his roots in the earth, even with a band of iron and brass, in the tender grass of the field; and let it be wet with the dew of heaven, and let his portion be with the beasts in the grass of the earth: Let his heart be changed from man's, and let a beast's heart be given unto him: and let seven times pass over him." – Daniel 4:15-16

<u>Daniel explains King Nebuchadnezzar's dream</u>

- The Great Tree = King Nebuchadnezzar

- Hewn or cut down = King Nebuchadnezzar would lose his position

- Leave the stump = King Nebuchadnezzar's loss would be temporary

- Let it be wet with the dew of heaven = King Nebuchadnezzar would be driven into the fields like the wild beasts

- Changed from a man's to a beast's heart = King Nebuchadnezzar would lose his sanity

- Seven times = Seven years (One time = One year)

- Time = 1 Year; Times = 2 Years; ½ Time = ½ Year

- Time, Times, ½ Time = 3½ Years

One day King Nebuchadnezzar said within his heart that Babylon the Great was built by his own power and majesty. By thinking he was a god, King Nebuchadnezzar committed the sin of Hubris. We all know there is only one God. Only God establishes and only God destroys. Only God opens that which no man can close, and only God closes that which no man can open. This was the lesson King Nebuchadnezzar needed to learn.

In Daniel Chapter Four verses 29 to 33 Daniel's interpretation came true. For seven years King Nebuchadnezzar lost his sanity and was driven out to live among the beasts of the field. The hair on his body grew like the fur on a bear and his nails grew like claws on an eagle. After the seven years had ended King Nebuchadnezzar's mind returned to him. He fell on his knees and blessed the Most High God. His counselors and lords sought him out and eventually he was restored to his kingdom.

<u>69 Prophetic Weeks</u>

Daniel was an Israelite that was taken into captivity by the Babylonian Empire when King Nebuchadnezzar destroyed Jerusalem. Daniel was also a great prophet. Daniel who had spent most of his life in captivity prayed and inquired of God when the nation of Israel would be allowed to return to Jerusalem to rebuild its' city, streets, and walls. In Daniel 9:20-27, God sent the angel Gabriel to reveal when this would occur. Gabriel gave Daniel much more than he requested, also revealing end time events concerning the House of Jacob.

"Seventy weeks are determined upon thy people and upon thy holy city, to finish the transgression, and to make an end of sins, and to make reconciliation for iniquity, and to bring in everlasting righteousness, and to seal up the vision and prophecy, and to anoint the most Holy." – Daniel 9:24

- Determined = God will be dealing with Israel for a period of 490 years

- Finish the transgression = Make atonement for all sin

- Seal up the vision = This will not happen for many years

- Anoint = Consecrate or ordain Jesus as Messiah

"Know therefore and understand, that from the going forth of the commandment to restore and to build Jerusalem unto the Messiah the Prince shall be seven weeks, and threescore and two weeks; the street shall be built again, and the wall, even in troublous times." – Daniel 9:25

Gabriel was telling Daniel from the time the decree is made granting the Israelis freedom to return and rebuild Jerusalem all the way to the death of Jesus' crucifixion would be 483 years or 69 prophetic weeks. In total there are 70 prophetic weeks. One prophetic week (seven years) remains.

- 1 Prophetic Hour = One Month
- 1 Prophetic Day = One Year
- 7 Prophetic Weeks or 7×7 = 49 years
- Threescore (score = 20×3 = 60) * (60×7) = 420 years
- 2 Weeks (2 Prophetic Weeks or 2×7) = 14 years
- 49 + 420 + 14 = 483 Years or 69 Prophetic Weeks

Eventually the Babylonian Empire fell to the Persian Empire. Around 537 B.C. under King Cyrus a decree was ordered allowing the Israelites to return and rebuild Jerusalem. For matters not understood, the city of Jerusalem was not totally rebuilt under this decree, but was still in the restoration process. Around 518 B.C. under King Darius, a follow up decree was issued allowing the Israelites to return and rebuild Jerusalem. For matters not understood, once again the city of Jerusalem was not totally rebuilt under this decree, but was still in the restoration process. Perhaps there was not enough manpower to rebuild, or enough money to buy materials to pay the laborers, or enough military protection. I am not sure why Jerusalem was not totally rebuilt under the two previous decrees.

Around 444 B.C. King Artaxerxes issued a third decree allowing the Israelites to return and rebuild Jerusalem under Nehemiah. Under Nehemiah's leadership the city of Jerusalem, its' streets and walls had finally been rebuilt (**ibid, Britannica.com/biography/Nehemiah**).

"After threescore and two weeks shall Messiah be cut off, but not for himself: and the people of the prince that shall come shall destroy the city and the sanctuary, and the end thereof shall be with a flood, and unto the end of the war desolations are determined." – Daniel 9:26

- And the prince of the people shall come and shall destroy the sanctuary is referring to Vespasian the Emperor who sent his son Titus. In 70 AD Titus led a large-scale campaign that resulted in the destruction of Jerusalem and the Jewish Temple, killing hundreds of thousands, once again scattering the Jewish Nation **(Saint Matthew 24:1-2)**.

- Unto the end of the war desolations are determined = Once again the Jews would be dispersed into different regions of the world having no place to call home for 1,800 years because they did not recognized the visitation of their true Messiah.

- Desolations are the Jewish wars that were fought during the silent years after 70 A.D. On May 14, 1948, the nation of Israel was reborn as a Jewish State by way of the United Nations.

209

After 62 weeks is actually the end of 483 years.

49 + 420 + 14 = 483 Years (69 Prophetic Weeks)

Messiah shall be cut off...but not for himself .

483   – <u>Years later Jesus is crucified</u>

– <u>444 BC</u> – <u>Final decree to rebuild Jerusalem</u>

39   – **Jesus was 39 years old when he was murdered.**

The Bible is not complicate. People make the Bible complicated just. You have scholars on one side saying Jesus died on this date and other scholars saying Jesus died on that date. You have scholars on one side saying Jesus was born in this B.C. and other scholars saying Jesus was born in that B.C. Most scholars date the birth of Jesus around 6 BC, his ministry around 29 AD, lasting three and one-half years. The Bible and secular history gives us the variables we need to calculate the exact date of Jesus' age, birth, and crucifixion.

Jesus died for our sins exactly 483 years later based on Gabriel's information. 6 BC + 29 AD + 3½ year ministry would make Jesus about 39 years old when he was crucified. Let us do the math and put this controversy to rest. First, we will solve for the year Jesus was crucified. It is a historical fact, exactly 39 years after Jesus' crucifixion, Jerusalem was scattered, and its' temple destroyed. If you subtract 39 years from 70 AD, you will get 31 AD. If you subtract 31 AD from 70 AD, you will get Jesus' age when he was crucified.

70 AD – The Jewish Temple is Destroyed

– (39) – <u>Age of Jesus when he was Crucified</u>

31 AD – Year of Jesus when he was Crucified

70 AD – The Jewish Temple is Destroyed

– 31 AD – <u>Year of Jesus when he was Crucified</u>

(39) – Age of Jesus when he was Crucified

Lastly, let us solve for the birth of Jesus. Jesus was born between 8 BC – 7 BC.

- 8 BC = Jesus is born – Saint Matthew 1:18-25
- 6 BC = Herod the Great tries to murder Jesus – Saint Matthew 2:13-20
- 4 AD = Jesus gets separated from his parents – Saint Luke 2:41-52
- 27 AD – 28 AD = Jesus starts his ministry – Saint Luke 4:13-14
- 31 AD = Jesus is crucified – Saint Luke 23:44-46

8 BC – 6 BC =	**2 years,**
6 BC – 4 AD =	**10 years**
4 AD – 28 AD =	**24 years**
27-28 AD – 31 AD =	**3.5 years**
TOTAL	**39 ½ Years**

According to ResearchGate.net, the deduced date of Nisan (Jewish equivalent of March-April) put the Passover on Nisan 14 (Tuesday, March 27th 31 AD). The Jewish day begins at sundown between 6PM–9PM. Jesus did celebrate Passover Tuesday night after 9PM, making it the next Jewish day (Wednesday) March 28, 31 AD. After Jesus' crucifixion Joseph of Arimathea went before Pilate to beg for the body of Jesus that Wednesday. Joseph and Nicodemus wrapped Jesus' body in linen with myrrh and aloe according to Jewish burial custom. There was a garden with a brand new sepulcher. The body of Jesus was placed there and branded with the Roman Seal.

Preparation Day to prepare for Shabbat would begin on Thursday evening and end Friday evening. Shabbat or the Sabbath day would begin on Friday evening and end Saturday evening. Sabbath is the day of rest: which means no work or related activities. During Preparation Day all the cooking, cleaning, organizing, prayer schedules, etc. needed to be done in one day. Thus, the dead needed to be buried that Wednesday.

Jesus' Death and Burial	Preparation Day	Shabbat or Sabbath
WEDNESDAY	**THURSDAY - FRIDAY**	**FRIDAY - SATURDAY**
Sometime between 3PM-9PM	9:01PM - 9:00PM	9:01PM - 9:00PM

Died	–	–	–	Resurrection
Passover °	°	°	°	°
Wednesday	**Thursday**	**Friday**	**Saturday**	**Sunday**
°	°	°	°	°
Btw 3pm - 6pm	6am to	6am to	6am to	6am
Buried Btw 6pm - 9pm	NIGHT ONE	DAY ONE NIGHT TWO	DAY TWO NIGHT THREE	DAY THREE

Wednesday night to Thursday night is night #1. Thursday night to Friday night is night #2. Friday night to Saturday night is night #3. Thursday morning to Friday morning is day #1. Friday morning to Saturday morning is day #2. Saturday morning to Sunday morning is day #3. Jesus rose from the grave early Sunday morning.

"For as Jonah was three days and three nights in the whale's bell; so shall the Son of man be three days and three nights in the heart of the earth." – Saint Matthew 12:40

The Bible confirms Jesus' Sunday morning resurrection.

"The first day of the week cometh Mary Magdalene early, when it was yet dark, unto the sepulcher, and seeth the stone taken away from the sepulcher." – Saint John 20:1

"Now upon the first day of the week, very early in the morning, they came unto the sepulcher, bringing the spices which they had prepared, and certain others with them. And they found the stone rolled away from the sepulcher. And they entered in, and found not the body of the Lord Jesus." – Saint Luke 24:1-3

"Now when Jesus was risen early the first day of the week, he appeared first to Mary Magdalene..." – Saint Mark 16:9

"In the end of the Sabbath, as it began to dawn toward the first day of the week, came Mary Magdalene and the other Mary to see the sepulcher." – Saint Matthew 28:1

Sunday	Monday	Tuesday	Wednesday	Thursday	Friday	Saturday
1ST DAY	2ND DAY	3RD DAY	4TH DAY	5TH DAY	6TH DAY	Sabbath DAY

Died & Buried On Passover	–	–	–	RESURRECTION
		1ST DAY	2ND DAY	3RD DAY
○	○	○	○	○
Wednesday	Thursday	Friday	Saturday	Sunday
○	○	○	○	○
March 28th	March 29th	March 30th	March 31st	April 1st, 31 AD
○	1ST NIGHT	2ND NIGHT	3RD NIGHT	

Antichrist's Seven Year Covenant Calculated

To calculate the date of the peace armistice, all we need to do is count backwards 1,260 days from the great tribulation period (October 23, 2057). Let us do the math.

Tuesday October 23nd, 2057		25th Tishrei	YEAR 5818
○		○	○
Jewish Month	**Year**	**Gregorian Month**	**Days**
Cheshvan – Tishrei	2057	November – October	22
Tishrei – Elul	2057	October – September	30
Elul – Av	2057	September – August	31
Av – Tammuz	2057	August – July	31
Sivan – Iyar	2057	June – May	30
Iyar – Nissan	2057	May – April	31
Nissan – Adar II	2057	April – March	30
Adar I – Adar II	2057	Jewish Leap Year	31
Adar I – Shevat	2057	March – February	28
Shevat – Tevet	2057	February – January	31
○		○	○
Totals			**295**

213

Jewish Month	Year	Gregorian Month	Days
Tevet – Kislev	2057	January – December	31
Kislev – Cheshvan	2056	December – November	30
Cheshvan – Tishrei	2056	November – October	31
Tishrei – Elul	2056	October – September	30
Elul – Av	2056	September – August	31
Av – Tammuz	2056	August – July	31
Tammuz – Sivan	2056	July – June	30
Sivan – Iyar	2056	June – May	31
Iyar – Nissan	2056	May – April	30
Nissan – Adar	2056	April – March	31
Adar I – Adar II	2056	Jewish Leap Year	X
Adar – Shevat	2056	March – February	29
Shevat – Tevet	2056	February – January	31
Totals			366

Jewish Month	Year	Gregorian Month	Days
	○	○	○
Tevet – Kislev	2055	January – December	31
Kislev – Cheshvan	2055	December – November	30
Cheshvan – Tishrei	2055	November – October	31
Tishrei – Elul	2055	October – September	30
Elul – Av	2055	September – August	31
Av – Tammuz	2055	August – July	31
Tammuz – Sivan	2055	July – June	30
Sivan – Iyar	2055	June – May	31
Iyar – Nissan	2055	May – April	30
Nissan – Adar	2055	April – March	31
Adar I – Adar II	2055	Jewish Leap Year	X
Shevat	2055	February	28
Shevat – Tevet	2055	February – January	31
○		○	○
Total			365

Jewish Month	Year	Gregorian Month	Days
	°	°	°
Kislev – Cheshvan	2054	December – November	31
Cheshvan – Tishrei	2054	November – October	30
Tishrei – Elul	2054	October – September	31
Elul – Av	2054	September – August	30
Av – Tammuz	2054	August – July	31
Tammuz – Sivan	2054	July – June	31
Sivan – Iyar	2054	June – May	30
Iyar – Nissan	2054	May – April	20
°	°	°	°
		12/31/2054 - 5/12/2054	234
°	°	°	°
Year	2055	12/31/2055 - 1/1/2055	365
Year	2056	12/31/2056 - 1/1/2056	366
Year	2057	10/22/2057 - 1/1/2057	295
°	°	°	°
Total			1,260 Days
Peace Armistice		Calm Before The Storm	3½ years of Peace
Begins * Iyar 4, 5814		May 12th, 2054	Tuesday

The Peace Armistice will begin sometime in the month of of May 2054.

216

And All These Things Shall Be Finished

"And I heard the man clothed in linen, which was upon the waters of the river, when he held up his right hand and his left hand unto heaven, and swear by him that liveth forever that it shall be for a time, times, and a half; and when he shall have accomplished to scatter the power of the holy people, all these things shall be finished." – Daniel 12:7

"And the angel which I saw stand upon the sea and upon the earth lifted up his hand to heaven, and swear by him that liveth forever and ever, who created heaven, and the things that therein are, and the earth, and the things that therein are, and the sea, and the things which are therein, that there should be time no longer: <u>But in the days of the voice of the seventh angel,</u> when he shall begin to sound, the mystery of God should be finished, as he hath declared to his servants the prophets." – Revelation 10:5-7

Daniel 12:7 is the first 3½ year installment of the last prophetic week. The scattering is the Abomination of Desolation or the Great Tribulation. After the desolation of Jerusalem it will be the beginning of the end of our era. All these things will be finished when God's wrath cometh. The Great Tribulation will last for a time, times, and a half which is 1,260 days, or 42 months, or 3½ years. There is no shortening or lengthening the great tribulation period. One thousand two hundred sixty days is written in stone. If you shorten or lengthen the 1,260 days you are making the Bible fit your theology.

- Daniel 12:7 – Time, times, and a half (3½ years)
- Revelation 11:2 – Forty and two months (3½ years)
- Revelation 13:5 – Forty and two months (3½ years)
- Revelation 12:14 – Time, and times, and half a time (3½ years)
- Daniel 7:25 – Time and times, and the dividing of time (3½ years)
- Revelation 12:6 – A thousand two hundred threescore days (3½ years)
- Revelation 11:3 – A thousand two hundred threescore days (3½ years)
- 30 Days × 42 Months = A thousand two hundred threescore days (3½ years)

*"And from the time that the daily sacrifice shall be taken away, and the abomination that maketh desolate **set up, there** shall be a thousand two hundred and ninety days. Blessed is he that waiteth, and cometh to the thousand three hundred and five and thirty days." – Daniel 12:11-12*

When you read Daniel 12:11-12, it sounds as though the Great Tribulation will last 1,290 days. This is not the case. Daniel 12:7 made it clear Antichrist will scatter the Jewish People for 3½ years (1,260 days). What do 1,290 days represent and why is it 1,290 days instead of 1,260 days?

217

Because of Daniel Chapter 12:7, inference would imply any number more than 1,260 days is not part of the great tribulation period. The Bible is giving us two different set of days because it is two different set of days. Daniel 12:11 is giving us the second (3½ year) installment of the last prophetic week of Daniel. "*...there shall be a thousand two hundred and ninety days.*"

The angel gives us the first half of Daniel's Seventieth Week in Daniel 12:7. Did anyone ever stop and think about the 490 year prophecy and how there is a gap between 483–490 years? Did anyone ever stop to consider that maybe; just maybe, there is a gap in the final prophetic week of Daniel? Daniel and Jesus gave us the gap in scripture: 3½ years or 1,260 days of great tribulation will occur in the midst of the seven-year peace armistice. This gap in the final week of Daniel occurs on the day of the total lunar eclipse or Blood Moon. There will be a fifteen day interval. God will literally stop the prophetic time clock for fifteen days. Fifteen days may not seem significant to you, but it is more significant than you may realize. You will understand when I do the math at the end of this chapter. After the fifteenth day God's wrath will fall on humankind and all hell will break loose.

As I mentioned earlier, we must view the seven year peace armistice as a gauge or reference point for when the Abomination of Desolation would occur, how long it would last, and when the Rapture would take place. The first half of Daniel's last prophetic week is the wrath of the Beast upon the elect of God. The wrath of Antichrist upon the elect of God is the 5th Seal. The second half of Daniel's last prophetic week is God's wrath upon Antichrist's world system. This will occur with the Seven Sealed Judgments (7th Seal).

The one thousand two hundred and ninety days is the second half of Daniel's Seventieth Week plus an additional thirty days. Contrary to what is taught by some, Jesus does not immediately return to earth to establish his millennial reign when God's wrath ends. It will be an additional thirty days before we return with Jesus at his second coming. The angel is telling Daniel that Jesus will return to earth on the 1,290th day, and will establish his millennial reign on the 1,335th day from the total lunar eclipse.

If you look closely in Daniel 12:11-12, there is a comma between (**set up, there**). When you have a sentence with a comma you are introducing a new idea. For example; Billy went to the store to buy milk, bread, cheese, and popcorn. Whenever you have a comma, you are no longer speaking of the previous idea in a sentence, but introducing a new idea. As I explained before, the King James 1611 was not translated into English smoothly. However, they were smart enough to put the comma there so we would be able to distinguish a new idea.

218

To paraphrase, *"And from the time the daily sacrifice shall be taken away and the abomination of desolation is set up, there will be another 1,290 days left, and then it will all be over."*

Did you ever wonder how long the Wrath of God is going to last? If 3½ years is assigned to the Great Tribulation, how much time remaining in Daniel's final week? The answer is 3½ years, or 1,260 days. From the Great Tribulation to the end of God's Wrath will be about seven years. We exclude the first 3½ years of the covenant because it will be peaceful. The second 3½ years of the covenant will start Jacob's Trouble. The remaining 3½ years will be the Wrath of God. The remaining thirty days in heaven is reserved for the Marriage of the Lamb. The Marriage of the Lamb & Supper occurs after the wrath of God. Revelation 11:15, 16:17 and 19:7 show the chronology.

Antichrist's	Covenant		1290	Days
Peace	Great Tribulation		Wrath of God	Marriage of the Lamb
3½ years	3½ years	Rapture	3½ years	
	1,260 DAYS		1,260 DAYS	30 Days
	Daniel's 70th Week (7 YEARS)			

*

DANIEL'S 70TH WEEK	LENGTH
FIRST-HALF *DESOLATION* = 3½ Years (OR 1,260 DAYS)	OR TIME, TIMES, & ½ TIME (OR 42 MONTHS)
○	○
○	○
○	○
SECOND-HALF *GOD'S WRATH* = 3½ Years (OR 1,260 DAYS)	OR 1 YEAR + 2 YEARS + ½ YEAR (OR 42 MONTHS)
○	○
○	○
○	○
THE 70th WEEK (ABOUT 7 YEARS)	OR 2,520 DAYS OR 84 MONTHS
○	○

Convert = 2,520 Days ÷ 365.25 Gregorian Days = 6 Years, 10 Months, 24 Days

219

The Beast will be given power to rule with impunity for 42 months or 1,260 days. The Beast will still be on his throne during the second half of Daniel's Seventieth Week, but he will be powerless just as Pharaoh of Egypt was powerless in Exodus.

D a n i e l 's 70th Week - Supplemental

Global Peace Armistice	**Daniel 9:27**		**N/A**
Great Tribulation	**Daniel 7:25**		**5th SEAL**
Revelation 6:9	**3½ Years**	**OR**	**1,260 Days**
○	○	○	○
The Rapture	**Syzygy Eclipse**		**6th SEAL**
Revelation 6:12			**15 Days**
○	○	○	○
Wrath Of GOD	**Revelation 16:1**		**7th SEAL**
Revelation 8:1	**3½ YEARS**	**OR**	**1,260 Days**
○	○	○	○
TOTAL			**2,535 Days**

These are the seven years Antichrist will reign
2,535 Days ÷ 365.25 (Gregorian Days) = 6 years, 11 Months, and 9 Days.

Just to be clear, the Abomination of Desolation initiates the Seventieth Week of Daniel. The Seventieth Week of Daniel is the last prophetic week of the 490 year prophecy. The last week will be a period of seven years. These seven years will be divided into two-halves.

It will be three and one-half years of **great tribulation** and three and one-half years of **God's wrath**, separated by fifteen days. The final seven years of Daniel's 490 year prophecy is just one of many links in the prophetic chain. The Rapture Equation and the last prophetic week of Daniel is the cornerstone for many of my calculations. Without these I would not have been able to bring this information to you.

The Fig Tree: Saint Matthew 24:32-35

"Now learn the parable of the fig tree; when his branch is yet tender, and putteth forth leaves, ye know that summer is nigh: So likewise ye when ye shall see all these things, know that it is near, even at the doors. Verily I say unto you, this generation shall not pass, till all these things be fulfilled. Heaven and earth shall pass away, but my words shall not pass away." – Saint Matthew 24:32-35

Jesus told us the end of our era would begin with the rebirth of the Israeli Nation, which is symbolic of the fig tree in Saint Matthew Chapter 24. This means all the prophecies leading up to Christ's 'Second Coming' will be fulfilled in our lifetime. The countdown to Christ's 'Second Coming' began in May 1948. We are the last generation.

According to the Bible a generational span is eighty years; great grandfather, grandfather, father, son (*4 generations*). But, for the benefit of the doubt I will include Old Testament length of age which is around one-hundred twenty years. God promised us seventy to eighty years, but there are some that live to be about one-hundred twenty years old. The oldest person on record was Jeanne Calment; born February 21, 1875 and died August 4, 1997. She was 122 years old.

"The days of our years are threescore years and ten; and if by reason of strength they be fourscore years, yet is their strength labor and sorrow; for it is soon cut off, and we fly away." – Psalm 90:10

Variable #1 = May 1948 and Variable #2 = 80 years to 120 years. We cannot add to or take away from these variables. Based on these two variables given by the Bible, the world as we know it must come to an end sometime between the years **2028 to 2068**.

Variable #1	Variable #2
1948 + 80 Years = 2028	1948 + 120 Years = 2068

This also means the Rapture must occur sometime between the years 2028 to 2068.

The end of the world will occur 1,335 days after the Rapture. By 'end of the world' I mean the end of our era beginning with the Millennial Reign of Christ. When we look at the eclipse data between the years 2028 to 2068 there are only 5 syzygy eclipses out of 954 eclipses when the Rapture can occur. These dates are:

BLACK SUN	BLOOD MOON
March 30th, 2033	April 14th, 2033
April 9th, 2043	March 25th, 2043
August 23rd, 2044	September 7th, 2044
May 20th, 2050	May 6th, 2050
April 20th, 2061	April 5th, 2061

April 14, 2033 is an interesting date because it falls on the day of a total lunar eclipse and Passover. If you like you can reserve this date, but remember, before the Rapture can happen the third Jewish Temple must be built. We will see if this comes to fruition in the next 11 years.

March 25, 2043 is the Jewish Holy day Purim, but it is not one of the Divine Appointments. September 7, 2044 and May 6, 2050 do not fall on any Divine Appointment. And we exclude any eclipse date after 2068.

The only two dates left are April 11, 2033 and April 5, 2061 for the end of our era. April 11, 2033 has a little problem though. The problem is the total solar eclipse (Black Sun) is March 30, 2033. The order of the syzygy eclipse is backwards. The total lunar eclipse must occur first. That leaves us with only one date on the eschatological calendar for the Rapture. But do not forget the Millennial Reign of Christ will begin 1,335 days after the Rapture. 1,335 days is almost 4 years later. 2061 plus an additional four years puts us at the year 2065 for the Millennial Reign of Christ.

April 5th, 2061 plus 4 years = 2065

The question many Eschatologists, biblical teachers and people are asking is, *"How long is a generation?"* I am not asking, *"How long is a generation?"* The question I asked myself was, *"Is God going to use the same requisite to end our era as he did with Noah's?"* God told Noah judgment would come based on the age and death of the oldest man (Genesis 6:3). The name of this man was Methuselah. Noah was Methuselah's grandson and the great grandfather of Noah's sons Shem, Ham and Japheth (*4 generations*). Methuselah lived to the age of 969 years old and he died, making Noah and his sons the last generation of that era.

If God uses the same requisite and base the end of our era on the lifespan of the oldest man to die in the 21st Century, our era will come to an end around the year 2065. The oldest person, Chiyo Miyako of Japan, died in 2018 at the age of 117 years old (**ibid, http://wiki/oldestpeople**). Let us do the math.

- Fig Tree = Israeli State established in the year 1948 AD
- Chiyo Miyako = Our modern day Methuselah died at the age of 117
- 1948 + 117 = The year **2065** A.D. = Start of the Millennium

From what you have read so far you might think I have some extraordinary or uncanny insight. I do not. As you can see for yourself all my calculations are based on **scriptural data**. I am taking the variables the Book of Revelation provides and doing the math. As I stated before, *"There is no date setting or pulling numbers out of the air."* The Book of Revelation is mathematical. Remove the emotion, theology and deeply engrained preconceived ideas, and just do the math.

There should be time no longer

"And the seventh angel sounded; and there were great voices in heaven, saying, the kingdoms of this world are become the kingdoms of our Lord...And the nations were angry, and thy wrath is come, and the time of the dead, that they should be judged, and that thou <u>shouldest give reward unto thy servants the prophets, and to the saints, and them that fear thy name, small and great</u>..." – Revelation 11:15-18

Whoever survives the Wrath of God and makes it to the 1,335[th] day will go into the millennial period as Jesus sits on the throne of David in Jerusalem. Nearly four years after the Rapture, the Millennium will come into fruition under the leadership of Jesus Christ. Time no longer means there will be no more time left in our era. The Millennium will start one thousand three hundred thirty-five (1,335) days after the Rapture. Jesus gives us three different set of days to distinguish the Great Tribulation, God's wrath, Marriage Supper of the Lamb, and the end of our era.

1,260 DAYS	1,290 DAYS	1,335th DAY
Great Tribulation	1,260 Days of Wrath	End of our Era
Abomination of Desolation	30 Days - Marriage & Supper of the Lamb	Millennium Begins

223

After the Battle of Armageddon is over and evil vanquished, there will be a thirty day period of celebration and restoration. During this thirty day period survivors will begin to come out of their hiding places, their desert places, the mountains, and out of the wilderness. A worldwide earthquake will have toppled all the magnificent skyscrapers and buildings. The technological earth we knew, gone! Cars, trains, planes, video games, television programs, and suchlike, gone! God is going to dismantle planet earth and throw civilization back to the stone ages. The bodies of the dead must be buried. The waters, streams, oceans, and seas are polluted with blood, feces, and radiation. There is no green grass and little tree life. The ozone layer is fractured. The earth is off its' axis. Planet earth is in urgent need of repairs.

Jesus will walk onto the shore of an ocean and kneel down to touch the ocean water with his index finger. At that moment, the bloody ocean waters will begin to cascade into pure water. The dead carcasses of fish, whales, dolphins, sharks, and such will start to twitch and wiggle and the odor of their dead carcasses will dissipate rapidly. Their skin, gills, scales, and flesh will seemingly come back together whole as they once were, and they will come back to life. Jesus is going to dazzle us with his display of power! Not only will we have a glorified body, but we will also have access to one hundred percent of our brain's potential. We will be, for the lack of a better word; superheroes.

"Beloved, now are we the sons of God, and it doth not yet appear what we shall be: but we know that, when he shall appear, we shall be like him; for we shall see him as he is." – I John 3:2

Superman is a fictional superhero in movies, animation, and comic books. His powers are so radical he can even move planets. The glorified body we will have will be compared to Superman, only with none of his weaknesses. Based on a person's reward(s) at the Judgment Seat of Christ there will be some with abilities so radical, they will be able to move objects up to and including planetary objects. Some may use the verse below in a symbolic sense, but I use it in a literal sense.

"And Jesus answering saith unto them, have faith in God. For verily I say unto you, that whosoever shall say unto this mountain, be thou removed, and be thou cast into the sea; and shall not doubt in his heart, but shall believe that those things which he saith shall come to pass; he shall have whatsoever he saith." – Saint Mark 11:22-23

With the capacity to access one-hundred percent of our brain's potential, there will be no room for doubt. Our newfound powers will manifest from our gifts, our will, and our thoughts. You will do things inconceivable in your new body you could not do in your old body.

224

According to God's will nothing will be impossible. Jesus will teach us how to do many things. When we come back with Jesus in our glorified bodies, we will not be eating apples and petting the lions. Jesus is going to put us to work. In our new bodies we are going to help Jesus restore and heal the planet. There will be no more doctors; no more nurses; no more physicians; no more clinics; no more urgent care; no more hospitals; no more emergency rooms; no more intensive care units.

We will anxiously wait for Jesus' every command. It will give us a chance to test the limits of our new abilities. Can you image a family of billions of super-men, superwomen, and super-children? Billions of saints will be working to-gether 24/7 for 30 days terraforming the planet. The geography of earth will look quite different when we finish. We will:

- Preach Christ crucified
- Bury the dead bodies
- Heal the sick and injured
- Make the flowers bloom again
- Gather all the orphaned children
- Repair the ozone layer, Purify the air
- Remove the rubble of the former world
- Gather the 144,000 from their secret place
- Make the vegetables and fruits grow again
- Make the trees, grass, and grains grow again
- Teach men how to survive without technology
- Remove nuclear and biological waste from off this planet
- Remove nuclear and biological weapons from off this planet
- Decontaminate the waters of blood, rotting flesh, and radiation

LET'S DO THE MATH

Second ½ of Daniel's 70th week	Wrath of God	1,260 Days
Marriage & Supper of the Lamb	Consummation	30 Days
Restoration / Regeneration	Celebration	30 Days
Syzygy Eclipse		15 Days
Total		1,335 Days

"Blessed is he that waiteth, and cometh to the thousand three hundred and five and thirty days." – Daniel 12:12

225

1st Seal	↓
2nd Seal	↓
o	= Beginning of Sorrows
3rd Seal	↑
4th Seal	↑
o	o
Interim	Rise of the New World Order
o	
5th Seal	Great Tribulation Period
o	
6th Seal	Rapture of the Church
o	
Sygyzy Eclipse	God stops the prophetic time clock
o	
7th Seal	7 Trumpets & 7 Vials
o	
Armageddon	Return of Jesus Christ

Links in the Prophetic Chain

ABOMINATION OF DESOLATION

RAPTURE OF THE CHURCH

WRATH OF GOD

SEVEN TRUMPETS BLOWN

SEVEN VIALS POURED

- GREAT TRIBILATION PERIOD = 5TH SEAL

- BLOOD MOON = 6TH SEAL

- BLACK SUN = THE 7TH SEAL

- SEVEN TRUMPETS = PLAGUES

- SEVEN VIALS = PLAGUES

Links in the Prophetic Chain Overlay

DAY OF THE LORD COMPONENT #1

15 DAY GRACE PERIOD

DAY OF THE LORD COMPONENT #2

SEVEN TRUMPETS

SEVEN VIALS

?

- EPISUNAGOGE (RAPTURE) = 6TH SEAL

- SYZYGY ECLIPSE = BLOOD MOON / BLACK SUN

- WRATH OF GOD = 7TH SEAL

- 7 TRUMPETS BLAST & 7 VIALS POURED

- THE CONSUMMATION = THE MISSING 30 DAYS

FINAL THOUGHT

Revelation's timeline is like a plate of pancakes topped on one another. Some layers overlap each other and there are layers within layers because of intervals, fragmentation, continuations, parentheticals, and narratives. Because the timeline of Revelation is so interwoven I used bullets, pictures, and charts.

The first Four Seals have already been opened. These changes taking place now will culminate with the beginning of sorrows. Humankind will pull itself up by the bootstraps with the help of the Antichrist, but it will be all lies and illusion. When they say peace and safety sudden destruction will result with the great tribulation period.

As it stands today, God is furious because humanity has gone off to serve false gods. The Day of the Lord upon the wicked will culminate with fourteen judgments. After God's wrath Jesus will return and make the kingdoms of this world his own when he rules on earth for one-thousand years.

After one-thousand years the devil will be allowed to deceive the world once again. Lucifer will once again bring the nations of the world together to try to destroy the nation of Israel. God will rain fire and brimstone from heaven and devour them all. The devil will finally meet his end when he is thrown into the Lake of Fire.

After this, God will resurrect all either to the Resurrection of Life or to the Resurrection of Damnation. Afterward, God will destroy planet Earth. By this time Jesus would have created a new planet earth and a New Jerusalem for us. He will give this to us as a gift for our faithfulness to Him. We will live and serve Jesus forever and ever. In the Book of Revelation Jesus revealed to his servants everything that will happen.

Do you have car insurance? Do you have homeowner's insurance? Do you have dental insurance? Do you have medical insurance? Do you have life insurance? If so, why not invest in eternal life insurance through Jesus Christ. As we speak there are many people walking around that have no clue they are separated from God, and many really do not care. They do not realize they are already condemned to an eternity separated from God. Unless they choose to accept Jesus Christ into their heart, all hope is lost to them (Saint John 3:18).

Many people will not enter into heaven because they absolutely hate God, but chose to be uninformed about God and his Christ. The real issue is people prefer excuses over integrity, ignorance over truth, and the created thing over the Creator. Human beings think too highly of themselves.

Regardless of the many haircuts you get, Rolex watches you wear, or Stuart Hughes suits you wear; you are not clean enough to get into heaven. Human beings are hopelessly, hilariously, pathetically, morally, lost creatures before Holy God.

The truth is we are hopelessly and eternally lost without Jesus Christ. My friend, all your good works, righteous deeds, and religion cannot save you. The only thing that can cleanse your sins is what Jesus Christ did on the cross for you. Jesus died in your place to save you from Hell. Hell is a choice. Heaven is a choice. Jesus is a choice.

Heaven is a gift and there is only one-way to heaven – Jesus. Get on your knees and ask Jesus to forgive you for all your sins. Ask Jesus to give you a new heart and to remove the blinders off your eyes so you may see this Matrix for what it really is. Ask Jesus to give you everlasting life. Then go; stop practicing your sinful ways and live for Him. Repent, and be baptized in the name of The Father, and of the Son, and of the Holy Spirit. Serve only Him and do not look back. If you do this, you will be saved. There is no other name under heaven whereby any man, woman, or child can be saved. Jesus said,

"I am the way, the truth, and the life. No man can go directly to God the Father, except through me." – Saint John 14:6

– Amen –

Coming Soon
Revelation: God's Wrath Cometh

As a continuation of Revelation: The Rapture Equation, the sequel titled *"Revelation: God's Wrath Cometh"*, explains chapters 8–22 verse by verse.

By doing the math, I calculate the number of the Beast (666). As I explain the Seven Mountains on which the Woman sits in Revelation 17:9, you will discover its' meaning has absolutely nothing to do with the Seven Hills of Rome.

I explain the symbolism of the Great Red Dragon in Revelation 12:3, the symbolism of the Beast in Revelation 13:2, and the symbolism of the Scarlet Colored Beast in Revelation 17:3. I explain the meaning of their heads, horns, and crowns. All three of these Beasts are not the same.

I reveal the identity of the Woman clothed with the sun in Revelation 12:1; and the role the 144,000 will play in end time prophetic events.

I explain these and so many other things including the year, month, and day of Jesus Christ's Second Coming. Brothers and sisters, we do not have much time left.

If you have read any book on biblical prophecy, you must read this book!

Notes and Bibliography

Chapter 1

Zodhiates, S. (1992). *The Hebrew-Greek Key Word Study Bible/King James Version/Bonded Black Leather*. Amg Pubs.

Britannica, The Editors of Encyclopedia. "Moloch". Encyclopedia Britannica, 10 Mar. 2020, https://www.britannica.com/topic/Moloch-ancient-god. Accessed 2 September 2021.

Sanderson, Peter and Roach, David. "The Flash". *Encyclopedia Britannica*, 19 Jan. 2018, https://www.britannica.com/topic/the-Flash. Accessed 2 September 2021.

Chapter 2

Wikipedia. *(n.d.). List of English Bible translations*. Retrieved March 30, 2021, from https://wiki.org

British Library, Leipzig University Library, St. Catherine's Monastery at Sinai, and the National Library of Russia. (2009, July). *Codex Sinaiticus. Experience the oldest Bible.* Codesinaiticus.Org. Retrieved March 30, 2021, from https://codexsinaiticus.org

Chabad-Lubavitch Media Center. (n.d.). *Jewish/Hebrew Date Converter*. Chabad.Org. Retrieved April 1, 2021, from https://chabad.org

Wikipedia. (n.d.). *Great Disappointment*. Retrieved March 30, 2021, from https://wiki.org

Dawahmaterials.Com. (n.d.). *Bible Versions List & Manuscripts*. Retrieved March 30, 2021, from https://dawahmaterials.com

Cs McGill.Ca. (n.d.). *Metonic Cycle*. Retrieved March 30, 2021, from https://csmcgill.ca/Hebrew/calendar

Sadinoff, D., & Michael, R. (n.d.). *Jewish holiday calendars & Hebrew Date Converter*. Hebcal.Com. Retrieved March 30, 2021, from https://hebcal.com

Parkinson, M and Mc Rae, D. (Directors). (2007). *David Koresh: The Final 24 Hours* [Documentary]. Popcornfilx

Myers, S. (Director). (2017). *Heavens Gate - The Untold Story* [Documentary]. Prime Video

Nelson, S (Director). (2006). *American Experience: Jonestown: The Life and Death of Peoples Temple* [Documentary]. Netflix

U.S. Naval Observatory Astronomical Applications Dept. (n.d.). *Passover dates 26–34 A.D.* Intercontinentalcog.Org. Retrieved April 1, 2021, from https://intercontinentalcog.org

Lohnes, Kate. *Siege of Jerusalem*. Encyclopedia Britannica, 29 Aug. 2018, https://www.britannica.com/event/Siege-of-Jerusalem-70. Accessed 31 March 2021.

Wachowski Bros. (Directors). (1999). *The Matrix* [Film]. Warner Bros

Chapter 3

Wikipedia. (n.d.). *No-fault divorce*. Retrieved March 30, 2021, from https://wiki.org

Wikipedia. (n.d.). *McCreary County v. American Civil Liberties Union*. Retrieved March 30, 2021, from https://wiki.org

Wikipedia. (n.d.). *Stone v. Graham*. Retrieved March 30, 2021, from https://wiki.org

Prison Policy.Org (n.d.). *Prison Policy Initiative*. Retrieved March 30, 2021, from https://prisonpolicy.org

Hamiltonproject.org (n.d.). *The Hamilton Project*. (2021). Retrieved March 30, 2021, from https://hamiltonproject.org

Cherry, K., & Gans, MD, S. (2020, March 19). *A List of Psychological Disorders*. Very Well Mind. Retrieved March 30, 2021, from https://verywellmind.com

Sorge, J. (Director). (2014). Divorce Corp. [Documentary]. Netflix

DuVernay, A. (Director). (2016). 13th [Documentary]. Netflix

Chapter 4

Cox, J. (2020, May 5). *Consumer debt*. Cnbc. https://cnbc.com

Hess, A. J. (2020, December 22). *Student debt*. Cnbc. https://cnbc.com

Positive Money. (n.d.). *How Banks Create Money*. Retrieved April 1, 2021, from https://positivemoney.org

Maki, S. (2021, February 17). *World's $281 Trillion Debt Pile Is Set to Rise Again in 2021*. Cnbc. https://bloomberg.com

Peter G. Peterson Foundation. (n.d.). *The National Debt is now more than $28 trillion. What does that mean?* Pgpf.Org/Info Graphic/National Debt. Retrieved April 1, 2021, from https://pgpf.org

University of Virginia. *Franklin D. Roosevelt – Key Events*. Retrieved April 2, 2021, from https://miller center.org

Gold Reserve Act of 1934. (n.d.). *Federal Reserve History*. Retrieved April 2, 2021, from https://federalreservehistory.org

(n.d.). *1929 Stock Market Crash and the Great Depression Part 1 & 2*. [Documentary]. Youtube_Nik TheSaint

(n.d.). *Transforming America: A New Deal*. [Documentary]. Youtube_John Varga

(n.d.). *The crash of 1929*. [Documentary]. Youtube_Oliver Bossard on Finance

U.S. National Archives. (n.d.). *Stories from the Great Depression*. [Documentary]. YouTube

Wikipedia. (n.d.). *Survival Kit*. Retrieved April 2, 2021, from https://wiki.org

Wikipedia. (n.d.). *Glass-Steagall Legislation*. Retrieved April 2, 2021, from https://wiki.org

Wikipedia. (n.d.). *Gramm-Leach-Biley Act*. Retrieved April 2, 2021, from https://wiki.org

Wikipedia. (n.d.). *List of Stock Exchanges*. Retrieved April 2, 2021, from https://wiki.org

Wikipedia. (n.d.). *Emergency Banking Relief Act*. Retrieved April 2, 2021, from https://wiki.org

Wikipedia. (n.d.). *Federal Deposit Insurance Corporation*. Retrieved April 2, 2021, from https://wiki.org

Wikipedia. (n.d.). *Securities & Exchange Commission*. Retrieved April 2, 2021, from https://wiki.org

Wikipedia. (n.d.). *Gold Reserve Act*. Retrieved April 2, 2021, from https://wiki.org

Wikipedia. (n.d.). *Federal Emergency Relief Administration*. Retrieved April 2, 2021, from https://wiki.org

Wikipedia. (n.d.). *Works Progress Administration*. Retrieved April 2, 2021, from https://wiki.org

Wikipedia. (n.d.). *Social Security Administration*. Retrieved April 2, 2021, from https://wiki.org

Wikipedia. (n.d.). *Civilian Conservation Corp*. Retrieved April 2, 2021, from https://wiki.org

Wikipedia. (n.d.). *National Industry Recovery Act*. Retrieved April 2, 2021, from https://wiki.org

Wikipedia. (n.d.). *National Recover Administration*. Retrieved April 2, 2021, from https://wiki.org

Wikipedia. (n.d.). *Agricultural Adjustment Administration*. Retrieved April 2, 2021, from https://wiki.org

Wikipedia. (n.d.). *Farm Mortgage Refinancing Act*. Retrieved April 2, 2021, from https://wiki.org

Wikipedia. (n.d.). *Tennessee Valley Authority*. Retrieved April 2, 2021, from https://wiki.org

Andersen, K and Kuhn, K. (Director). (2017) *What the Health*. [Documentary]. Prime Video

National Library of Medicine. (n.d.). *2016 Alzheimer's Disease-Fact and Figures*. PMID:27570871/Abstract. Retrieved April 1, 2021, from https://Pubmed.ncbi.nlm.nih.gov

ASCO.org. (n.d.). *Sarcoma-Kaposi*. Cancer.Net. Retrieved April 2, 2021, from https://cancer.net

Epstein-Barr virus and the elderly host. (n.d.). Duke University - Schol-ars@Duke. Retrieved April 2, 2021, from https://Dukeuniversity.com

Erba, H. P., Eddy, R., Shows, T., Kedes, L., & Gunning, P. (1988, April 8). *Structure, chromosome location, and expression of Human gamma. . .*Pubmed. https://pubmed.gov

National Institute of Neurological Disorders and Stroke. (n.d.). *Shingles Information Page*. US Department of Health and Human Services. Retrieved April 2, 2021, from https://Nih.gov

National Library of Medicine. (1993, December 2). *Molecular Biology of Human Herpesviruses 6A and 6B*. Pubmed. https://pubmed.gov

Saleh, D., Yarrarapu, S., & Sharma, S. (2021, January 5). *Herpes Simplex Type 1*. National Institute of Health. https://Nih.gov

U.S. Department of Health and Human Services. (2009, August 17). *Why genital herpes boosts the risk of HIV infection*. National Institute of Health. https://Nih.gov

U.S. National Library of Medicine. (2021, September 29). *Cytomegalovirus Infections*. Medline Plus. https://Medlineplus.com

U.S. Department of Health and Human Services. (n.d.). *Diabetes*. National Diabetes Statistics Report 2020. Retrieved April 1, 2021, from https://cdc.gov

U.S. Department of Health and Human Services. (n.d.). *Overweight & Obesity*. National Obesity Statistics Report 2020. Retrieved April 1, 2021, from https://cdc.gov

U.S. Department of Health and Human Services. (n.d.). *Chronic Kidney Disease in the United States*. National Kidney Statistics Report 2020. Retrieved April 1, 2021, from https://cdc.gov

U.S. Department of Health and Human Services. (n.d.). *Colorectal (Colon) Cancer*. National Colorectal Cancer Statistics Report 2020. Retrieved April 1, 2021, from https://cdc.gov

U.S. Department of Health and Human Services. (n.d.). *COPD*. National Chronic Obstructive Pulmonary Disease Statistics Report 2020. Retrieved April 1, 2021, from https://cdc.gov

U.S. Department of Health and Human Services. (n.d.). *Arthritis*. National Arthritis Statistics Report 2020. Retrieved April 1, 2021, from https://cdc.gov

U.S. Department of Health and Human Services. (n.d.). *Tuberculosis* (TB) National Tuberculosis Statistics Report 2020. Retrieved April 1, 2021, from https://cdc.gov

U.S. Department of Health and Human Services. (n.d.). *Cholesterol*. National Cholesterol Statistics Report 2020. Retrieved April 1, 2021, from https://cdc.gov

U.S. Department of Health and Human Services. (n.d.). *HIV*. National HIV & AIDS Statistics Report 2020. Retrieved April 1, 2021, from https://cdc.gov

U.S. Department of Health and Human Services. (n.d.). *Viral Hepatitis*. National Diabetes Statistics Report 2020. Retrieved April 1, 2021, from https://cdc.gov

U.S. Department of Health and Human Services. (n.d.). *Heart Disease*. Interactive Atlas of Heart Disease and stroke. Retrieved April 1, 2021, from https://cdc.gov/stats

U.S. Department of Health and Human Services. (n.d.). *Leading causes of death*. Retrieved April 1, 2021, from https://cdc.gov

U.S. Department of Health and Human Services. (n.d.). *Increase in Kidney Disease*. National Library of Medicine. Retrieved April 1, 2021, from https://Pubmed.ncbi.nlm.nih.gov/table 4-6

U.S. Department of Health and Human Services. (n.d.). *National Library of Medicine*. Accessed April 1, 2021, from https://Pubmed.gov

American Cancer Society. (n.d.). *Cancer Facts and Figures*. Cancer Statistics Center. Retrieved April 1, 2021, from https://cancer.org

Chapter 5

Wikipedia. (n.d.). *Mein Kampf*. Retrieved March 30, 2021, from https://wiki.org

Wikipedia. (n.d.). *NSDAP 25 points manifesto*. Retrieved March 30, 2021, from https://wiki.org

Wikipedia. (n.d.). *Allies of World War I.* Retrieved March 30, 2021, from
https://wiki.org

UN.Org. (n.d.). *Model United Nations.* Retrieved March 31, 2021,
from https://un.org

Wikipedia. (n.d.). *Extermination camp.* Retrieved March 30, 2021, from
https://wiki.org

Griffin, S. (Director). (2016). Hitler - The Opportunist. S1.E1. Hitler - The Actor. S1E2. Hitler - The Fuhrer. S1.E3. Hitler - The Victor. S1.E4. Hitler - The Monster. S1.E5. Hitler - The Downfall.S1.E5 [Documentary]. AHC Channel

Chapter 6

Wikipedia. (n.d.). *Internet of things.* Retrieved March 30, 2021, from
https://wiki.org

Shah, A. (2013, January 7). *Poverty Facts and Stats.* Retrieved March 30, 2021,
from https://globalissues.org

United Nations. (n.d.-a). *PEACE BUILDING.* UN.Org. Retrieved March 31,
2021, from https://un.org

United Nations. (n.d.-b). *Sustainable Development Goals - 17 Goals to Transform Our World.* UN.Org. Retrieved March 31, 2021, from https://un.org

US Department of the Interior. (n.d.-a). *Earthquake Hazards.* Usgs.Gov. Retrieved March 31, 2021, from https://usgs.gov

US Department of the Interior. (n.d.-b). *Greenhouse Gases.* Usgs.Gov. Retrieved March 31, 2021, from https://usgs.gov

Fighter,A and Le Meir, H. (Writer). (2015). *Dream the Future. Episodes 1-20* [Documentary]. CuriosityStream Inc.

Chapters 7, 8 and 9

U.S. Naval Observatory Astronomical Applications Dept. (n.d.). *Passover dates 26–34 A.D.* Intercontinentalcog.Org. Retrieved April 1, 2021,
from https://intercontinentalcog.org

Britannica, The Editors of Encyclopedia. *Nehemiah*. Encyclopedia Britannica, 8 Dec. 2017, https://www.britannica.com/biography/Nehemiah. Accessed 31 March 2021.

Lohnes, Kate. *Siege of Jerusalem*. Encyclopedia Britannica, 29 Aug. 2018, https://www.britannica.com/event/Siege-of-Jerusalem-70. Accessed 31 March 2021.

Wikipedia. (n.d.). *VY Canis Majoris*. Retrieved March 31, 2021, from https://wiki.org

Wikipedia. (n.d.). *Time Dilation*. Retrieved March 31, 2021, from https://wiki.org

Fairchild, M. (2020, April 16). *Percentage of Christians Worldwide*. Retrieved March 31, 2021, from https://learnreligions.com

One Plus One. (n.d.). *Jewish Calendar*. JCal.Com. Accessed March 31, 2021, from https://jcal.com

Time and Date AS. (1995). *Find Solar and Lunar Eclipses Worldwide*. Time and Date.com. Accessed March 31, 2021, from https://timeanddate.com

Wikipedia. (n.d.). *List of the verified oldest people*. Accessed October 24, 2021, from https://wiki.org

Additional Sources

Zodhiates, S. (1992). *The Hebrew-Greek Key Word Study Bible/King James Version/Bonded Black Leather*. Amg Pubs.

Miller Jr., B. (Director). (2017). *The Coming Convergence* [Documentary]. Gravitas Ventures

Weiss, T. G., Forsythe, D. P., Coate, R. A., & Pease, K. (2016). *The United Nations and Changing World Politics* (8th ed.). Westview Press.

Bullinger, E. W. (1969). *Number in Scripture*. Kregel Publications

Strong, J. (2009). *Strong's Exhaustive Concordance of the Bible*. Macmillan Publishers.

Britannica, The Editors of Encyclopedia. *List of Roman emperors*. (2015, November 11). Retrieved March 31, 2021, from https://www.britannica.com/topic/list-of-Roman-emperors-2043294.

Bolt, Bruce A. "*Earthquake*". *Encyclopedia Britannica*, 1 Feb. 2021, https://www.britannica.com/science/earthquake-geology. Accessed 3 April 2021.

Area Calculator. (n.d.). *Calculator.Net*. Retrieved April 3, 2021, from https://calculator.net

Cooking Measurement Conversion Calculator. (n.d.). Good Calculators Free Online. Retrieved April 3, 2021, from https://goodcalculators.com

Length, Width & Height to Volume Calculator. (n.d.). Sensor One. Retrieved April 3, 2021, from https://sensorone.com

National Heart, Lung, and Blood Institute. (n.d.). *Calculate Your Body Mass Index*. NIH. Retrieved April 3, 2021, from https://nih.gov

Time and Date AS. (n.d.-a). *Find Solar & Lunar Eclipses*. Time and Date. Retrieved April 3, 2021, from https://timeanddate.com

Time and Date AS. (n.d.-b). *Time Zones, Calendars, Calculators & Timers*. Time and Date. Retrieved April 3, 2021, from https://timeanddate.com

Underdog projects. (n.d.). *Computer Value In Gematria Calculator*. Gematrix. Retrieved April 3, 2021, from https://gematrix.org

Worldtime Buddy. (n.d.). *Worldtime Buddy*. Retrieved April 3, 2021, from https://worldtimebuddy.com

Wittenberger, P. (Director). (2013). The Book of Revelation. Episodes 1-22. [Documentary Teaching]. Framing the World Productions.

Faithful Teachings of Pastor Charles Stanley. In Touch ministries. PO Box 7900. Atlanta, GA 30357. 3836 Dekalb Technology Pkwy. Atlanta GA 30340

Cover by: Askorbin. [Fiverr.com/Graphics and Design/Illustration]

Edited by: Mr. Anonymous and Ms. Anonymous, - GOOGLE SEARCH :)

Four Horsemen of the Apocalypse: By Asya Saliy [saradovask@gmail.com]